Verbal Homework

Verbal Lesson: 1 M T W Th F Sa Su Time: Date:	
Verbal Lesson: 2 M T W Th F Sa Su Time: Date:	
Verbal Lesson: 3 M T W Th F Sa Su Time: Date:	
Verbal Lesson: 4 M T W Th F Sa Su Time: Date:	
Verbal Lesson: 5 M T W Th F Sa Su Time: Date:	
Verbal Lesson: 6 M T W Th F Sa Su Time: Date:	
Verbal Lesson: 7 M T W Th F Sa Su Time: Date:	
Verbal Lesson: 8 M T W Th F Sa Su Time: Date:	

Math Homework

Math Lesson: 1 M T W Th F Sa Su Time: Date:	
Math Lesson: 2 M T W Th F Sa Su Time: Date:	
Math Lesson: 3 M T W Th F Sa Su Time: Date:	
Math Lesson: 4 M T W Th F Sa Su Time: Date:	
Math Lesson: 5 M T W Th F Sa Su Time: Date:	
Math Lesson: 6 M T W Th F Sa Su Time: Date:	
Math Lesson: 7 M T W Th F Sa Su Time: Date:	
Math Lesson: 8 M T W Th F Sa Su Time: Date:	

SAT Unlocked II

vocabulary edition

SAT Unlocked II

SAT Unlocked II (vocabulary edition)

Copyright © 2013 Elegus Corp. All rights reserved.
ISBN-13: 978-0-9838460-3-1
ISBN-10: 0983846030

All information contained herein is provided "AS IS", for information purposes only.
The changing nature of the topic and reliance on outside sources for information prevents us from giving any warranty or guarantee either expressed or implied that the information appearing herein or accessible through links to outside sources will be accurate, complete, current, relevant, or timely in content. We further make no warranties either expressed or implied as to the quality or accuracy of any information contained herein and do not make any claims as to the use of this information for any particular purpose(s). Although reasonable effort has been taken to ensure the accurate presentation of reliable and useful information in this book, neither the publisher nor the author assumes any responsibility for errors or omissions. Further no liability is assumed for any damages resulting from the use of information contained herein.

SAT Unlocked is a trademark of Elegus Corp. SAT and SAT Reasoning Test are registered trademarks of the College Board. PSAT/NSMQT is a registered trademark of the College Board and National Merit Scholarship Corp. Neither the College Board nor National Merit Scholarship Corp. has endorsed nor is in any way affiliated with this publication or Elegus Corp.

The Official SAT Study Guide, 2nd ed. is © 2009 by the College Board and Educational Testing Service, and is not a publication of Elegus Corp.

Written by: Adam Piacente
Editorial Assistant: Brette Connolly
Student essay reprinted with permission of the author.

Published by:
Elegus Corp.
San Rafael, CA
Email: info@elegus.com

For my Dad.

Table of Contents

How to Use This Guide (Read Me First!) — 11
    What is *SAT Unlocked II*? — 11
    Purchasing *The Official SAT Study Guide, 2nd ed.* (OSSG) — 12
    How does *SAT Unlocked II* work? — 13
    How is *SAT Unlocked II* organized? — 14

SAT Basics — 15
    How is the SAT organized? — 16
        What is the Equating Section? — 17
    Can I go back to previous sections if I have time? — 18
    How is the PSAT organized? — 18
    How is the SAT scored? — 20
        SAT Scaled Score — 20
        SAT Raw Score — 20
    When should I guess on multiple choice questions? — 21
        What about guessing on Math Grid-In questions? — 21
    How does the Essay affect my SAT score? — 22
    What if I get the same answer multiple times in a row? — 22
    Are all questions the same difficulty? — 23
    Does every question count the same? — 23
    What are Percentiles? — 24
    Why should I study for the SAT? — 24

SAT Reading — 25
    Introduction to SAT Reading — 26
        How to Finish a Critical Reading Section — 27
        Alternatively, leave Sentence Completions for last — 27
    Sentence Completions — 28
        How much time should I spend on vocabulary? — 28
        When should I skip Sentence Completion questions? — 29
        Strategies for Sentence Completions — 30
            Look for Key Words — 30
            Play Positive/Negative — 31
            Double-Blank Sentence Completion Questions — 32
    Passage Reading — 35
        Passage Reading Strategy — 35
            Part 1: Reading the Passage — 35
            Part 2: Answer the Questions — 38
        Answering Double Passage Sets — 48
            Double Passage Questions — 61
        Short Passage Questions — 66
    SAT Critical Reading Quick Review — 67

Get more help online at: SATunlocked.com

SAT Math	**69**
Introduction to SAT Math	70
SAT Math question types	70
In what order do SAT Math questions appear?	71
What math subjects does the SAT test?	71
Is SAT Math very advanced?	72
Know your capabilities	72
What formulas do I need to know?	73
Can I use a calculator?	74
Calculators you CANNOT use:	74
When should I use my calculator?	74
What are Grid-Ins?	75
How do I enter Grid-Ins?	76
Fractions vs. Decimals	77
Numbers & Operations	79
SAT Numbers Terminology	79
Plugging in Answers	81
Plugging in Numbers	83
Plugging in Numbers (basic)	83
Plugging in Numbers (word problems)	87
Number Lines	89
Sets	91
SAT Set Terminology	91
Venn Diagrams	93
Sequences	95
Consecutive Integers	97
Sum of Consecutive Integers	97
Lists of Consecutive Integers	98
Logic Questions	100
Logic Puzzles	100
Logic Word Problems	102
Fractions	104
Fractions (basic)	104
Fractions (Word Problems)	106
Percentages (basic)	108
Calculating Percentage Increase/Decrease	110
Calculating a Series of Percentage Increases/Decreases	111
Ratios & Proportions	113
Cross Multiplying	113
Ratios (word)	115
Ratios (parts)	117
Direct and Inverse Proportions	119
Geometry	122
Angles	123
Angles of Parallel Lines	126
Sum of Polygon Angles	128
Triangle Sides & Angles	130
Triangle Equation Writing	135
Right Triangles	137
Similar Triangles	141
Triangle Area	143
Circles	145
Circle Circumference & Area	145
Circle Arc Length & Sector Area	150

Rectangles & Squares	152
Volume	156
Box Volume	156
Cylinder Volume	158
Internal Lines	160
Coordinate Graphing	162
Coordinate Graphing (basic)	162
Coordinate Geometry	165
Coordinate Formulas	167
Slope	169
Slope (basic)	169
Slope: Perpendicular Lines and Reflections	172
Algebra & Functions	**176**
Equations	176
Solving Equations	176
Writing Equations (basic)	178
SAT Equation Writing Terminology	178
Writing Equations (Word Problems)	181
Rate x Time = Distance (RT = D)	183
Exponents & Roots	185
Exponent Rules	185
Roots Rules	185
Simplifying Exponents & Roots	185
Equalizing Exponent Bases	191
Inequalities	193
Absolute Value	195
Absolute Value and Inequalities	196
Substitution	198
Substituting Numbers	198
Substituting Variables	200
Substituting Combinations	202
Substituting Combinations and Factoring	204
Substituting Difference of Two Squares	206
Functions	208
Function Tables	208
Values of Functions	210
Function Word Problems	212
Symbol Functions	214
Graphing Functions	216
Graphing Function Shifts	220
Graphing Function Shapes	222
Data & Statistics	**225**
Average (Arithmetic Mean)	225
Median & Mode	227
Data Analysis	229
Tables	229
Bar Graphs	231
Line Graphs	233
Circle Graphs (Pie Charts)	235
Scatter Plots	237
Pictographs	239
Combinations	241
Probability	244
SAT Math Quick Review	**246**

SAT Writing	**247**
SAT Writing Introduction	248
WARNING: Don't go hunting for rules not tested!	251
Improving Sentences	252
Improving Sentences Strategies	253
Improving Sentences Grammar Rules & Questions	254
Wordy Sentences	254
Using 'Because'	256
Sentence Fragments	257
Combining Sentences	259
Rewriting Sentences	261
Introductory Phrases	262
Spotting Contrasts	264
Error IDs	265
Error ID Strategies	266
Error ID Grammar Rules & Questions	267
Adverbs	267
Word Choice	268
Dual Phrases	268
'Verby' Words with Prepositions	269
Other Phrases	271
Grammar Rules for Both Improving Sentences & Error IDs	272
Parallelism	272
Parallelism & Lists	272
Parallelism & Dual Phrases	273
Verbs	275
Verb Agreement	275
Verb Agreement & Prepositional Phrases	276
Verb Agreement & Parenthetical Expressions	278
Verb Agreement & Compound Subjects	279
Verb Agreement & Inverted Subjects	280
Verb Tense	281
Verb Tense & Dates	283
Verb Tense & '-ing'	284
Pronouns	285
Ambiguous Pronouns	286
Pronoun Number Agreement	288
Pronoun Consistency	290
Who vs. Which	291
Pronoun Case	292
Noun Agreement	294
Comparisons	295
Faulty Comparisons	295
Comparing Two vs. Three or More Things	297
Redundancies	298
Improving Paragraphs	299
Improving Paragraphs Strategies	299
Improving Paragraphs Question Sets	301
SAT Writing Multiple Choice Quick Review	302

SAT Essay	**303**
Frequently Asked Questions	304
Where does the essay appear on the test?	304
How much time do I have to write the essay?	304
How much do I have to write?	305
How is the essay scored?	305
Who grades the essay?	305
Can I get a zero on the essay?	305
How does the essay affect my SAT score?	306
What am I graded on?	308
What about spelling mistakes?	308
What can I write about?	309
Can I write about personal experiences?	309
What should I write about?	309
What if I can't remember a specific name or date?	310
Can I just make something up?	310
Analyzing the Question	311
Brainstorming Exercises	312
Writing Your Essay	314
Organizing Your Essay	315
Paragraph 1: Short Introduction.	315
Paragraph 2: Your BETTER example.	316
Paragraph 3: Transition, then your second example.	317
Paragraph 4: Conclusion.	317
Essay Example	318
Timing Your Essay	320
SAT Essay Quick Review	321
SAT Test Day	**323**
The Night Before	324
The Morning Before	326
At the Test	327
During the Test	327
After the Test	328
SAT Quick Review	**329**
SAT Vocabulary	**337**
Definitions	337
Work Sheets	360
About the Author	**364**

Get more help online at: SATunlocked.com

How to Use This Guide (Read Me First!)

Thank you for purchasing *SAT Unlocked II (vocabulary edition)*. This complete SAT training program shows you step-by-step how to master all of the subjects tested on the SAT Reasoning Test (SAT I).

What is *SAT Unlocked II*?

Developed over many years of SAT tutoring with hundreds of individual students, *SAT Unlocked II* is a proven and uniquely effective program that will maximize your SAT score.

> ***SAT Unlocked II* shows you a simple, straightforward strategy for Critical Reading that is effective with students at every reading level.**

A hands-on tutorial guides you step by step through actual passages as you learn a strategy that systematically targets the fundamental reason students most often miss passage reading questions. *SAT Unlocked II* also shows you easy and effective strategies for handling vocabulary-based questions.

> ***SAT Unlocked II* organizes every SAT Math and Writing multiple choice question in *The Official SAT Study Guide, 2nd ed.* (OSSG) by topic and difficulty.**

By reading the topic descriptions, practicing the exercises, and answering the OSSG questions, you will quickly and efficiently learn how to answer any type of Math or Writing question you are likely to see on the actual SAT.

> ***SAT Unlocked II's* Essay chapter shows you an easy way to write high scoring essays using an SAT-optimized format.**

Brain storming exercises, timing strategies, and an example essay are also included to get you ready.

> **Day-of-Test preparation tips help ensure you score your best.**

SAT Unlocked II also includes many useful test taking strategies, tips, and tricks to give you that extra edge.

SAT Unlocked II

Purchasing *The Official SAT Study Guide, 2nd ed. (OSSG)*

To get the most out SAT Unlocked II, you will also need to purchase *The Official SAT Study Guide (OSSG) 2nd ed.*

Published by the College Board, *The Official SAT Study Guide, 2nd ed.* (OSSG) is the only SAT prep book containing authentic questions actually written by the test makers themselves.

The print version of *The Official SAT Study Guide, 2nd ed.* (OSSG) is your best source for practice SAT questions.

Tip:
The Official SAT Study Guide (OSSG), 2nd ed. is essential to understanding the exact type and format of each question, you are likely to see on the actual SAT. *'Fake' SAT books from non-official publishers do not do a good job of simulating actual SAT questions, while answering question from online question services simply cannot give you the same test taking experience you get by answering printed SAT questions like those you will see on the actual paper exam.*

***The Official SAT Study Guide, 2nd ed.* (OSSG) is available at all major bookstores as well as online.**

Remember!
SAT Unlocked II works <u>only</u> with The Official SAT Study Guide (OSSG) 2nd ed. Other books do not work with this program.

Get more help online at: SATunlocked.com

How does *SAT Unlocked II* work?

SAT Unlocked II works by organizing questions in *The Official SAT Study Guide, 2nd ed.* (OSSG) by subject and difficulty. By answering the questions in the order listed, you progressively hone your skills on each topic.

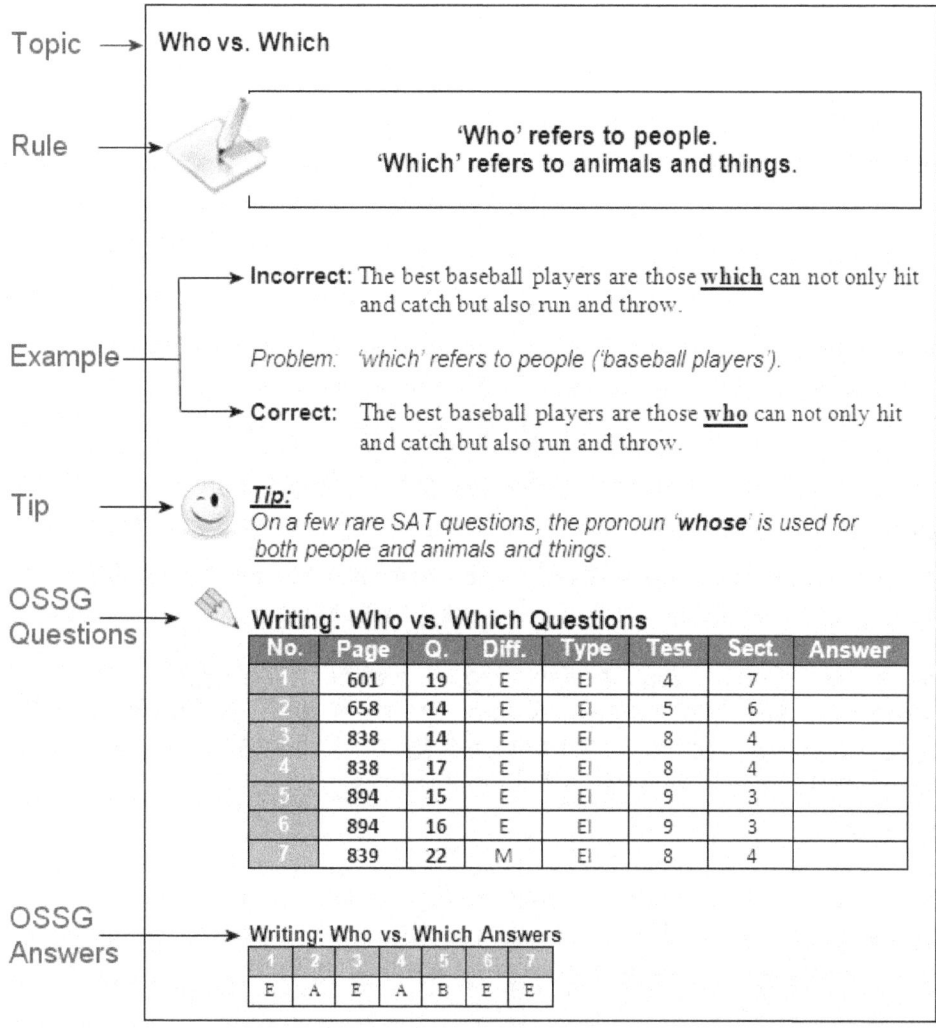

For each question topic:
1. Read the rule, the example, and any tips.
2. Answer each OSSG practice question *in the order listed.*

Start with the easy questions and move to the harder ones to progressively develop your skills for each topic. By the time you get to the end of each question list, you will have a good grasp of the topic and how it is tested.

How is *SAT Unlocked II* organized?

SAT Basics
This section gives you a brief overview of the test and includes information about SAT structure, scoring, percentiles, and why studying for the SAT is so important. The introduction also provides general test taking tips and strategies to help maximize your score.

SAT Reading
This section breaks down the Critical Reading portion of the SAT by question and passage type. A hands-on tutorial shows you a uniquely effective strategy to use on any type of passage reading question. The SAT Reading section also includes useful techniques for dealing with even the hardest, vocabulary-based questions.

SAT Math
The Math section organizes all of the questions in *The Official SAT Study Guide, 2nd ed.* by subject and difficulty. By reading the explanations, practicing the exercises, and answering the OSSG questions in order they appear in this book, you progressively learn the reasoning skills necessary to master any SAT Math question.

SAT Writing
Like the Math section, the Writing section also organizes every OSSG question by subject and order of difficulty, so you know exactly which grammar rules are tested and on which types of questions. Also included are effective tips for answering each of the three types of SAT Writing questions: Improving Sentences, Error IDs, and Paragraph Improvements, as well as an overall strategy that assures you will be able answer many questions other students miss.

SAT Essay
Don't sweat the SAT Essay! This section shows you step-by-step how to write high scoring essays using descriptive examples and concise language within an SAT-optimized format. Brain storming exercises, timing strategies, and an example essay are also included.

SAT Test Day
We review everything you'll need for the big day. This includes a checklist for what to bring, as well as tips on what to eat and drink beforehand, what to wear, how to keep your own time, and more. You'll also learn valuable day-of-test techniques that improve focus and concentration while reducing test fatigue and anxiety.

SAT Quick Review & Vocabulary
The SAT Quick Review boils all of the *SAT Unlocked II* strategies down to a few convenient pages, which is great for last minute study and review. The Vocabulary section includes definitions for over 1000 SAT vocabulary words along with handy worksheets to use while practicing.

Good Luck!!!

How is the SAT organized?

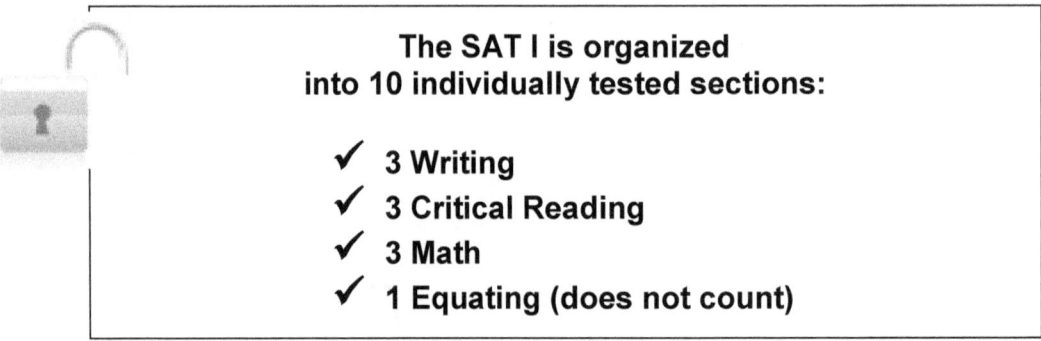

The SAT I is organized
into 10 individually tested sections:

✓ 3 Writing
✓ 3 Critical Reading
✓ 3 Math
✓ 1 Equating (does not count)

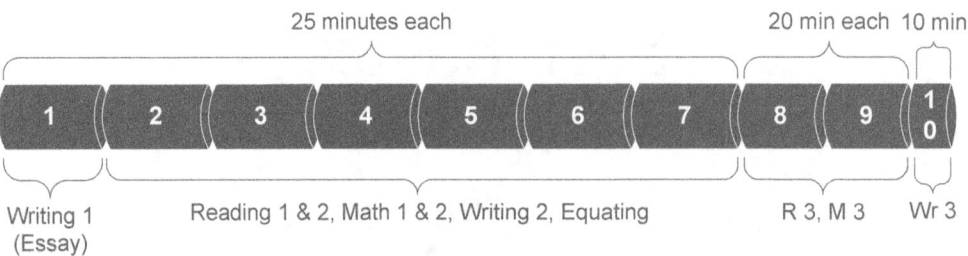

1. **Section 1:**
   Writing 1 (Essay) is always the FIRST section.

2. **Sections 2-7:**
   Six 25-minute multiple choice sections in random order -
   Critical Reading 1 & 2, Math 1& 2, Writing 2, and Equating.

3. **Sections 8 & 9:**
   Two 20 minute sections - Critical Reading 3 and Math 3.

4. **Section 10:**
   One 10 minute Writing section is always the LAST section.

SAT Basics

The chart below shows you the total number of each question type for each subject as well as how each section is organized.

SAT I Questions by Subject		
Total Critical Reading	**Total Math**	**Total Writing**
67 Questions 19 Sentence Completions 8 Short Passage 40 Long Passage **in 70 minutes**	**54 Questions** 44 Multiple Choice 10 Grid-In **in 70 minutes**	**1 Essay & 49 Questions** 25 Improving Sentences 18 Error IDs 6 Para Improvements **in 60 Minutes**
Critical Reading 1	**Math 1**	**Writing 1** *(always Section 1)*
24 Questions 5 Sentence Completions 4 Short Passage 15 Long Passage **in 25 minutes**	**20 Questions** 20 Multiple Choice **in 25 minutes**	**1 Essay** **in 25 minutes**
Critical Reading 2	**Math 2**	**Writing 2**
24 Questions 8 Sentence Completions 4 Short Passage 12 Long Passage **in 25 minutes**	**18 Questions** 8 Multiple Choice 10 Grid-In **in 25 minutes**	**35 Questions** 11 Improving Sentences 18 Error IDs 6 Para Improvements **in 25 minutes**
Critical Reading 3	**Math 3**	**Writing 3** *(always Section 10)*
19 Questions 6 Sentence Completions 13 Long Passage **in 20 minutes**	**16 Questions** 16 Multiple Choice **in 20 minutes**	**14 Questions** 14 Improving Sentences **in 10 minutes**

What is the Equating Section?

The SAT also includes an additional experimental section that does not count toward your score.

The Equating Section is designed to test out new questions and to compare the performances of current students with those of previous test takers. The Equating section can test any of the three subjects and can appear anywhere on the SAT, although it usually appears as one of the 25 minute sections.

SAT Unlocked II

Tip:
Do NOT try to guess which section is the Equating section.
Trying to 'game' which section doesn't count can get you into real trouble. When taking the SAT, always assume every section counts.

Can I go back to previous sections if I have time?

> You can NOT answer questions from a previous section once time has been called for that section.

How is the PSAT organized?

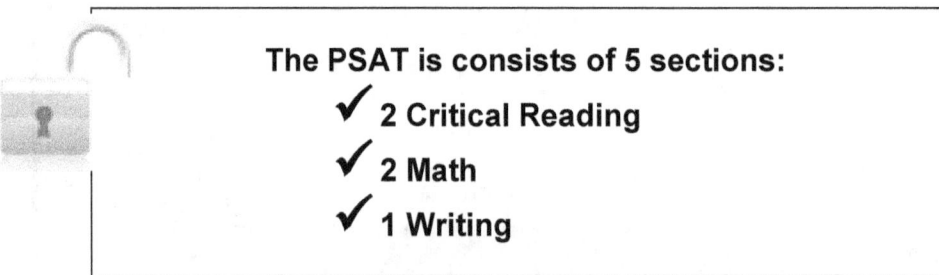

> The PSAT is consists of 5 sections:
> ✓ 2 Critical Reading
> ✓ 2 Math
> ✓ 1 Writing

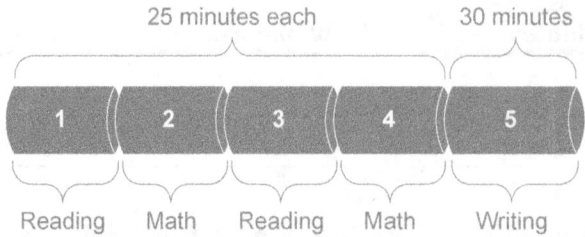

1. **Sections 1-4:**
   Four 25-minute multiple choice sections in random order - Critical Reading 1 & 2, Math 1 & 2.

2. **Section 5:**
   One 30 minute Writing Section.

SAT Basics

PSAT Questions by Subject		
Total Critical Reading	**Total Math**	**Total Writing**
48 Questions 19 Sentence Completions 8 Short Passage 40 Long Passage **in 50 minutes**	**38 Questions** 28 Multiple Choice 10 Grid-In **in 50 minutes**	**40 Questions** 25 Improving Sentences 18 Error IDs 6 Para Improvements **in 30 Minutes**
Critical Reading 1	**Math 1**	**Writing 1**
24 Questions 5 Sentence Completions 4 Short Passage 15 Long Passage **in 25 minutes**	**20 Questions** 20 Multiple Choice **in 25 minutes**	**39 Questions** 20 Improving Sentences 14 Error IDs 5 Para Improvements **in 30 minutes**
Critical Reading 2	**Math 2**	
24 Questions 8 Sentence Completions 4 Short Passage 12 Long Passage **in 25 minutes**	**18 Questions** 8 Multiple Choice 10 Grid-In **in 25 minutes**	

Tip:
There is no Essay or Equating Section on the PSAT.

How is the SAT scored?

SAT Scaled Score

Each subject is scored on a 200-800 point scale.

SAT Subject	Possible Points
Critical Reading	200 - 800
Math	200 - 800
Writing	200 - 800
Total SAT Score	**600 - 2400**

SAT Raw Score

Your scaled score is determined by comparing your **Raw Score** on each subject with those of other students.

For *multiple choice* questions,
your raw score is calculated using this formula:

+ 1 point for each CORRECT answer

- ¼ point (minus!) for each INCORRECT answer

0 points for each SKIPPED answer

Remember!
The SAT SUBTRACTS ¼ point from your raw score each for incorrect multiple choice answer. Since each multiple choice question has 5 possible answers, subtracting a ¼ point for each incorrect answer prevents you from receiving extra points by randomly guessing on questions you otherwise can't answer.

That's why it's **called the 'guessing penalty'.**

SAT Basics
When should I guess on multiple choice questions?

Don't worry about the 'Guessing Penalty'. GUESS!

The so called 'guessing Penalty is not actually a 'penalty'.
If you skip five questions or randomly guess at five questions, you are statistically likely to get the same score (0 points). But, **if you can eliminate answer choices for any of those five questions, you are statistically likely to be in positive points for the group.**

So answer as many questions as you can, while eliminating as many incorrect answers along the way.

What about guessing on Math Grid-In questions?

The 54 SAT I Math questions include 10 'Student Produced Response' questions, commonly known as 'Grid-In' questions. Grid-In questions require you to fill in actual numbers on your score sheet, rather than simply choosing from different lettered answers.

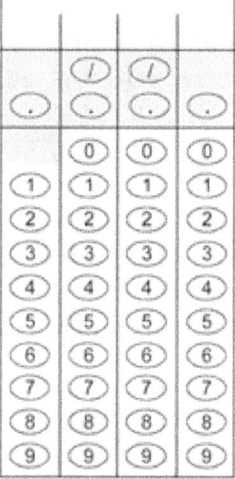

Always guess on Math Grid-In questions.

Unlike multiple choice questions, you do not lose a ¼ point when you answer incorrectly on a Math Grid-In question.

Remember!
ALWAYS guess on Math Grid-In questions! *Because the SAT does not subtract points for incorrect Grid-In answers, you have nothing to lose by* <u>always</u> *answering every Grid-In question – even if you have no idea what a particular question is asking.*

How does the Essay affect my SAT score?

The Essay counts for 30% of your Writing <u>scaled</u> score.

Although 30% sounds like a lot, in practice your essay score will usually only affect your overall SAT Writing scaled score by about 20 or 30 points. For more on the impact the essay has on your SAT Writing score, see the SAT Essay section later in this book.

What if I get the same answer multiple times in a row?

Students sometimes ask whether they should change answers if the same answer choice comes up multiple times in a row.
The answer is **NO**.

Never let your answer sheet affect how you answer a question.

The SAT often repeats the same answer choice multiple times in a row, so relying on your answer sheet for clues about what the next answer will be is simply asking for trouble.

For example, take a look at this answer sheet from an *actual* SAT:

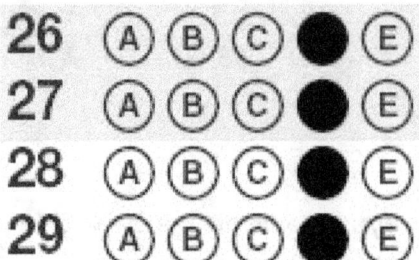

See that? Four answer choices in a row are (D).
In fact, questions 24 & 31 were also (D)!

The SAT often repeats the same answer choice multiple times, so you should never try to game your answers based on what your answer sheet looks like.

SAT Basics

**Ignore answer patterns.
Instead circle the numbers of any questions
you are not sure of in your test booklet.**

Then, if you have time left over, go back and review those circled questions again.

Remember!
If you decide to change an answer choice, always be sure you have a reason other than how it appears on your answer sheet.

Are all questions the same difficulty?

No.

**The SAT ranks questions
on a five point scale by difficulty:**

**1 - easiest
2 - easy
3 - medium
4 - hard
5 - hardest**

Most SAT question types tend to appear in order of difficulty, with the easiest coming at the beginning and the hardest questions at the end. As we'll see, knowing which questions are easy, medium and hard is very important in helping you plan your strategy for each section.

Does every question count the same?

Yes!

**Regardless of difficulty,
every question counts ONE point.**

Tip:
If you get stuck on a hard question, skip it and come back to it.
Don't waste time pondering hard questions when there are easier questions that are worth just as much.

What are Percentiles?

**Percentiles tell you the percentage of
SAT test takers you performed better than.**

For example, if your overall SAT Scaled Score is in the 75th percentile, you performed better than approximately 75 percent of students who have taken the SAT.

Although each test and subject varies, SAT scaled scores for each subject generally break down into the following percentiles:

SAT Score	SAT Percentile
800	99th
700	95th
600	75th
500	45th
400	15th
300	3rd
200	1st

Tip:
Notice that there is a 60 percentile jump between 400 and 600.
In this range, improving your SAT score by even just a few points can have a big impact on your overall percentile ranking.

Why should I study for the SAT?

Finding extra time to study for the SAT can really put a crimp in your schedule. Yet in terms of your college application, the extra time spent studying for the SAT can pay big dividends.

**In terms of your college application,
the SAT is worth as much as
ALL of your GRADES from ALL of your CLASSES!**

Most colleges give the same weight to your SAT scores as they give to your entire grade point average. When you look at it this way, studying for the SAT suddenly seems like a pretty smart use of your time.

SAT Unlocked II

Introduction to SAT Reading

SAT Critical Reading (CR) consists of 67 total questions tested in three sections.

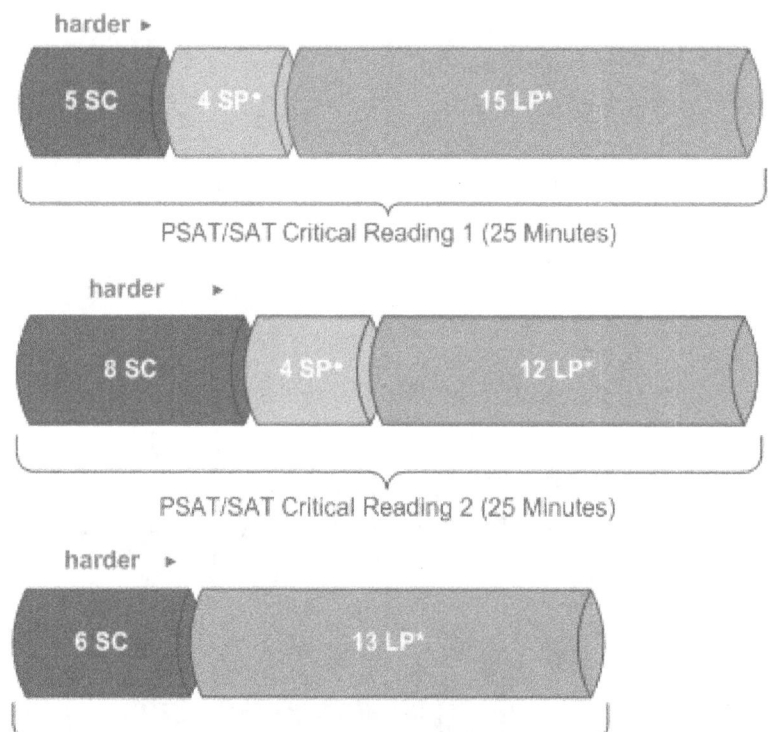

Critical Reading (CR) tests THREE types of questions:

✓ **19 Sentence Completions (SC)**
A sentence with one or two words missing. Choose which missing word(s) that best complete the sentence.

✓ **8 Short Passage (SP)***
One paragraph passages to read and interpret.
Questions can also compare two separate short passages.

✓ **40 Long Passage (LP)***
A multiple paragraph passage to read and interpret.
Questions can also compare two separate long passages.

** Passage Reading questions do **NOT** appear in order of difficulty.*

SAT Reading

Tip:
Always make sure to finish the entire Critical Reading section so you can answer easy questions that may be at the end of the section. *The big temptation on the Critical Reading section is to spend too much time on the shorter Sentence Completion questions at the beginning of the section, and not leave enough time for the Passage Reading questions, which take more time to read but can include easier questions near the end of the section.*

How to Finish a Critical Reading Section

The way to be sure to finish each Critical Reading section is to limit the amount of time you spend on the earlier, shorter questions.

Try to spend about:

✓ **30 seconds on each Sentence Completion question**

✓ **60 seconds on each Short Passage question (includes passage)**

Tip:
By limiting the amount of time you spend on the shorter questions, you buy time for the Long Passage questions. *This way you are far more likely to complete each Critical Reading section and score more points.*

Alternatively, leave Sentence Completions for last

If you are still having trouble finishing: start with Passage Reading questions FIRST, and end with Sentence Completions LAST.

By saving Sentence Completion questions for last, you finish up with shorter questions at the end when you are running out of time. Remember also that Sentence Completions DO appear in order of difficulty, so if you run out of time, you can at least be sure that the questions you don't get to will be hard questions anyway.

Now let's take a closer look at the Critical Reading question types.

Sentence Completions

Sentence Completions omit either one or two words from a sentence, and ask you to choose from a list of possible word choices to complete the sentence.

Remember!
Sentence Completions appear in order of difficulty from easiest at the beginning to hardest at the end. *You always know where the hardest of these questions lie – at the end of each Sentence Completion question group.*

How much time should I spend on vocabulary?

While a few reading passage questions are vocabulary based, the bulk of questions that test your vocabulary on the SAT are Sentence Completions. Especially with more difficult Sentence Completions, a well developed vocabulary will certainly help you on these questions. However...

Studying a lot of raw vocabulary words is probably not the best use of your limited SAT study time.

Remember that Sentence Completions make up only 19 out of 67 Critical Reading questions. Moreover, less than half of all Sentence Completions contain answer choices with difficult vocabulary words you may not already know.

For these reasons, spending hours memorizing vocabulary words is not an efficient use of your time. Better to spend that time practicing actual questions!

Important Tip!
In the back of this book are vocabulary worksheets and a list of definitions for over 1000 OSSG words. While practicing Critical Reading questions, use the worksheets to write down any words that you do not know. When you are finished answering the questions, look up and write down the definitions of the words so you remember them.

SAT Reading

When should I skip Sentence Completion questions?

**If you DO NOT KNOW the answer
and/or CANNOT confidently
ELIMINATE ANY answer choices,
SKIP the Sentence Completion question.**

Hard sentence completion questions can be some of the most difficult questions on the entire SAT. The sentences are difficult to interpret and the vocabulary answer choices are even tougher.

What's more, hard Sentence Completion questions often include trick answers (known as 'Attractors') that sound like they could be the correct answer, but in reality mean something completely different than the word the question is looking for.

Remember, is far more important to finish the Critical Reading section than to waste too much time trying to answer some of the hardest questions on the whole test – especially if you can't eliminate any incorrect words.

__Beware!__
__Hard Sentence Completion questions can really mess up your Reading score.__ The temptation is to waste valuable time pondering vocabulary words you don't know, only then to desperately guess. When you do this, not only are you likely to answer incorrectly, but also, and more importantly, you lose precious time you need to answer later Passage Reading questions that make up the bulk of Critical Reading points.

__If you can't eliminate any Sentence Completion answers, it's almost always better simply to skip the question, rather than waste time you will need to answer easier Passage Reading questions later in the section.__

Strategies for Sentence Completions

Now let's take a look at how to approach Sentence Completion questions. First, we'll look at single-blank questions and then tackle double-blanks.

Look for Key Words

The SAT is very particular about the words used in each question.

Look for KEY WORDS in the QUESTION that give you an idea of what the answer should be.

The answer choices always relate to key words in the question. It is up to you to spot the key words and see the relationship.

Tip:
When practicing, cover the answer choices and try to guess, in your own words, what the correct answer should be.

Sentence Completions Tutorial 1 (Key Words):

Turn to page 402.

For the question below, cover the answer choices and try to guess what the correct word should be.

Then uncover the answer choices and answer the question.

No.	Page	Q.	Diff.	Type	Test	Sect.	Answer
1	402	1	E	MC	1	5	

SAT Reading

Sentence Completions Tutorial 1 (Key Words) Answer:

No.	A	Answer Word	Key Word(s)
1	C	hospitality	'eagerly welcomes anyone', 'home'

Tip:
Key words often follow a comma (,), colon (:) or semi-colon (;).

Play Positive/Negative

Even if you can't figure out exactly what the word is, you can often still figure out whether the word is POSITIVE or NEGATIVE.

This is often a useful strategy that helps you can quickly eliminate incorrect answer choices not similarly positive or negative.

Sentence Completions Tutorial 2 (Positive/Negative):
For the question below, cover over the answer choices and decide whether the correct answer should be a positive or negative word. Then answer the question.

No.	Page	Q.	Diff.	Type	Test	Sect.	Answer
1	402	2	E	MC	1	5	
2	402	3	E	MC	1	5	
3	402	7	H	MC	1	5	
4	402	8	H	MC	1	5	

Remember!
*For **harder Sentence Completion questions** near the end of the set, it's **often better simply to skip the question** if you either don't know the answer or can't eliminate any of the answer choices.*

Sentence Completions Tutorial 2 (Positive/Negative) Answers:

No.	A	Answer Word	Positive/Negative	Key Word(s)
1	B	derailed	negative	'disappointed'
2	C	stimulus	positive	'increase brain activity' 'promote learning'
3	D	supercilious	negative	'haughty'
4	C	perfidy	negative	'synonymous with disloyalty'

Double-Blank Sentence Completion Questions

To answer most double-blank Sentence Completions:

<u>First</u>, cross out as many words as you can on ONE SIDE of the answer choices.

<u>Next</u>, cross out words on the OTHER SIDE from the remaining answer choices.

By crossing out words that are obviously incorrect on one side of the answer choices, it is much easier to narrow down the final answer from the remaining choices on the other side.

Tip:
BOTH words must fit WELL.
No matter how well one word may fit as an answer,
both words must fit <u>well</u> to properly complete the sentence.

Sentence Completions Tutorial 3 (Double-Blank):

For the question below, answer by eliminating incorrect answers for one blank and then the other.

No.	Page	Q.	Diff.	Type	Test	Sect.	Answer
1	402	5	M	MC	1	5	

SAT Reading

Sentence Completions Tutorial (Double-Blank) Answers

No.	A	Answer Words	Pos./Neg.	Key Word(s)
1	D	derivative/inept	neg./neg.	'taken from another artist' /'poorly executed'

Tip:
Clues appear in the same order as the blanks.
In the question above, the clue 'taken from another artist', appears before 'poorly executed', which means 'taken from another artist' is the clue for the first blank and 'poorly executed' is the clue for the second blank.

Sometimes, the two words in the correct Sentence Completion answer have to WORK TOGETHER in the sentence.

For these questions, be sure to read the question carefully for clues as to how the answers fit.

Sentence Completions Tutorial 4 (Double-Blank):
Answer each question below.

No.	Page	Q.	Diff.	Type	Test	Sect.	Answer
2	402	4	M	MC	1	5	
3	402	6	M	MC	1	5	

Sentence Completions Tutorial (Double-Blank) Answers

No.	A	Answer Words	Pos./Neg.	Keyword(s)
2	D	negotiate/ concessions	neg./neg.	'ambassador' 'diplomacy'
3	B	transformed/ viable	pos/pos.	'inexpensive' 'nascent'

Sentence Completion Sets

Page	Questions	Test	Section	Answers Page
390	1 - 5	1	2	432
402	1 - 8	1	5	432
425	1 - 6	1	9	432
458	1 - 8	2	4	494
475	1 - 5	2	7	494
487	1 - 6	2	9	494
520	1 - 8	3	4	556
537	1 - 5	3	7	556
549	1 - 6	3	9	556
576	1 - 8	4	2	618
587	1 - 5	4	5	618
605	1 - 6	4	8	618
644	1 - 5	5	3	680
662	1 - 8	5	7	680
672	1 - 6	5	9	680
706	1 - 5	6	3	742
724	1 - 8	6	7	742
735	1 - 6	6	9	742
762	1 - 5	7	2	804
780	1 - 8	7	5	804
791	1 - 6	7	8	804
824	1 - 5	8	2	866
842	1 - 8	8	5	866
853	1 - 6	8	8	866
898	1 - 8	9	4	928
909	1 - 5	9	6	928
920	1 - 6	9	9	928
960	1 - 8	10	4	990
971	1 - 5	10	6	990
982	1 - 6	10	9	990

SAT Reading

Passage Reading

For many students, Passage Reading questions can initially seem like the some of the most difficult questions on the SAT, but once you have a strategy for approaching Passage Reading, these questions can often be quite easy.

Passage Reading Strategy

To get a handle on Passage Reading, you need a strategy you can apply to both the passages and the questions.

Part 1: Reading the Passage

Step 1: Mark line numbers and circle key words.

Quickly scan questions for line numbers (shown in parentheses) and mark these with a check or bracket in the margin next to the appropriate line(s) in passage. This way, you know where to focus your greatest attention when reading the passage.

Also, line number questions often ask about "key words" (shown in quotes in the question). If you see a "key word" in quotes in a line number question, circle that same word in the passage.

 Passage Reading Tutorial 1:

*Turn to OSSG **page 477**.*

Quickly scan questions 10-15.

In the passage, mark question line numbers in the margin and circle the key words.

Page	Q.	Line nos.	Key Words
477	10	-	-
477	11	11-14	("in size…so")
477	12	22-31	-
478	13	28-30	("There would…dragonflies")
478	14	32-34	("In 1962…information")
478	15	43-44	("The answer…Sun")

Step 2: Read the passage, <u>underlining</u> the one or two most important sentences in each paragraph.

Don't worry about absorbing every detail of the passage. Just read each paragraph quickly and underline the most important parts.

Tip:
Even if you are not sure what is truly important, always be sure to underline SOMETHING in each paragraph. Underlining keeps you focused on the passage as well as marks information that can help you answer the questions. Most importantly, the more you practice underlining, the better your reading comprehension will become and, believe it or not, the faster you will actually read.

Passage Reading Tutorial 2:

Read the passage on OSSG page 477.

As you read, **underline** *the one or two most important sentences in each paragraph.*

SAT Reading

Page	Para-graph	Important Sentence(s)
477	1	Despite that proximity, for a long time it was generally termed "the planet of mystery."
477	2	In size and mass, Venus is almost the equal of Earth, and its gravitational field is only slightly weaker than ours, so that logically it might be expected to have the same kind of atmosphere – but this is emphatically not so.
477	3	According to one theory, the clouds contained a great deal of water. Another intriguing theory made Venus very similar to the Earth of over 200 million years ago.
477	4	In 1962, the American probe Mariner 2 bypassed Venus at less than 22,000 miles and gave us our first reliable information. The scene – a rocky scorched landscape – could hardly be more hostile.
477	5	Why is Venus so unlike Earth? The answer can only lie in its lesser distance from the Sun.

Tip:
Before answering the questions, quickly re-read your underlining to give yourself a 'mental map' of the passage.
This quick and easy strategy helps you sum up the passage and put the various parts in context.

Part 2: Answer the Questions

Step 3: Read the question CAREFULLY.

The secret to passage reading is not so much about understanding the passage as it is about understanding the *questions*.

Step 4: Cross out three INCORRECT answers.

IMPORTANT!
Nearly every Passage Reading question includes:

✓ **Three INCORRECT answers.**
  Answers that are clearly wrong.

✓ **One ATTRACTOR answer.**
  An answer that can appear correct, but is not.

✓ **One CORRECT answer.**
  Score.

Get rid of the clearly wrong answers first, so you can isolate the most likely answers and compare them side-by-side.

SAT Reading

Passage Reading Tutorial Note:
Don't worry if you cross out a different combination of incorrect answers than the ones listed here. That's OK as long as you don't cross out the correct answer.

 Passage Reading Tutorial 3:

On OSSG **page 477**, carefully **read question 10**.

Then **cross out three answers** that are clearly <u>incorrect</u>.

Page	Q.	Choices	Answer?
477	10	(~~A~~)	<u>Cross out:</u> While the passage does mention a lack of reliable information prior to 1962, criticizing that prior lack is not the overall point of the passage.
477	10	(~~B~~)	<u>Cross out:</u> The passage does not 'speculate' about life on another world. On the contrary, it attempts to <u>prove</u> that life does NOT exist on that world.
477	10	(~~C~~)	<u>Cross out:</u> Emotional terms like 'lament' are usually signs of an incorrect answer.
477	10	(D)	<u>Keep.</u>
477	10	(E)	<u>Keep.</u>

 <u>Tip:</u>
For questions that ask about the 'primary purpose' look for an answer that sums up the entire passage as whole. Answers that only talk about <u>part</u> of the passage or that include <u>emotional</u> terms are NOT correct.

Step 5:   IMPORTANT! Re-read the question.

Before deciding which is the attractor answer and which is the correct answer, always re-read the question to be sure exactly what it is asking. Most answers simply complete the sentence started by question. Re-reading the question helps you figure out which answer better finishes the sentence.

**Step 6:   Cross out the ATTRACTOR answer
           to find the CORRECT answer.**

The ATTRACTOR (incorrect) answer will look like the correct answer, but there will be something about it that isn't quite right. Once you spot the problem, you know the other answer is CORRECT one.

SAT Reading

Primary purpose questions focus on the 'big picture'

Look for the statement that best describes the passage as a <u>whole</u>.

Passage Reading Tutorial 4:
On OSSG page 477, carefully <u>re-read</u> question 10.
Then find the attractor answer (the INCORRECT answer)
and choose the other answer (the CORRECT answer).

Page	Q.	Choices	Answer?
477	10	(A)	<u>Cross out:</u> While the passage does mention a lack of reliable information prior to 1962, criticizing that prior lack is not the overall point of the passage.
477	10	(B)	<u>Cross out:</u> The passage does not 'speculate' about life on another world. On the contrary, it attempts to <u>prove</u> that life does NOT exist on that world.
477	10	(C)	<u>Cross out:</u> Emotional terms like 'lament' are usually incorrect answers.
477	10	(D)	<u>ATTRACTOR:</u> While the passage does, "illustrate the principles of planetary research", the answer does not refer to anything specific in the passage and so is <u>too general</u>.
477	10	(E)	**CORRECT:** "Attempts to understand the astronomical enigma (or mystery)" of life on Venus is specifically discussed throughout the passage and is therefore its primary purpose.

<u>Tip:</u>
For primary purpose questions, the attractor answer will often be <u>too general</u>, *that is, talk about the basic topic but not refer to anything specific within the passage.*

SAT Unlocked II

Look for 'clunkers' in the incorrect answers.

An attractor answer often has a 'clunker' – a word or phrase that just doesn't sound right. Once you spot a clunker, you know the answer is INCORRECT.

Passage Reading Tutorial 5:
On OSSG **page 477**, **answer question 11**, following the strategy outlined above.

Page	Q.	Choices	Answer?
477	11	(A)	**CORRECT:** The sentence says that, "logically it might be expected to have the same kind of atmosphere" ('plausible supposition') but concludes this supposition is, "emphatically not so" ('dismiss').
477	11	(B)	Cross out: The statement does not 'mock' the idea of Venus having a similar atmosphere to Earth. It just denies that Venus does. Also, nowhere does the passage state the idea is an 'outrageous claim'.
477	11	(C)	Cross out: The statement does not 'bolster' (support) Venus having a similar atmosphere to Earth. Also, nowhere does the passage say the idea is an 'accepted opinion'.
477	11	(D)	Cross out: No experiment is yet mentioned in the passage.
477	11	(E)	ATTRACTOR: Although, the statement could be said to undermine the Venus atmosphere hypothesis, there is nothing here that suggests the statement is *'controversial'* (clunker).

SAT Reading

**Correct answers best describe
the 'plain meaning' of the passage text.**

Don't look for subtleties or 'hidden meanings'. The correct answer will almost always be one that has the most <u>straightforward</u> description of the text.

Passage Reading Tutorial 6:

*On OSSG **page 477**, **answer question 12**, following the strategy outlined above.*

Page	Q.	Choices	Answer?
477	12	(A)	<u>Cross out:</u> No 'evidence' is presented in the paragraph – only opinions.
477	12	(B)	<u>ATTRACTOR:</u> This paragraph merely describes two misconceptions, but does not seek to *'challenge'* (clunker) these theories.
477	12	(C)	<u>Cross out:</u> The paragraph simply describes <u>two</u> hypotheses (not a 'particular' one) and does not show why either is 'misguided'.
477	12	(D)	<u>Cross out:</u> The paragraph talks about various scientific hypotheses, not about romanticizing 'throughout history'.
477	12	(E)	**<u>CORRECT:</u> The simplest, most straightforward description of the paragraph.**

Where a question includes an ALL CAPS word like 'NOT' or 'EXCEPT', the <u>wrong</u> answer is the <u>right</u> one.

'ALL CAPS questions' include four answer choices that are factually correct and one that is <u>not</u> factually correct. For this type of question, the answer that is NOT factually correct is the CORRECT answer. In other words, the wrong answer is the right one.

Incorrect answers often include EXTREME (100%) words.

Words like always, never, solely, none, every, etc. are usually signs of an incorrect answer.

Passage Reading Tutorial 7:
On OSSG page 478, answer question 13.

Page	Q.	Choices	Answer?
478	13	(A)	<u>Cross out:</u> This part of the passage describes a warm and humid environment.
478	13	(B)	**ATTRACTOR (CORRECT!):** 'Pure' is an extreme (100%) word that points to a factually incorrect attractor answer, yet because the questions asks what 'could NOT be true', here the attractor answer is the correct answer.
478	13	(C)	<u>Cross out:</u> The possibility of evolution on Venus is discussed in this part of the passage.
478	13	(D)	<u>Cross out:</u> Since this part of the passage describes vegetation, light for photosynthesis is presumably present.'.
478	13	(E)	<u>Cross out:</u> Dragonflies are able to fly with ease.

SAT Reading

**The passage 'SUGGESTS' or 'IMPLIES'
and you, the reader, 'INFER'
something about the text that is
NOT SPECIFICALLY STATED.**

Passage Reading Tutorial 8:

On OSSG page 478, answer question 14.

Page	Q.	Choices	Answer?
478	14	~~(A)~~	Cross out: The sentence does not suggest the scientists' emotional reaction ('surprise').
478	14	(B)	**CORRECT: 'Our first reliable information' suggests the information that came before was untrustworthy.**
478	14	~~(C)~~	Cross out: Scientist did not 'rediscover' the records. Mariner 2 provided new information.
478	14	(D)	ATTRACTOR: 'Completely' is an extreme (100%) word and is therefore not the right answer. Also, nothing in the sentence suggests what theory probe's findings confirmed, let alone that the theory was new.
478	14	~~(E)~~	Cross out: The sentence does not suggest what, if anything, the data confirmed, only that the data was reliable.

Tip:
Even where a question asks what in the passage 'suggests',' implies', or can be 'inferred', still look for the plainest meaning, that is, the most basic, straightforward interpretation.

For questions that ask about 'tone' or 'attitude', avoid emotional and/or extreme answers.

Passage Reading Tutorial 9:

On OSSG page 478, answer question 15.

Page	Q.	Choices	Answer?
478	15	(A)	Cross out: Emotional term 'regretful' not the correct answer.
478	15	(B)	ATTRACTOR (opposite): The author is not 'guarded' (defensive) about his conclusion about Venus' atmosphere. He is confident.
478	15	(C)	Cross out: The author is not 'skeptical' since he does not question his own conclusion.
478	15	(D)	**CORRECT:** **"The answer can only lie" is a decisive statement.**
478	15	(E)	Cross out: Emotional term 'amused' not the correct answer.

Tip:
Attractor answers are often the OPPOSITE of the correct answer.

Long Single Passage Sets

Page Start	Questions	Test	Section	Answers Page
392	10 - 15	1	2	432
404	13 - 24	1	5	432
426	7 - 19	1	9	432
460	13 - 25	2	4	494
477	10 – 24	2	7	494
522	13 - 24	3	4	556
539	10 - 14	3	7	556
550	7 - 19	3	9	556
589	10 - 24	4	5	618
606	7 - 19	4	8	618
646	10 - 24	5	3	680
673	7 - 19	5	9	680
708	10 - 24	6	3	742
734	7 - 19	6	9	742
764	10 - 24	7	2	804
792	7 - 19	7	8	804
826	10 - 24	8	2	866
854	7 - 19	8	8	866
900	13 - 24	9	4	928
911	10 - 24	9	6	928
962	13 - 24	10	4	990
973	10 - 24	10	6	990

Answering Double Passage Sets

SAT Critical Reading always includes one long double passage question set somewhere on the test.

It is tough enough to interpret questions for a single passage. It is even harder when the question asks about two passages at the same time. When reading two passages back to back, students often get confused about what was said in each passage.

A better strategy is to break up the passages into manageable pieces.

To answer double passage questions:

1. **Read Passage 1**
2. **Answer questions for Passage 1**

3. **Read Passage 2**
4. **Answer questions for Passage 2**

5. **Answer questions asking about both passages.**

This strategy helps you to break down the passage by turning double passages into two single passages. Once you've read and analyzed each passage individually, it is a lot easier to answer questions that ask about both passages.

SAT Reading

Did you know?
All Passage 1 questions come before all Passage 2 questions.
*The SAT helps you out by always asking passage reading questions in order of line number. Because line numbers continue from one passage to the next, the Passage 1 questions always come before Passage 2 questions. That means **once you hit the Passage 2 questions you know you are done with Passage 1 questions.***

Skip questions that ask about both passages, and come back to them after you answer all of the single passage questions.

The SAT will sometimes place questions that ask about both passages at the beginning or in the middle of the question set. Leave these alone until you have answered the single passage questions.

Tip:
Circle the numbers of questions that ask about both passages, *so you don't forget to come back to them after you've answered the single passage questions.*

SAT Unlocked II

 Double Passage Reading Tutorial 1:

*Turn to OSSG **pages 921-23**.*

*Quickly **scan** the questions; **mark question line numbers** in the margins, and **circle the key words** for each passage.*

Circle the numbers of the questions that ask about BOTH passages, so you remember to save these for last.

Passage 1 Questions			
Page	Q.	line #	key word(s)
922	9	14	"gamble"
922	11	24 - 26	-
922	12	32	"fear"
922	13	-	-
Passage 2 Questions			
Page	Q.	line #	key word(s)
922	15	50	"pretty decent"
923	16	59 - 60	-
923	17	61	"marketing virus"
923	18	67 - 77	-
Double Passage Questions			
Page	Q.	line #	key word(s)
922	7	6 / 57	"great artists"/ "The Grateful Dead"
922	8	-	-
922	10	17 - 20	-
922	14	59 - 60	-
922	19	26 - 29	-

SAT Reading

Always read the italicized introduction and any asterisked (*) notes.

The introduction and notes are very helpful in giving context to the passage and filling in extra details that help you answer the questions more easily.

 Double Passage Reading Tutorial 2:

Read Passage 1 on OSSG page 921.

*As you read, **underline** one or two most important sentences in each paragraph.*

		Passage 1
Page	**Para-graph**	**Important Sentence(s)**
921	1	Over the next 50 years, Jerry and I composed many now-familiar songs like "Hound Dog," "Jailhouse Rock," and "Love Potion No. 9," in many different musical styles, from rhythm and blues to jazz and rock.
921	2	Each time a Napster user downloads a copy of a song that I have composed, I am deprived of the royalty that my work should have earned me.
921	3	Napster and companies like it are threatening not only my retirement, but the future of music itself.

SAT Unlocked II

> For line number questions,
> read a few lines above and below
> the line numbered portion of text
> to understand its context.

Reading a few lines above and below is often the key to getting the correct answer, because the information you need from the passage is usually located somewhere nearby (but not within) the text cited by line number.

 Double Passage Reading Tutorial 3:

On OSSG **page 922**, answer **question 9**.

Page	Q.	Choices	Answer?
922	9	(A)	**CORRECT:** The text just below line 14 explains the 'gamble': "A songwriter makes nothing until a song is marketed…, and unless that record of the song sells, a songwriter gets nothing for it". The 'gamble' is therefore <u>financial</u>.
922	9	(B)	ATTRACTOR: Reading only the line, one might assume the songwriter would be describing something 'artistic', but reading *in context* shows he is describing a financial gamble.
922	9	(C)	Cross out: There is nothing in the passage to suggest a 'legal' gamble.
922	9	(D)	Cross out: There is nothing in the passage to suggest a 'technological' gamble.
922	9	(E)	Cross out: There is nothing in the passage to suggest a 'psychological' gamble.

SAT Reading

 Double Passage Reading Tutorial 4:

On OSSG **page 922**, answer **question 11**.

Page	Q.	Choices	Answer?
922	11	(A)	Cross out: Nothing suggests the author is making an 'historical' argument.
922	11	(B)	Cross out: Nothing suggests the author is making a 'political' argument.
922	11	(C)	**CORRECT: The author's concern with how to 'make a living' presents a 'pragmatic' (practical) argument.**
922	11	(D)	ATTRACTOR: An 'idealistic' argument is the opposite of a 'pragmatic' one.
922	11	(E)	Cross out: Nothing suggests the author is being 'facetious' (sarcastic).

 Tip:
Pragmatic' means 'practical'.
The word 'pragmatic' is an SAT favorite and is often the correct answer on passage reading questions.

Look for themes in the question set.

SAT question sets often ask about the same theme over and over again in different ways.

Double Passage Reading Tutorial 5:

*On OSSG **page 922**, answer **question 12**.*

Page	Q.	Choices	Answer?
922	12	(A)	Cross out: Devotion to the craft of songwriting is not the issue here. Whether young songwriters can support themselves is.
922	12	(B)	Cross out: The passage does not discuss the popularity of young songwriters, nor does it say they are 'adolescent'.
922	12	(C)	ATTRACTOR: 'Increasing demand for music' (clunker) is not what the author argues will cause royalties to decline. Downloading songs for free is.
922	12	(D)	**CORRECT:** **The answer repeats the theme of previous Passage 1 questions that focus on the financial implications for songwriters of downloading.**
922	12	(E)	Cross out: The author does not fear 'music' will be rendered obsolete; just that songwriters will not be able to earn enough money to write the music.

SAT Reading

 Double Passage Reading Tutorial 6:

On OSSG **page 922**, answer **question 13**.

Page	Q.	Choices	Answer?
922	13	(A)	<u>Cross out:</u> The author does not 'challenge' a traditional 'ethical stance'. He supports a traditional financial arrangement.
922	13	(B)	<u>Cross out:</u> The passage does not describe the technological process of downloading – just the financial implications.
922	13	(C)	<u>Cross out:</u> The passage does not claim that downloading music is an 'adolescent impulse.'
922	13	(D)	<u>ATTRACTOR:</u> 'Radical' (clunker) is an extreme word that points to an incorrect answer.
922	13	(E)	**<u>CORRECT:</u> The author is arguing against the practice of downloading music.**

 Remember:
Primary purpose questions focus on the 'big picture'.
Look for the statement that best describes the passage as a <u>whole</u>.

Now that we've read and answered the questions for Passage 1, let's do the same for Passage 2.

 Double Passage Reading Tutorial 7:

Read Passage 2 on OSSG page 921.

*As you read, **underline** one or two most important sentences in each paragraph.*

Passage 2		
Page	Para-graph	Important Sentence(s)
921	1	. . . how will we be assured payment for the work we do with our minds?
921	2	Most white-collar jobs already consist of mind work.
921	3	The Grateful Dead, for whom I once wrote songs, learned by accident that if we let fans tape concerts and freely reproduce those tapes -...- the tapes would become a marketing virus that would spawn enough Deadheads to fill any stadium in America.
921	4	. . . the more a program is pirated, the more likely it is to become a standard.
921	5	All these examples point to the same conclusion: noncommercial distribution of information increases the value of information. For ideas, fame is fortune.

SAT Reading

 Double Passage Reading Tutorial 8:

*On OSSG **page 922**, answer **question 15**.*

Page	Q.	Choices	Answer?
922	15	(A)	<u>Cross out:</u> 'Solemn' (serious, sad) is an emotional term unlikely to be correct.
922	15	(B)	<u>Cross out:</u> 'Cheerful' is an emotional term unlikely to be correct.
922	15	(C)	**<u>CORRECT:</u> The author is "ironically understating" (falsely downplaying) the accomplishments of great artists in order to make the point that art survived and thrived in the 5000 years prior to the establishment of copyright law.**
922	15	(D)	<u>Cross out:</u> The author does not doubt the work of the artists mentioned.
922	15	(E)	<u>ATTRACTOR:</u> By itself, the phrase 'pretty decent' would seem to describe reluctant approval, but the <u>context</u> of the sentence shows a different meaning.

Double Passage Reading Tutorial 9:

On OSSG **page 922**, answer **question 16**.

Page	Q.	Choices	Answer?
923	16	(A)	<u>Cross out:</u> 'Ebullient' (bubbly) is an emotional term unlikely to be correct.
923	16	(B)	<u>Cross out:</u> 'Somber' (sad) is an emotional term unlikely to be correct.
923	16	(C)	ATTRACTOR: The author is not being 'quizzical' (questioning) the language of those who oppose downloading.
923	16	(D)	<u>Cross out:</u> 'Irate' (very angry) is an emotional term unlikely to be correct.
923	16	(E)	**<u>CORRECT:</u>** **The author is being 'satirical' by <u>making fun of</u> the language used by those who oppose downloading.**

<u>Tip:</u>
Irony and satire are SAT favorites and often correct answers on passage reading questions.

SAT Reading

> **Authors take stands.**
> On the SAT, neutral or 'ambivalent' (undecided) attitudes are usually signs of an incorrect answer.

 Double Passage Reading Tutorial 10:

*On OSSG **page 922**, answer **question 17**.*

Page	Q.	Choices	Answer?
923	17	(A)	**CORRECT:** The author shows a positive attitude when he says the marketing virus "would spawn enough Deadheads to fill any stadium in America" because the virus made the band more popular.
923	17	(B)	Cross out: While positive, there is nothing in the passage that talks about the sophistication of the band's worldview.
923	17	(C)	ATTRACTOR: A neutral attitude is usually a sign of an incorrect answer. Also, the views of music critics are not discussed in the passage.
923	17	(D)	Cross out: The author's attitude toward the marketing virus is positive. Also, the passage is not concerned with tension between monetary gain and artistic integrity.
923	17	(E)	Cross out: The author's attitude toward the marketing virus is positive. Also, the author does not appear to consider 'too many fans' to be a problem.

Double Passage Reading Tutorial 11:

On OSSG **page 922**, answer **question 18**.

Page	Q.	Choices	Answer?
923	18	(A)	Cross out: 'The vast influence of technology in contemporary life' is too general and does not relate specifically to the author's argument about downloading.
923	18	(B)	**CORRECT: The author cites the experiences of VCR's, CD's and software to bolster (support) his primary argument that downloading helps sales.**
923	18	(C)	Cross out: The author does not relate anything personal ('I') about his own experience with these technologies.
923	18	(D)	ATTRACTOR: Just because the author argues for downloading does not mean he wishes to discourage the purchasing of CD's and software.
923	18	(E)	Cross out: 'The wide scope of the entertainment industry today' is too general and does not relate specifically to the author's argument about downloading.

SAT Reading

Double Passage Questions

Once you've answered questions for Passage 1 and Passage 2, it is then time to go back and answer the questions about both passages.

For questions that ask about BOTH passages, make sure the correct answer applies equally well to each author's point of view.

Double Passage Reading Tutorial 12:

*On OSSG **page 922**, answer **question 7**.*

Page	Q.	Choices	Answer?
922	7	(A)	Cross out: The authors mention the artists because they both wrote songs for these artists, not because they want to illustrate their ranges of musical taste.
922	7	(B)	Cross out: The authors mention the artists because they both wrote songs for these artists, not because they want to illustrate their appreciation of the musicians' talent.
922	7	(C)	Cross out: The authors mention the artists because they both wrote songs for these artists, not because they want to illustrate their appreciation of the musicians' talent.
922	7	(D)	ATTRACTOR: The author of Passage 2 does use irony, but the author of Passage 1 does not. Also, neither author discuses the quality of the music they wrote.
922	7	(E)	**CORRECT: The songwriters both mention the musicians they wrote for to show their experience with the music business.**

Double Passage Reading Tutorial 13:

On OSSG **page 922**, answer **question 8**.

Page	Q.	Choices	Answer?
922	8	(A)	<u>Cross out:</u> The Passage 2 author would likely agree, the Passage 1 author would likely not.
922	8	(B)	<u>ATTRACTOR:</u> 'Solely' is an extreme word (clunker) that likely points to an incorrect answer.
922	8	(C)	<u>Cross out:</u> The Passage 1 author would likely agree, the Passage 2 author would likely not.
922	8	(D)	**<u>CORRECT:</u>** While the authors disagree about whether downloading will increase or decrease sales, they both agree about the need for commercial sales to sustain the professional songwriter.
922	8	(E)	<u>Cross out:</u> Both authors would likely disagree with this statement.

Double Passage Reading Tutorial 14:

*On OSSG **page 922**, answer **question 10**.*

Page	Q.	Choices	Answer?
922	10	(A)	**CORRECT:** The Passage 2 author would probably contend the statement is 'shortsighted', since he believes downloading increases sales.
922	10	(B)	ATTRACTOR: The Passage 2 author would probably NOT contend the statement is 'cynical', since he too believes artists should be compensated.
922	10	(C)	Cross out: The Passage 2 author would probably NOT contend the statement is 'unreasonable', since he does not argue that music buyers would be forced to purchase music they don't like.
922	10	(D)	Cross out: The Passage 2 author would probably NOT contend the statement is 'discouraging', since he does not argue that downloading drives a wedge between technical innovation and artistic creation. Indeed, he probably believes quite the opposite.
922	10	(E)	Cross out: The Passage 2 author would probably NOT contend the statement is 'patronizing' (condescending), since 'the function of the Internet' is not discussed in either passage.

For questions about text in quotation marks (" "), interpret the text in an ironic or other non-typical way.

Double Passage Reading Tutorial 15:

On OSSG **page 922**, answer **question 14**.

Page	Q.	Choices	Answer?
922	14	(A)	<u>Cross out:</u> Neither passage discusses 'musical theories'.
922	14	(B)	<u>Cross out:</u> 'Respected authorities' are not mentioned in the quoted terms.
922	14	(C)	<u>ATTRACTOR:</u> The author of Passage 2 may mock the practices of the music industry, but the author of Passage 1 does not. On the contrary, he defends the practices. Also, 'mock' (clunker) is too extreme to be the correct answer.
922	14	(D)	<u>**CORRECT:**</u> **Both authors use the quotation marks to show that the terms are not 'apt' (appropriate) for the circumstances in which they are used.**
922	14	(E)	<u>Cross out:</u> The phrases are not unusual. They are just used in a different way.

Double Passage Reading Tutorial 16:

*On OSSG **page 923**, answer **question 19**.*

Page	Q.	Choices	Answer?
922	19	(A)	Cross out: The Passage 2 author does not argue that downloading provides 'artistic freedom'.
922	19	(B)	Cross out: The Passage 2 author does not argue that downloading creates 'musical elitism'.
922	19	(C)	**CORRECT:** **The author of Passage 2 argues throughout that downloading makes the artist more famous (or 'renown').**
922	19	(D)	ATTRACTOR: 'Financial injury' is the opposite of what the Passage 2 author argues would happen if users download.
922	19	(E)	Cross out: The Passage 2 author does not argue downloading increases 'technical knowledge'.

More Long Double Passage Sets

Page Start	Questions	Test	Section	Answers Page
394	16 - 24	1	2	432
488	7 - 18	2	9	494
541	15 - 24	3	7	556
578	13 - 24	4	2	618
664	13 - 24	5	7	680
726	13 - 24	6	7	742
782	13 - 24	7	5	804
844	13 - 24	8	5	866
921	7 - 19	9	9	928
983	7 - 19	10	9	990

SAT Unlocked II

Short Passage Questions

Answer short double passage questions the very same way you answer long ones.

Short passage questions are excellent practice, especially if you are having trouble with double passage questions.

Tip:
You know when a short passage question set asks double passage questions because the passages will appear on top of each other rather than side by side.

Short Single Passage Sets

Page	Questions	Test	Section	Answers Page
391	6 - 9	1	2	432
476	6 - 9	2	7	494
538	6 - 9	3	7	556
577	9 - 12	4	2	618
645	6 - 9	5	3	680
725	9 - 12	6	7	742
763	6 - 9	7	2	804
843	9 - 12	8	5	866
910	6 - 9	9	6	928
961	9 - 12	10	4	990

Short Double Passage Sets

Page	Questions	Test	Section	Answers Page
403	9 - 12	1	5	432
459	9 - 12	2	4	494
521	9 - 12	3	4	556
588	6 - 9	4	5	618
663	9 - 12	5	7	680
706	6 - 9	6	3	742
781	9 - 12	7	5	804
825	6 - 9	8	2	866
899	9 - 12	9	4	928
972	6 - 9	10	6	990

SAT Critical Reading Quick Review

SAT Critical Reading

Sentence Completions
- Don't waste time (30-45 seconds per Q).
- Qs appear in order of difficulty (easy to hard).
- Look carefully for clues in question.
- Play positive/negative.
- Right answer fits <u>well</u>.
- On double answer Qs, work one side then the other.
- Skip hard Qs if you can't eliminate any answers.

Passage Reading

<u>Reading the Passage:</u>
1. Mark question line numbers and circle key words.
2. *Always read the italicized introduction and any asterisked (*) notes.*
3. Read the passage, <u>underlining</u> one or two things in each paragraph.

<u>Answering the Questions:</u>
4. Read the question carefully.
5. Eliminate the three DUMB answers first.
6. Re-read the question.
7. Eliminate ATTRACTOR answer (look for 'clunker').
   Extreme words ('all', 'never', 'always', 'none', etc.) usually attractors.
8. Whatever remains is CORRECT answer.
   ('pragmatic' usually correct.)

<u>Double Passage Sets:</u>
1. Mark line numbers & circle Q #s that ask about BOTH passages.
2. Read Passage 1.
3. Answer the questions for Passage 1.
4. Read Passage 2.
5. Answer the questions for Passage 2.
6. Answer questions that ask about both passages.

<u>Question Tips:</u>
- Primary Purpose Qs: Look for 'big picture' that mentions <u>facts</u> of passage.
- Most nearly means Qs: Substitute answer for word in the passage.
- Line # Qs: Always read a few lines above and below.
- Tone Qs: Avoid: emotional words and words that don't take a stand ('ambivalent').

Introduction to SAT Math

SAT Math consists of 54 total questions tested in three sections.

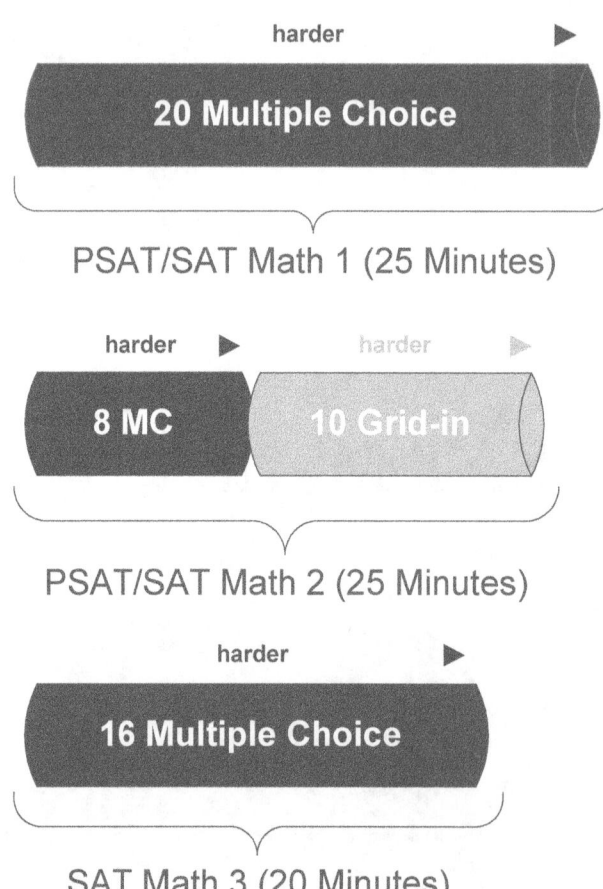

SAT Math question types

Math includes 2 types of questions:

✓ **44 Multiple Choice (MC)**
Typical SAT question with 5 possible answer choices.

✓ **10 Grid-In (GI)**
Enter an actual value on your answer sheet, instead of simply filling in a multiple choice oval.

SAT Math

In what order do SAT Math questions appear?

Math questions tend to appear in order of difficulty with the easiest question at the beginning and the hardest questions at the end of each section.

NOTE:
In the section with Grid-In questions, the Multiple Choice questions start easy and end with hard questions and then the **Grid-Ins start over with easy questions and end with hard questions.**

Tip:
The harder the question, the less obvious the answer.
Because questions at the beginning of the section are easier, the answer choices tend to be straightforward. As the section progresses however, the test makers throw in trick answers to try to fool you.

What math subjects does the SAT test?

SAT Math tests four subjects:

- ✓ **Numbers and Operations**
- ✓ **Algebra & Functions**
- ✓ **Geometry**
- ✓ **Statistics and Probability**

Tip:
Don't get hung up trying to figure out in which area a specific SAT question is supposed to belong. It's better to focus on the math concepts the SAT tests, and let the test takers worry about what they call each question.

Is SAT Math very advanced?
No. The concepts tested on SAT math sections are all fairly basic.

The most advanced math you need to know is basic Geometry (no proofs) and some Algebra II.

A lot of students actually find that the biggest difficulty on the math section is remembering some of the basic concepts they learned in grade school, but have now forgotten (like 'remainders').

The SAT uses basic math concepts to test *reasoning* skills. This may sound funny, but the SAT does not really test your overall knowledge of math. Instead, the SAT primarily tests your ability to figure out which basic math concepts to apply and how to apply them.

Know your capabilities
Many students rush too quickly through the math section to finish, and so miss earlier, easier questions simply because they are not careful enough.

On SAT Math, it is more important to be accurate than to be complete.

It's far more important to answer SAT Math questions you know *correctly*, than to worry about finishing the entire section. Failing to finish the very last questions on the SAT math section simply means that you haven't been able to answer the very hardest questions. Better to take a little bit of extra time checking your work on the earlier questions than rush and lose easy points.

__Remember!__
What hurts your score are not so much the questions you don't know, but rather the questions you know how to answer but answer incorrectly because you make dumb mistakes.

SAT Math

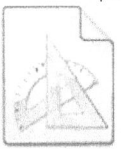

**Concentrate on correctly answering
the first 2/3 of the questions on each Math section.
Then cherry-pick the hard questions.**

Given enough time, most students can answer many of the first 2/3 of SAT math questions in any given section, which are mostly easy to medium difficulty questions. Be sure you are scoring as many points as you can on these earlier questions, and then work on the hard questions at the end to add to your total.

Did you know?
You only need about 2/3 of the total points to earn a scaled score of 600 on SAT Math.

If you get stuck on a question, skip it and come back.

Every question counts the same regardless of difficulty, so there is no point wasting too much time on any single question when there are other points to the earned.

Remember:
Math questions tend to appear in order of difficulty.
On the section with both multiple choice and Grid-In questions, the questions at the beginning of each of the multiple choice and Grid-In parts are the easy questions, while the questions at the end of each part are the hard ones.

What formulas do I need to know?

**On the first page of every math section,
the SAT prints all of the formulas
you need to answer nearly every geometry question.**

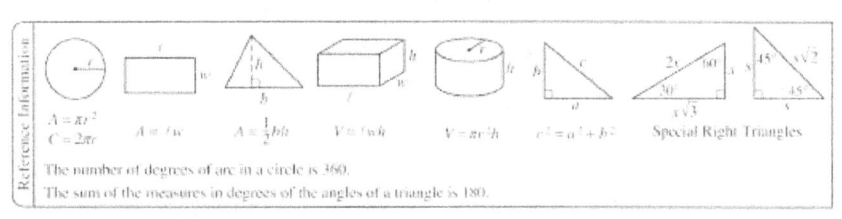

We will also learn a few also formulas that help with a few specific problems, but in general these formulas are what you need to know.

Can I use a calculator?

Calculators the SAT allows:
- ✓ four-function calculators
- ✓ scientific calculators
- ✓ graphing calculators

Tip:
A 'super-fancy' calculator is not necessary for the SAT I.
A simple, four-function (=, -, X, /) calculator is all you really need.

Tip:
You never have to calculate π or square roots.
Where necessary, answer choices will always include the symbols.

Calculators you CANNOT use:
- ☒ pocket organizer
- ☒ hand-held or laptop computer
- ☒ electronic writing pad or pen input device
- ☒ calculator with a QWERTY (typewriter-like) keypad
- ☒ calculator with paper tape
- ☒ calculator that makes noises or "talks"
- ☒ calculator that requires an outlet

When should I use my calculator?
Generally, most SAT questions do not require a calculator at all, and many students take the entire the SAT without even turning one on.

Use your calculator to:
- ✓ multiply or divide large numbers
- ✓ calculate percentages
- ✓ answer Grid-In questions

SAT math questions rarely ask you to calculate big numbers. Still, if you tend to make silly math errors, a calculator can help ensure you don't miss questions – especially on Grid-Ins.

SAT Math

What are Grid-Ins?

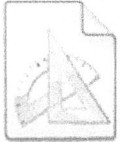

Grid-In questions require you to enter an actual numerical value on your answer sheet, instead of simply filling in a multiple choice oval.

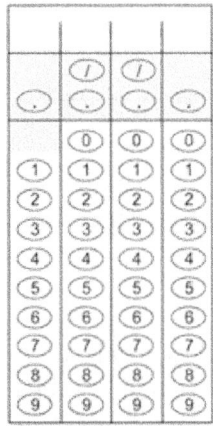

Tip:
Don't rush Grid-Ins.
Take extra time and make sure that your arithmetic is correct to avoid giving back points you should otherwise earn. Students often miss Grid-Ins because of simple arithmetic errors, even though they actually know how to answer. Be careful.

There is no guessing penalty on Grid-In questions.

ALWAYS ANSWER!

Always make sure to put something down for every Grid-In answer, even if you don't have a clue what the question is asking. You have nothing to lose.

Tip:
On Grid-In questions, if you have absolutely no idea what the answer is, write the number of the question. *For some reason, 5 out of 10 tests in the Official SAT Study Guide include a Grid-In question whose number is also its answer. So if you've got nothing else....*

How do I enter Grid-Ins?

Enter Grid-Ins by writing in a numerical value at the top and then filling in the ovals below.

The ovals are what count.
The SAT scores your answer based on the filled in ovals and not the numbers you write at the top of the column. Still, it's always a good idea to write the numbers in first to make sure you remember which ovals to fill in.

Position does not technically matter. You can enter a Grid-In value beginning in any of the four columns as long as you can fit in the entire number.

Tip:
While position within the columns does not technically matter, it is a good idea to **always start in the far left column** *to avoid problems with repeating decimals (see below).*

Grid-In answers will ALWAYS be:

✓ **POSITIVE NUMBERS including:**
- **Improper Fractions (reduce!)**
- **Decimals (including repeating decimals)**

✓ **ZERO (no negatives!)**

Remember!
Grid-In answers are **never negative**.
If you ever get a negative answer on a Grid-In question, go back and check your work.

SAT Math

**Grid-In questions sometimes have
more than one correct answer.**

Grid-In question can sometimes have two correct values.
For example: 2 or 9.
You only need to enter one of these values to get credit.

Grid-Ins answers can also be within a range.
For example: any number between 0 and 1.
In this case, any value entered within this range will be correct.
(Just remember to reduce your fractions!)

Fractions vs. Decimals

**The SAT does not care whether the value
you enter is a decimal or a fraction.**

Either way is correct.

**For repeating decimals,
START ALL THE WAY ON THE LEFT
and grid-in as many columns over as you can.**

For example, the repeating decimal $.\overline{666}$ should be started all the way on the left and entered as .666.

Remember!
For repeating decimals, if you do not grid-in your answer all the way over to the right it will be marked <u>incorrect</u>.

Tip:
Don't round.
The SAT allows you to round. So technically $.\overline{666}$ could be entered as .667. It's better not to round, however, as rounding just adds another opportunity to make a mistake.

  Convert mixed fractions to IMPROPER factions.

For example:

If you enter the value $2\frac{2}{3}$ as 2 2/3, it will appear to the scoring machine as 22/3 and will be scored as incorrect.

Instead, convert the mixed fraction to an improper fraction (8/3).

Remember!
Improper fractions are *proper* on the SAT. Just remember to reduce!

Grid-In Exercise:

Grid-In the following values:

0.333...   2 ¼   1.666...   - 5.4

Grid–In Exercise Answers:
1/3 or .333, 9/4 or 2.25, 1.66 or 1.67, no answer (negative value).

SAT Math

Numbers & Operations

SAT Numbers Terminology

Term	Definition	Examples
Number	Any positive or negative real value including fractions, decimals and zero.	-4/5, 0, 1.23, 4,...
Integer	Any positive or negative whole number or zero.	...-3, -2,-1, 0, -1, 2, 3,...
Positive Integer	Any integer greater than zero	1,2,3,4,...
Negative Integer	Any integer less than zero	... -4, -3, -2, -1
Non-negative Integer	Positive integers plus zero	0,1,2,3,4,...
Even Integer	Integer with NO remainder when divided by 2 **0 is an even integer.**	... -6, -4, -2, **0**, 2, 4, 6, ...
Odd Integer	Integer with a remainder of 1 when divided by 2	...-5, -3, -1, 1, 3, 5, ...
Consecutive Integers	Integers in numerical order	1, 2, 3, 4, 5
Consecutive Even Integers	Even integers in numerical order	-4, -2, 0, 2, 4
Consecutive Odd Integers	Odd integers in numerical order	11, 13, 15, 17
Prime number	Number > 1 divisible only by 1 & itself	2,3,5,7,11,13,17,19,23,... **0, 1 NOT Prime**
Factor	Number that divides evenly into another number	Factors of 10: 1, 2, 5, 10
Prime factor	Prime number that divides evenly into another number	Prime factors of 10: 2, 5
Divisible by	Number that can be divided evenly into another number	15 is divisible by 3 & 5
Multiple of	Result of a number multiplied by another number	15 is a multiple of 3 & 5
Remainder	Amount left over when a number is divided by another	10 ÷ 3 = 3 with rem **1** 9 ÷ 3 = 3 with **no** rem
Rounding	shortening longer decimal	1.44 rounds to 1.4 1.45 rounds to 1.5
Digit	Place within a number NOTE: a '3 digit number' is a number made up of Hundreds, Tens, and Ones digits	432 Place / Digit Hundreds / 4 Tens / 3 Ones / 2

Tip:
Be careful not to confuse <u>even</u> integers with <u>positive</u> integers.

Math: OSSG Factors Questions

No.	Page	Q.	Diff.	Type	Test	Sect.	Answer
1	785	1	E	MC	7	7	
2	585	15	M	MC	4	3	
3	713	6	M	MC	6	4	
4	773	17	H	GI	7	3	
5	969	14	H	MC	10	5	
6	919	14	H	MC	9	8	
7	468	16	H	GI	2	5	

Math: OSSG Remainders Questions

No.	Page	Q.	Diff.	Type	Test	Sect.	Answer
1	399	11	M	MC	1	3	
2	611	9	M	MC	4	9	
3	949	6	M	MC	10	2	
4	643	20	H	MC	5	2	

Math: OSSG Digits Questions

No.	Page	Q.	Diff.	Type	Test	Sect.	Answer
1	464	4	E	MC	2	5	
2	715	9	E	GI	6	4	
3	850	13	M	MC	8	7	
4	731	9	M	MC	6	8	
5	418	16	H	GI	1	7	

Math: OSSG Rounding Questions

No.	Page	Q.	Diff.	Type	Test	Sect.	Answer
1	416	10	E	GI	1	7	

Math: OSSG Factors Answers

1	2	3	4	5	6	7
C	C	A	8	D	B	9

Math: OSSG Remainders Answers

1	2	3	4
B	B	D	C

Math: OSSG Digits Answers

1	2	3	4	5
C	990	A	E	5940

Math: OSSG Rounding Answers

1
.2 or 1/5

SAT Math

Plugging in Answers

Unlike most math tests, SAT multiple choice questions put the correct answer right in front of you.

Any time a question asks:

"which of the following"
OR
"what is the value"

plug the answer choices into the question.

Example:

If $a^2 - 16 = 0$, which of the following could be a value for a?

(A) -8
(B) -4
(C) 0
(D) 8
(E) 16

Tip:
When plugging in answers, STOP when you get to the right answer. There is only one correct answer, so no sense wasting time with other answer choices after you find the one that works.

Answer: (B)
Since the question asks, "which of the following", plug each of the answer choices in for *a* until you find the value that satisfies the equation.
Since $(-4)^2 - 16 = 0$, (B) is the correct answer.

Math: OSSG Plugging In Answers Questions

No.	Page	Q.	Diff.	Type	Test	Sect.	Answer
1	396	1	E	MC	1	3	
2	796	5	E	MC	7	9	
3	857	1	E	MC	8	9	
4	904	6	E	MC	9	5	
5	915	2	E	MC	9	8	
6	456	16	M	MC	2	2	
7	518	14	M	MC	3	2	
8	787	8	M	MC	7	7	
9	787	10	M	MC	7	7	
10	798	12	M	MC	7	9	
11	905	9	M	MC	9	5	
12	968	12	M	MC	10	5	

Math: OSSG Plugging in Answers Answers

1	2	3	4	5	6	7	8	9	10	11	12
A	D	A	C	B	D	C	C	D	A	B	C

Plugging in Numbers

Plugging in Numbers (basic)

Plugging in numbers is a simple and very effective technique that can help you answer even some of the hardest 'Numbers and Operations' questions.

**Whenever you see VARIABLES
in *either*
the question or the answer choices:**

1) **PICK a NUMBER that fits the variable's description**
   (for example, 'a positive, even integer *x*' might = '2')
   and SOLVE the question using that number.

2) **If the ANSWER contains variables, plug that same number into the variables of the answer choices to find the same solution.**

Remember!
Pick EASY numbers.
1, 2, 3, 4, 5, 10, and 100 are often best, depending on the question.

Check ALL answers
Occasionally, the number you plug in may be correct for more than one answer choice. Be sure to check all answers to make sure only one is correct. If you get more than one correct answer, plug in a different number for the remaining choices.

Example 1:

If x and y are positive numbers and $x + y = 9$, then $\dfrac{9-x}{y} =$

(A)   -1
(B)   0
(C)   1
(D) x
(E) $y - 1$

Example 2:

An integer x is multiplied by 3 and the result is decreased by 3. This result is divided by 3. Finally, that result is increased by 3. In terms of x, what is the final result?

(A) $x + 3$
(B) $x - 3$
(C) $x + 2$
(D) $3x - 3$
(E) x

Answer 1: (C)
Because the question mentions 'positive numbers', we should pick our own positive numbers that work for the equation $x + y = 9$.

For instance, let's choose $x = 4$ and $y = 5$.

Now plug those x and y values into the equation $\dfrac{9-x}{y}$

to find the correct answer choice:

$\dfrac{9-4}{5} = \dfrac{5}{5} = 1$, or (C).

Answer 2: (C)
Because the question contains variables in our answer choices, we should pick a number for x.

For this example, let's pick **2**.

2 multiplied by 3 = 6
6 decreased by 3 = 3
3 divided by 3 = 1
1 increased by 3 = 4

So when we pick 2, our answer is 4.

Now plug 2 (our original number) into the answer choices for x, to see which variable combination also gives us a value of 4.

$x + 2 = 4$, or (C).

Math: OSSG Plugging in Numbers (basic) Questions

No.	Page	Q.	Diff.	Type	Test	Sect.	Answer
1	454	7	E	MC	2	2	
2	483	6	E	MC	2	8	
3	796	4	E	MC	7	9	
4	848	3	E	MC	8	7	
5	516	9	M	MC	3	2	
6	583	8	M	MC	4	3	
7	641	14	M	MC	5	2	
8	642	16	M	MC	5	2	
9	670	13	M	MC	5	8	
10	670	14	M	MC	5	8	
11	716	11	M	GI	6	4	
12	770	7	M	MC	7	3	
13	797	9	M	MC	7	9	
14	851	16	M	MC	8	7	
15	907	15	M	MC	9	5	
16	916	6	M	MC	9	8	
17	918	12	M	MC	9	8	
18	979	7	M	MC	10	8	
19	485	13	H	MC	2	8	
20	613	16	H	MC	4	9	
21	733	16	H	MC	6	8	
22	832	8	H	MC	8	3	
23	888	7	H	MC	9	2	
24	970	20	H	MC	10	5	

Math: OSSG Plugging in Numbers (basic) Answers

1	2	3	4	5	6	7	8	9	10	11	12
A	C	E	E	C	E	A	E	C	E	8,10,12	C
13	14	15	16	17	18	19	20	21	22	23	24
D	E	D	D	E	B	B	D	C	A	D	E

Plugging in Numbers (word problems)

Plugging in numbers works well for word problems, especially ones that use variables in answer choices.

Example:

A lawn mower costs x dollars, and this cost is shared equally by a group of people. In terms of x, how many dollars less will each person contribute if there are five people in the group instead of four?

(A) $\dfrac{x}{20}$

(B) $\dfrac{x}{5}$

(C) $\dfrac{x}{4}$

(D) $\dfrac{9x}{20}$

(E) $9x$

Remember!
Always plug your numbers into every answer choice.
If you happen to get the same correct value for more than one answer, pick new numbers for the remaining correct answers and try again until you get only one correct value.

Answer: (A)

Because the question contains equations in our answer choices, we should pick a number for *x* (the price of the mower). For this example, let's pick **100**.

If the price of a $100 mower is shared equally by a group of 4 people, the contribution per person is $\frac{100}{4}$ or $25.

If the price of the $100 mower is shared equally by a group of 5 people, the contribution per person is $\frac{100}{5}$ or $20.

So, when five people share the cost instead of four, each person pays $5 less.

We now plug 100 (our original number) into the answer choices for *x*, to see which variable combination also gives us a value of 5.

$\frac{100}{20} = $ **5**, or (A).

Math: OSSG Plugging in Numbers (word problems) Questions

No.	Page	Q.	Diff.	Type	Test	Sect.	Answer
1	482	4	E	MC	2	8	
2	526	3	E	MC	3	5	
3	786	3	E	MC	7	7	
4	640	8	M	MC	5	2	
5	702	10	M	MC	6	2	
6	787	9	M	MC	7	7	
7	797	10	M	MC	7	9	
8	905	7	M	MC	9	5	
9	401	20	H	MC	1	3	
10	519	20	H	MC	3	2	
11	585	18	H	MC	4	3	
12	981	16	H	MC	10	8	

Math: OSSG Plugging in Numbers (word problems) Answers

1	2	3	4	5	6	7	8	9	10	11	12
C	D	D	A	E	A	B	E	A	B	A	E

SAT Math

Number Lines

Once or twice per test, the SAT will ask you to interpret a number line.

When a number line question includes UNDEFINED POINTS (labeled by variables), ESTIMATE the VALUES of those points before answering the question.

Example:

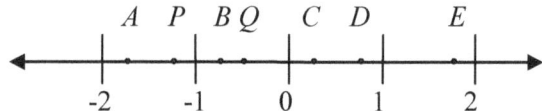

Which of the lettered points on the number line above could represent the result when the coordinate of point P is subtracted from the coordinate of point Q?

(A) A
(B) B
(C) C
(D) D
(E) E

Tip:
Number line questions often include fractions and negatives:

- *Multiplying a number by a fraction makes the number smaller.*

- *Subtracting a negative number moves the value to the right on the number line (positively).*

Answer: (D)
When shown undefined points on a number line, the first step is to estimate values for these points.

Point *P* looks to be around $-1\frac{1}{4}$ or -1.25

Point *Q* looks to be around $-\frac{1}{2}$ or -.5

Subtracting -1.25 from -.5, we get $\frac{3}{4}$ or .75

The point on the number line whose value is closest to **.75** is (D).

Math: OSSG Number Lines Questions

No.	Page	Q.	Diff.	Type	Test	Sect.	Answer
1	516	8	E	MC	3	2	
2	596	10	E	GI	4	6	
3	639	6	E	MC	5	2	
4	700	2	E	MC	6	2	
5	978	6	E	MC	10	8	
6	398	9	M	MC	1	3	
7	417	12	M	GI	1	7	
8	484	11	M	MC	2	8	
9	701	6	M	MC	6	2	
10	797	8	M	MC	7	9	
11	834	11	M	GI	8	3	
12	859	8	M	MC	8	9	
13	423	12	H	MC	1	8	
14	655	17	H	GI	5	4	

Math: OSSG Number Lines Answers

1	2	3	4	5	6	7	8	9	10	11	12	13	14
D	57.5	E	D	D	D	0<X<1.5	A	D	C	1,11	C	B	4/9 or .444

SAT Math

Sets

Set questions ask you to compare overlapping groups to determine which members are in each set.

SAT Set Terminology

Term	Definition	Examples
Set	any group	Set A: {1, 2, 4, 6} Set B: {2, 3, 6, 9}
Member	Individual item in a set	Member Set A: 1 Member Set B: 3
Union	members in <u>either</u> set.	Union of A & B: {1, 2, 3, 4, 6, 9}
Intersection	members in <u>both</u> sets.	Intersection of A & B: {2, 6}
Common members	same as Intersection	Common A & B: {2, 6}

Example:

If J and K are two sets of numbers, and if every member in J is also in K, which of the following CANNOT be true?

(A) 1 is in neither J nor K.
(B) 4 is in J, but not in K.
(C) 5 is in both J and K.
(D) 6 is in K, but not in J.
(E) If 9 is not in K, then 9 is not in J.

Answer: (B)

This question asks which answer CANNOT be true- that is, which answer is NOT possible based on what the question tells you.

Here, if every number in Set J is also in Set K, it is not possible for the number 4 to be in Set J but not be in Set K.

Every other answer choice is at least possible based on what the question tells you, so (B).

Math: OSSG Sets Questions

No.	Page	Q.	Diff.	Type	Test	Sect.	Answer
1	667	1	E	MC	5	8	
2	886	1	E	MC	9	2	
3	713	4	M	MC	6	4	
4	789	15	M	MC	7	7	
5	905	10	M	MC	9	5	
6	967	8	M	MC	10	5	

Math: OSSG Sets Answers

1	2	3	4	5	6
B	A	E	E	A	C

Venn Diagrams

 **Venn Diagrams represent sets as overlapping circles.**

Example:

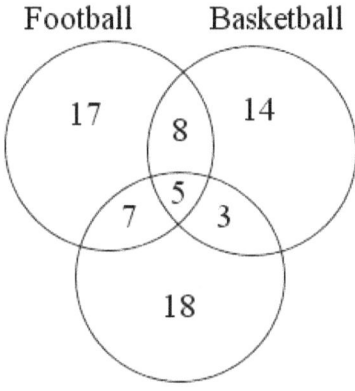

The Venn diagram above shows the distribution of 72 students who play football, baseball, and basketball. How many students play *both* football and baseball?

(A) 5
(B) 7
(C) 12
(D) 23
(E) 58

 Tip:
Trace the circles with your pencil to see where they overlap.

Answer: (C)
To find the number of students who play both football and baseball, we need to see where those circles overlap.

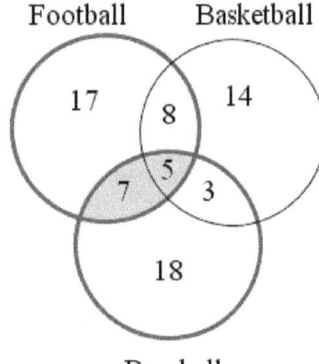

Tracing the circles for football and baseball shows that the overlap includes 7 and 5 students. Thus, the total number of students who play both football and baseball is 7+5 = **12**, or (C).

Math: OSSG Venn Diagrams Questions

No.	Page	Q.	Diff.	Type	Test	Sect.	Answer
1	397	5	E	MC	1	3	
2	455	13	M	MC	2	2	
3	517	12	M	MC	3	2	

Math: OSSG Venn Diagrams Answers

1	2	3
C	C	D

SAT Math

Sequences

The SAT will sometimes include a question that asks you to figure out the pattern of a sequence of numbers.

Write out the numbers of the sequence until you get to the term you need.

Example:

The first term in a sequence is 24 and each term after the first is determined by dividing the preceding term by 3 and then subtracting 2. Which term is the first term the sequence that is <u>not</u> an integer?

(A) 3rd term
(B) 4th term
(C) 5th term
(D) 6th term
(E) 7th term

Remember!
A number is not necessarily the same thing as an integer.
A number can be a fraction (or decimal), while an integer can only be a <u>whole</u> number (not a fraction or decimal).

Answer: (C)

1st term: 24

2nd term: $24 \div 3 = 8$, $8 - 2 = 6$

3rd term: $6 \div 3 = 2$, $2 - 2 = 0$

4th term: $0 \div 3 = 0$, $0 - 2 = -2$

5th term: $-2 \div 3 = -\frac{2}{3}$, $-\frac{2}{3} - 2 = -2\frac{2}{3}$, or (C).

Math: OSSG Sequences Questions

No.	Page	Q.	Diff.	Type	Test	Sect.	Answer
1	452	1	E	MC	2	2	
2	638	2	E	MC	5	2	
3	833	10	E	GI	8	3	
4	903	1	E	MC	9	5	
5	399	13	M	MC	1	3	
6	583	9	M	MC	4	3	
7	597	14	M	GI	4	6	
8	769	5	M	MC	7	3	
9	952	13	M	GI	10	2	
10	417	14	H	GI	1	7	
11	530	16	H	GI	3	5	
12	548	15	H	MC	3	8	

Math: OSSG Sequences Answers

1	2	3	4	5	6	7	8	9	10	11	12
D	B	6/25 or .24	E	E	D	5	D	25/2 or 12.5	117	67	C

SAT Math

Consecutive Integers
Consecutive Integers are those which occur in numerical order (like 3, 4, 5, 6, . . .).

Sum of Consecutive Integers
One type of consecutive integer question tells you the sum total of a list of consecutive integers and asks you to find one of these integers.

To answer Sum of Consecutive Integer questions:

1) Divide the sum of the integers by the number of integers to find the <u>middle number</u> (or median) of the list.

2) Count up or down from this middle number to find the integer asked for by the question.

Example:

What is the greatest of 5 consecutive integers whose sum equals 565?

Answer: 115
To find the greatest of 5 consecutive integers whose sum is 565, divide the sum by the number of integers to get the midpoint of the list.

Here $565 \div 5 = 113$, which means **113 is the midpoint** of the 5 integer list.

This means the full list of consecutive integers is: 111, 112, <u>113</u>, 114, **115**.

So **115** is the greatest integer in this list.

Lists of Consecutive Integers

Another type of Consecutive Integer question shows you a long list of consecutive integers, and asks you to figure out the sum of all the integers.

**For long lists of consecutive integers,
there will always be pairs that cancel each other out,
so you don't have to add all the integers up.**

For instance, the sum of consecutive integers from -3 to 3
(-3, -2, -1, 0, 1, 2, 3) = 0, since each negative value is cancelled out by a positive value.

Example:

What is the sum of consecutive integers from -10 to 13 inclusive?

(A)   3
(B)   13
(C)   23
(D)   36
(E)   48

Answer: (D)
The sum of consecutive integers from -10 to 10 = 0.
(Pairs 10 & -10, 9 & -9, 8 & -8, etc all cancel each other out.)

Adding up the remaining integers in the list we get:

11+12+13=**36**, or (D).

Math: OSSG Consecutive Integers Questions

No.	Page	Q.	Diff.	Type	Test	Sect.	Answer
1	547	12	M	MC	3	8	
2	654	12	M	GI	5	4	
3	834	12	M	GI	8	3	
4	907	17	M	MC	9	5	
5	789	18	H	MC	7	7	

Math: OSSG Consecutive Integers Answers

1	2	3	4	5
B	46	39	D	B

Logic Questions
Logic questions basically test your common sense.

Logic questions come in two types: puzzles and word problems.

Logic Puzzles

Example:

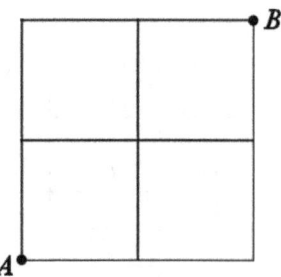

In the figure above, a path from point A to point B is determined by moving upward or to the right along the grid lines. How many paths can be drawn from A to B?

(A) Two
(B) Four
(C) Six
(D) Eight
(E) Twelve

Answer: (C)

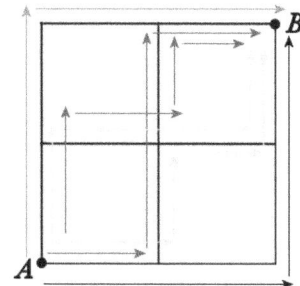

Six paths, or (C).

Math: OSSG Logic Puzzles Questions

No.	Page	Q.	Diff.	Type	Test	Sect.	Answer
1	453	5	E	MC	2	2	
2	515	3	E	MC	3	2	
3	526	4	E	MC	3	5	
4	582	4	E	MC	4	3	
5	582	5	E	MC	4	3	
6	785	2	E	MC	7	7	
7	702	11	M	MC	6	2	
8	852	18	M	MC	8	7	
9	968	13	M	MC	10	5	
10	486	16	H	MC	2	8	

Math: OSSG Logic Puzzles Answers

1	2	3	4	5	6	7	8	9	10
D	B	B	E	B	D	B	D	C	E

Logic Word Problems

Example:

Emily has four cats, each a different color: Tan, Grey, Black, and Calico. Tan is neither the smallest nor the largest. Calico is one of the two smaller cats. Black is the largest. Grey sometimes bullies two of the smaller cats. Which cat is the smallest?

(A) Tan
(B) Grey
(C) Black
(D) Calico
(E) It cannot be determined from the information given.

Answer: (D)

Smallest to Largest

"Tan is neither the smallest nor the largest."

   _   T   T   _

"Calico is one of the two smaller cats."

   C   C   _   _

"Black is the largest."

   _   _   _   B

"Grey sometimes bullies two of the smaller cats."

   _   _   G   _

Final order:

   C   T   G   B

Calico is smallest, or (D).

Math: OSSG Logic Word Problems Questions

No.	Page	Q.	Diff.	Type	Test	Sect.	Answer
1	420	5	E	MC	1	8	
2	847	1	E	MC	8	7	
3	468	15	M	GI	2	5	
4	703	15	M	MC	6	2	
5	788	13	M	MC	7	7	
6	849	7	M	MC	8	7	
7	891	17	H	GI	9	2	

Math: OSSG Logic Word Problems Answers

1	2	3	4	5	6	7
B	B	8	A	A	D	10/7, 1.42, 1.43

Fractions

About once per test, the SAT will test your knowledge of fractions.

Fractions (basic)

**To find a fraction 'OF' a value,
MULTIPLY the fraction by that value.**

Example:

If $\frac{2}{5}$ of k is 32, what is $\frac{4}{5}$ of k ?

(A) 80
(B) 64
(C) 36
(D) 20
(E) 10

Answer: (B)
Remember that 'of' means multiply, so:
"$\frac{2}{5}$ of k is 32" is the same as $\frac{2}{5}k = 32$

Solving for k we get:

$k = \frac{5(32)}{2} = \frac{160}{2} = 80$

"what is $\frac{4}{5}$ of k ?"

$\frac{4}{5}k = \frac{4(80)}{5} = \frac{320}{5} = 64$, or (B).

Math: OSSG Fractions (basic) Questions

No.	Page	Q.	Diff.	Type	Test	Sect.	Answer
1	582	6	E	MC	4	3	
2	651	4	E	MC	5	4	
3	830	1	E	MC	8	3	
4	952	14	M	GI	10	2	

Math: OSSG Fractions (basic) Answers

1	2	3	4
A	D	D	3/50, ,.06

Fractions (Word Problems)

'WHAT FRACTION' : $\dfrac{\text{number of things asked for}}{\text{total number of things}}$

Example:

At an ice cream store, 18 customers ordered a scoop of chocolate, 12 customers ordered a scoop of vanilla, and 10 customers ordered a scoop of strawberry. If everyone ordered only single scoops, what fraction of the store's customers ordered a scoop of vanilla?

(A) $\dfrac{2}{3}$

(B) $\dfrac{11}{20}$

(C) $\dfrac{9}{20}$

(D) $\dfrac{2}{5}$

(E) $\dfrac{3}{10}$

Remember!
Always reduce your fractions.

Answer: (E)

The *total* number of customers is 18 (chocolate) + 12 (vanilla) + 10 (strawberry) =

18 + 12 + 10 = 40, which is the <u>denominator</u> of the fraction.

Thus the fraction of customers who ordered vanilla (12 in the numerator) =

$\frac{12}{40} = \frac{3}{10}$, or (E).

Math: OSSG Fractions (word) Questions

No.	Page	Q.	Diff.	Type	Test	Sect.	Answer
1	481	1	E	MC	2	8	
2	544	4	E	MC	3	8	
3	668	3	E	MC	5	8	
4	889	9	E	GI	9	2	
5	655	15	M	GI	5	4	

Math: OSSG Fractions (word) Answers

1	2	3	4	5
B	A	A	2/3, .666	7/15, .466, .467

Percentages (basic)

To find 'PERCENT OF' a value:

1) CONVERT the percentage to a decimal or a fraction

2) MULTIPLY the converted percentage by that value

Convert to a fraction: 60% of $15 = \dfrac{60}{100} \times 15 = \dfrac{900}{100} = 9$

Convert to a decimal: 60% of $15 = .60 \times 15 = 9$

Example:

If 20 percent of n is 50, what is 10 percent of n ?

(A) 10
(B) 15
(C) 20
(D) 25
(E) 30

Tip:
Calculators can be helpful when answering percentage questions.

Answer: (D)

Remember that 'of' means multiplication, so:

"20 percent of n is 50" is the same as:

$\frac{20}{100} n = 50$ or $.20n = 50$

Solving for n we get:

$n = \frac{50(100)}{20} = \frac{5000}{20} = 250$

"what is 10 percent of n?"

$.10 (250) = $ **25**, or (D).

Shortcut: Since 10% is half of 20%, 25 is half of 50.

Math: OSSG Percentages (basic) Questions

No.	Page	Q.	Diff.	Type	Test	Sect.	Answer
1	796	3	E	MC	7	9	
2	518	15	M	MC	3	2	
3	670	12	M	MC	5	8	
4	655	16	H	GI	5	4	

Math: OSSG Percentages (basic) Answers

1	2	3	4
B	A	B	3

Calculating Percentage Increase/Decrease

The SAT will also sometimes give you the amount and ask you to find the percentage change.

To calculate change in percentage: (increase or decrease)

$$\frac{2^{nd} \text{ Amount} - 1^{st} \text{ amount}}{1^{st} \text{ amount}}$$

Then covert the fraction to a percentage.

Example:

A factory produced 200 cars the first week. If production increased to 250 cars the second week, by what percent did the number of cars increase from the first to the second week?

(A) 20
(B) 25
(C) 50
(D) 100
(E) 125

NOTE:
If you get a <u>negative</u> number, it simply means there was a <u>decrease</u> in the amount. Do not use the negative sign in your answer.

Answer: (B)

Applying the formula, we get $\dfrac{250-200}{200} = \dfrac{50}{200} = \dfrac{1}{4} = .25 = \mathbf{25\%}$, or (B).

Calculating a Series of Percentage Increases/Decreases

Sometimes the SAT asks about a *series* of percentage changes and asks you to find the final amount.

Where you have MORE THAN ONE percentage increase or decrease:

1) **CONVERT the first percentage to a decimal and MULTIPLY by the first amount.**

2) **ADD OR SUBTRACT this number from the original amount to find the new amount after the first percentage change.**

3) **CONVERT the second percentage to a decimal and MULTIPLY by the <u>new</u> amount.**

4) **ADD OR SUBTRACT this number from the new amount to find the final amount after the second percentage change.**

Example:

A music store is having a going out of business sale. The first week the store marked down all merchandise 30%. The second week the store marked down all merchandise an additional 20%. If the price of a CD was originally $15, how much did the CD cost in dollars after all store mark downs were taken?

(A) 7.50
(B) 8.40
(C) 9.10
(D) 10.50
(E) 12.00

Answer: (B)

The original price of $15 is marked down 30%:
.30 (15) = 4.50

Subtract 4.50 from 15:
15 - 4.50 = 10.50

This marked down price of $10.50 is then marked down 20%:
.20(10.50) = 2.10

Subtract 2.10 from 10.50:
10.50 – 2.10 = **8.40**, or (B).

Math: OSSG Percentages (word) Questions

No.	Page	Q.	Diff.	Type	Test	Sect.	Answer
1	517	13	M	MC	3	2	
2	613	13	M	MC	4	9	
3	834	13	M	GI	8	3	
4	415	8	H	MC	1	7	
5	586	20	H	MC	4	3	
6	861	15	H	MC	8	9	

Math: OSSG Percentages (word) Answers

1	2	3	4	5	6
D	C	6500	C	E	B

Ratios & Proportions

Ratios are really just another name for fractions that equal each other.
The SAT asks you to find values for variables within these equal fractions.

Cross Multiplying

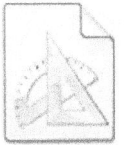

If $\dfrac{a}{b} = \dfrac{c}{d}$, then $ad = bc$

**To solve ratio problems,
cross-multiply to find missing value(s).**

Example:

If $\dfrac{2x-4}{x} = \dfrac{14}{9}$, what is the value of x?

Shortcut:
You can often figure out the value of a variable simply by comparing the numerators (top) or denominators (bottom) on each side of the = sign.

(See answer below for explanation.)

Answer: 9
By cross multiplying: $\dfrac{2x-4}{x} = \dfrac{14}{9}$, we get:

$9(2x - 4) = 14x$

$18x - 36 = 14x$

$18x - 14x = 36$

$4x = 36$

$x = 9$

Shortcut:
Here, by comparing the denominators, we see that $x = 9$.
(Yes, that really does work for this type of question!)

Math: OSSG Cross Multiplying Questions

No.	Page	Q.	Diff.	Type	Test	Sect.	Answer
1	730	5	E	MC	6	8	
2	965	1	E	MC	10	5	
3	978	4	E	MC	10	8	
4	467	12	H	GI	2	5	
5	705	19	H	MC	6	2	
6	981	15	H	MC	10	8	

Math: OSSG Cross Multiplying Answers

1	2	3	4	5	6
A	B	E	1/15, .066 ,.067	A	C

Ratios (word)

To solve ratio word problems, set up a ratio with the missing value as *x* and cross-multiply.

Example:

On a trail map, $\frac{1}{2}$ inch represents 4 miles. If a trail is 22 miles long, what is its length, in inches, on the map?

(A) $\frac{2}{11}$

(B) $\frac{4}{11}$

(C) 2

(D) $2\frac{3}{4}$

(E) 11

Answer: (D)

Set up the ratio: $\dfrac{inches}{miles} = \dfrac{1/2}{4} = \dfrac{x}{22}$

Cross multiply to get:

$4x = (22)\dfrac{1}{2}$

$4x = 11$

$x = \dfrac{11}{4} = 2\dfrac{3}{4}$, or (D).

Math: OSSG Ratios (word problems) Questions

No.	Page	Q.	Diff.	Type	Test	Sect.	Answer
1	639	5	E	MC	5	2	
2	715	10	E	GI	6	4	
3	768	1	E	MC	7	3	
4	849	8	M	MC	8	7	
5	918	11	M	MC	9	8	

Math: OSSG Ratios (word problems) Answers

1	2	3	4	5
E	30	A	B	C

Ratios (parts)

**When a question mentions
"the ratio of *x* to *y*" :**

**ADD *x* and *y* together to find
the TOTAL number of ratio PARTS.**

Example:

At a music store, the ratio of guitars to basses is 7 to 4.
Which of the following could be the total number guitars
and basses at the store?

(A)   4
(B)   7
(C)   22
(D)   28
(E)   56

Remember!
Finding the <u>total number of ratio parts</u> is almost always the key to answering this type of question.

Answer: (C)

"the ratio of guitars to basses is 7 to 4."

The total number of ratio parts = 7 + 4 = 11.

Since the total number of ratio parts is 11, the total number of guitars and basses at the store must be a multiple of 11.

The only answer that is a multiple of 11 is **22,** or (C).

Math: OSSG Ratios (parts) Questions

No.	Page	Q.	Diff.	Type	Test	Sect.	Answer
1	594	6	M	MC	4	6	
2	980	12	M	MC	10	8	
3	953	16	H	GI	10	2	

Math: OSSG Ratios (parts) Answers

1	2	3
B	C	8/7, 1.14

Direct and Inverse Proportions

Proportion	Question States:	Set up
Direct (think '<u>d</u>ivision')	"x varies **directly** as y" or "x is **directly proportional** to y"	$\dfrac{x}{y}$
Inverse	"x varies **inversely** with y" or "x is **inversely proportional** to y"	xy

Example (Direct):

If x is directly proportional to y and $x = 4$ when $y = 12$, what is the value of y when $x = 16$?

(A) $\dfrac{1}{4}$

(B) $\dfrac{1}{3}$

(C) 3

(D) 4

(E) 48

Answer (Direct): (E)

"If x is **directly** proportional to y" = $\dfrac{x}{y}$

"and $x = 4$ when $y = 12$"

$$\dfrac{x}{y} = \dfrac{4}{12}$$

"what is the value of y when $x = 16$?"

$$\dfrac{4}{12} = \dfrac{16}{y}$$

Cross multiply to solve for y:
$4y = (12)\, 16$

$4y = 192$

$y = 48$, or (E).

Example (Inverse):

If x is inversely proportional to y and $x = 4$ when $y = 12$, what is the value of y when $x = 16$?

(A) $\dfrac{1}{4}$

(B) $\dfrac{1}{3}$

(C) 3

(D) 4

(E) 48

Answer (Inverse): (C)

"If x is **inversely** proportional to y" = xy

"and $x = 4$ when $y = 12$"
$xy = 4(12) = 48$

"what is the value of y when x = 16 ?"
$48 = 16y$

$3 = y$, or (C).

Math: OSSG Direct & Inverse Proportion Questions

No.	Page	Q.	Diff.	Type	Test	Sect.	Answer
1	527	6	M	MC	3	5	
2	858	6	M	MC	8	9	
3	906	12	M	MC	9	5	
4	950	7	M	MC	10	2	

Math: OSSG Direct & Inverse Proportion Answers

1	2	3	4
E	B	D	C

Geometry

On the first page of every math section,
the SAT prints all of the formulas you need
to answer practically any geometry question.

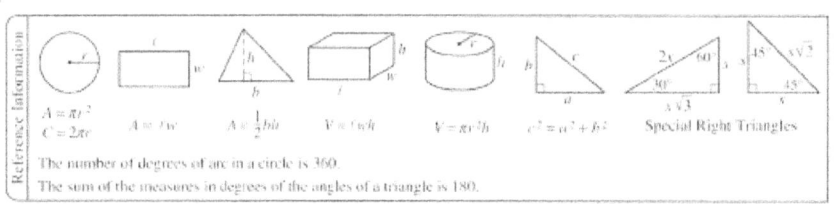

 Tip:
Write down everything the question tells you.
Mark up the figures with all of the information provided by the question, so you don't miss anything important.

 Tip:
Always assume you have been given enough information.
The answer, "It cannot be determined from the information given." is hardly, if ever, the correct answer.

**Figures are drawn to scale,
unless they say otherwise.**

Many times you can eliminate incorrect answer choices simply by 'eyeballing' the figure.

 Tip:
Never trust a figure with that says:

"*Note:* *Figure not drawn to scale.*"

Treat this caption as a warning that the figure has been purposefully drawn to confuse you.

**For irregular shapes, draw lines to create
simple triangles and/or rectangles**

Angles

Line angle rules you need to know:

The measure of a RIGHT ANGLE is 90 degrees.	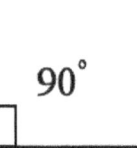
OPPOSITE angles are EQUAL.	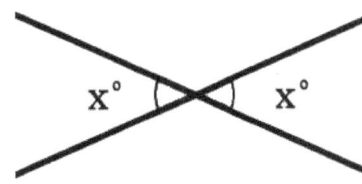
The SUM of the measures of angles on a STRAIGHT LINE is 180 degrees.	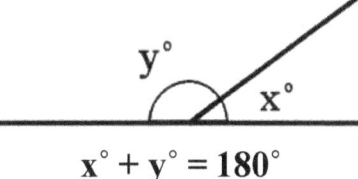 $x° + y° = 180°$
The SUM of the measures of angles around a SINGLE POINT is 360 degrees.	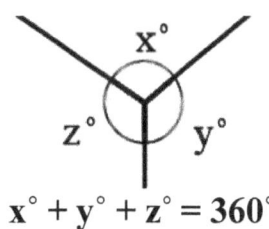 $x° + y° + z° = 360°$

Example:

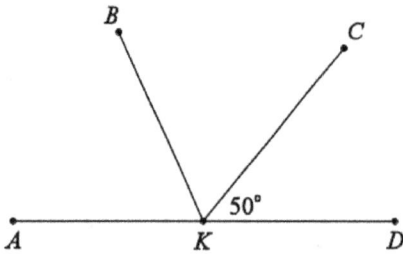

In the figure above, K lies on $\overline{AD}$ and $\overline{KB}$ bisects $\angle CKA$. What is the measure of $\angle BKC$?

(A) 50
(B) 55
(C) 60
(D) 65
(E) 70

 Tip:
A line that 'BISECTS' an angle cuts that angle in half.

Answer: (D)

The sum of the three angles along line $\overline{AD}$ equals 180 degrees.

Subtracting the measure of ∠CKD (50) from 180 we get:
180 − 50 = **130**, which is the measure of ∠CKA.

Since $\overline{KB}$ bisects (cuts in half) ∠CKA, then both ∠BKA and ∠BKC (the angle we want to find) are 130/2 = 65, or (D).

Math: OSSG Angles Questions

No.	Page	Q.	Diff.	Type	Test	Sect.	Answer
1	398	10	E	MC	1	3	
2	482	5	E	MC	2	8	
3	831	3	E	MC	8	3	
4	916	3	E	MC	9	8	
5	610	6	M	MC	4	9	
6	654	11	M	GI	5	4	
7	769	6	M	MC	7	3	
8	968	11	M	MC	10	5	
9	530	15	H	GI	3	5	

Math: OSSG Angles Answers

1	2	3	4	5	6	7	8	9
C	B	A	E	C	135	A	B	90

Angles of Parallel Lines

Where a third line crosses two PARALLEL lines,

the corresponding ANGLES on either parallel line are EQUAL.

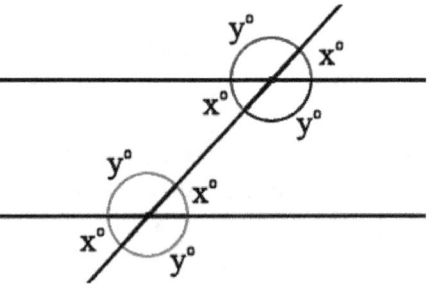

Example:

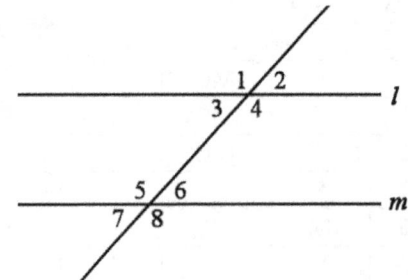

In the figure above, if $l \parallel m$, then the sum of the measures of which two angles must equal 180 degrees?

(A) 1 and 4
(B) 1 and 5
(C) 3 and 7
(D) 4 and 7
(E) 4 and 8

Answer: (D)
Remember that the sum of the measures of angles along a straight line is
180 degrees, so we are looking for two different angles who measures are equal to,
say, angles 1 and 2. The only pair of angles that fits this description is 4 and 7, or
(D).

Math: OSSG Angles of Parallel Lines Questions

No.	Page	Q.	Diff.	Type	Test	Sect.	Answer
1	593	2	E	MC	4	6	
2	730	6	E	MC	6	8	
3	858	3	E	MC	8	9	
4	421	6	M	MC	1	8	
5	466	10	M	GI	2	5	
6	584	11	M	MC	4	3	
7	640	9	M	MC	5	2	
8	772	14	M	GI	7	3	

Math: OSSG Angles of Parallel Lines Answers

1	2	3	4	5	6	7	8
D	A	A	E	135	A	A	$22.5 < x < 27.5$

Sum of Polygon Angles

SUM of the ANGLES of any POLYGON is:

180 [(number of sides or angles) – 2]

Example:

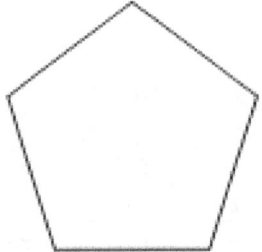

If all the interior angles of the polygon above are congruent, then what is the measure in degrees of each interior angle?

(A) 45
(B) 72
(C) 108
(D) 120
(E) 540

Tip:
Since the number of sides and angles of a polygon is always the same, the formula works using either sides or angles.

Answer: (C)

The sum of the angles of a pentagon (5 sides) =

$180(\#\,sides - 2) = 180(5 - 2) = 180(3) = 540$
or
$180(\#\,angles - 2) = 180(5 - 2) = 180(3) = 540$

Each of the five interior angles is congruent, so each angle is therefore:

$$\frac{540}{5} = 108$$

or (C).

Math: OSSG Sum of Polygon Angles Questions

No.	Page	Q.	Diff.	Type	Test	Sect.	Answer
1	918	10	M	MC	9	8	
2	952	12	M	GI	10	2	

Math: OSSG Sum of Polygon Angles Answers

1	2
C	105

Triangle Sides & Angles

Basic TRIANGLE side and angle rules you need to know:

The SUM of the ANGLES of a triangle is 180 degrees.

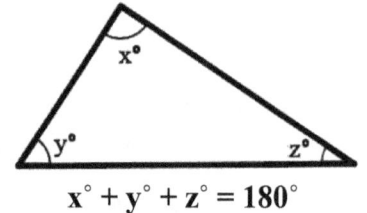

$x° + y° + z° = 180°$

TWO SIDES of a triangle are EQUAL, OPPOSITE ANGLES are also EQUAL.

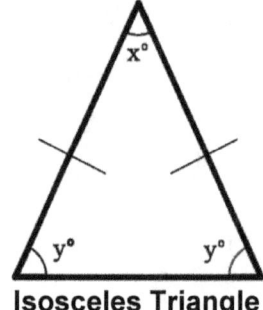

Isosceles Triangle

THREE SIDES of a triangle are EQUAL, each angle measures 60 degrees.

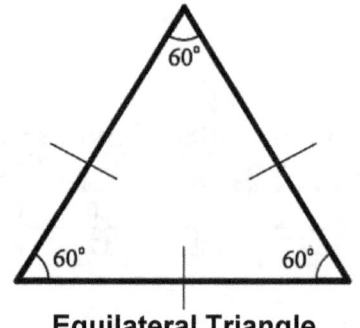

Equilateral Triangle

The SUM of lengths of any TWO SIDES of a triangle is always GREATER THAN the length of the THIRD SIDE.

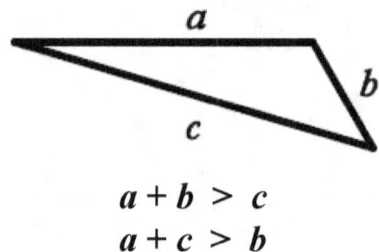

$a + b > c$
$a + c > b$
$b + c > a$

SAT Math

Example 1:

A square and an equilateral triangle have equal perimeters. If the length of one side of the square is 6, what is the length of one side of the triangle?

(A) 6
(B) 8
(C) 12
(D) 18
(E) 24

Example 2:

Which of the following CANNOT be the lengths of the sides of a triangle?

(A) 2, 3, 4
(B) 3, 3, 3
(C) 3, 4, 5
(D) 3, 5, 8
(E) 2, 45, 45

Example 3:

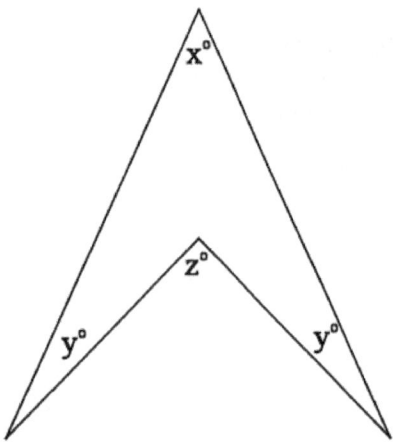

If $x = 50$ and $y = 20$ in the figure above, what is the value of z?

(A) 60
(B) 75
(C) 90
(D) 108
(E) It cannot be determined from the information given.

Remember!
For non regular shapes, <u>draw lines</u> to create simple triangles and/or rectangles.

Answer 1: (B)
If the length of one side of the square is 6, then the perimeter of the square (4 sides all being equal) is 6 x 4 = 24.

Since the perimeter of the equilateral triangle is equal to the perimeter of the square, the perimeter of the triangle is also 24.

Therefore, the length of one side of the three sides of the equilateral triangle is: 24 /3 = 8, or (B).

Answer 2: (D)
The sum of the lengths of any two sides of a triangle is always greater than the length of the third side. The sum of lengths 3 and 5 is not <u>greater than</u> 8.

Answer 3: (C)

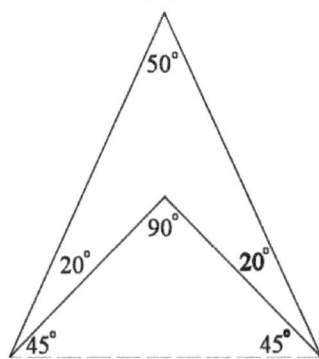

Create triangles by drawing a line connecting the two end points of the figure (shown by the dotted line in the figure above).

Now we have two triangles: a big triangle with a top angle of 50 and another smaller triangle with a top angle of z (which we want to find).

Since the top angle x = 50, and the sum of the angles of a triangle is 180, the sum of the lower angles of the big triangle must together be 180 -50 = 130.

Because angles y are both equal (20 degrees), we can infer that the lower angles of the big triangle we drew are also equal. Therefore, the measure of each of the lower angles of the big triangle is 130/2 = 65.

Subtracting 20 (angle y) from 65 will give us the measure of each of the lower angles of the smaller triangle, which is: 65 - 20 = 45.

The sum of the two lower angles of the smaller triangle is: 45 + 45 =90.

Therefore, the measure of angle z is:
180 (the sum of all the angles) – 90 (the sum of the two lower angles) = 90, or (C).

Math: OSSG Triangle Sides & Angles Questions

No.	Page	Q.	Diff.	Type	Test	Sect.	Answer
1	413	2	E	MC	1	7	
2	515	5	E	MC	3	2	
3	545	6	E	MC	3	8	
4	668	4	E	MC	5	8	
5	795	2	E	MC	7	9	
6	848	4	E	MC	8	7	
7	916	5	E	MC	9	8	
8	966	3	E	MC	10	5	
9	415	7	M	MC	1	7	
10	584	14	M	MC	4	3	
11	597	11	M	GI	4	6	
12	642	15	M	MC	5	2	
13	654	14	M	GI	5	4	
14	713	5	M	MC	6	4	
15	799	13	M	MC	7	9	
16	418	17	H	GI	1	7	
17	485	14	H	MC	2	8	
18	530	17	H	GI	3	5	
19	704	18	H	MC	6	2	
20	907	16	H	MC	9	5	

Math: OSSG Triangle Sides & Angles Answers

1	2	3	4	5	6	7	8	9	10
B	E	A	C	A	C	C	C	E	D
11	12	13	14	15	16	17	18	19	20
110	C	70	D	D	90	E	100	B	E

Triangle Equation Writing

Occasionally, the SAT will ask you to figure out the angles of a triangle in terms of the other angles.

Example:

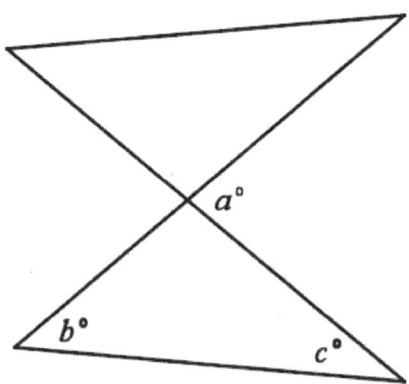

In the figure above, what does *c* equal in terms of *a* and *b*?

(A) $a - b$
(B) $a + b$
(C) $180 - a - b$
(D) $180 + a - b$
(E) $180 - a + b$

 Remember!
Whenever you see variables in your answer choices, you can always pick your own numbers for the variables and solve using those values. Then plug the same values into your answer choices to find the answer.

Answer: (A)

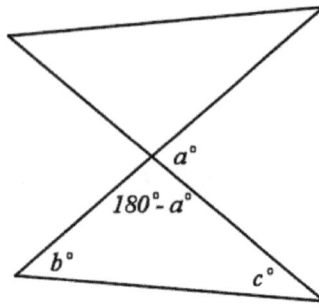 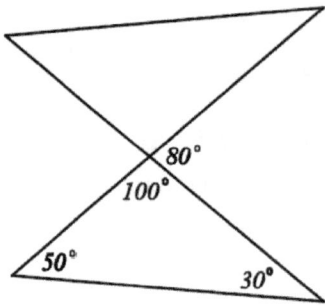

Since the sum of the measures of the angles of a triangle is 180, the measure of any one angle of triangle is 180 minus the sum of the other two angles.

Therefore:
$c = 180 - ((180 - a) + b)$
$c = 180 - 180 + a - b$
$c = a - b$, or (A).

Alternatively, a perhaps easier way to solve the question is to simply pick your own numbers for the variables.

For instance, let's say $a = 80$. In that case, the top angle of the triangle will equal $180 - 80 = 100$. Since the sum of the measures of the angles of a triangle is 180, the sum of b and c together will equal $180 - 100 = 80$.

Now let's pick a number for b. Since $b + c = 80$, let's call $b = 50$, which means c must now equal 30. So our numbers are: $a = 80$, $b = 50$, $c = 30$.

Now plug the numbers 80 and 50 into the answers for a and b to find 30, or c. Since $80 - 50 = 30$, or (A).

(For more, see 'Plugging in Numbers' earlier in this section).

Math: OSSG Triangle Equation Writing Questions

No.	Page	Q.	Diff.	Type	Test	Sect.	Answer
1	595	8	M	MC	4	6	
2	980	14	M	MC	10	8	
3	733	15	H	MC	6	8	

Math: OSSG Triangle Equation Writing Answers

1	2	3
E	E	B

SAT Math

Right Triangles

A triangle with one angle measuring 90 degrees is called a RIGHT triangle. The SAT will commonly provide the length of side(s) and/or angle(s) of a right triangle and ask you to figure out another side or angle.

	**Pythagorean Theorem** $$c^2 = a^2 + b^2$$ Use Pythagorean Theorem to figure out the sides of <u>any</u> right triangle.	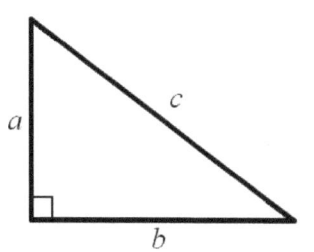
	30-60-90 Triangle	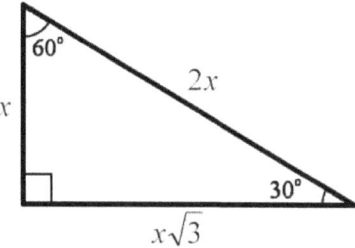
	45-45-90 Triangle	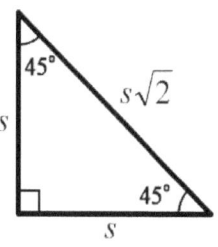

 TIP:

If a question shows $\sqrt{3}$ on one side of a right triangle, assume 30-60-90.

If a question shows $\sqrt{2}$ on the hypotenuse of a right triangle, assume 45-45-90.

 <u>**Remember!**</u>

The Pythagorean Theorem ($c^2 = a^2 + b^2$) and the two other 'special' right triangle formulas are always printed at the beginning of every SAT math section.

Example 1:

Phil leaves his house and walks to Frank's house by walking due west for four miles and then due north for three miles. What is the straight-line distance, in miles, between Phil's house and Frank's house?

(A) 5
(B) 6
(C) 7
(D) 9
(E) 12

Example 2:

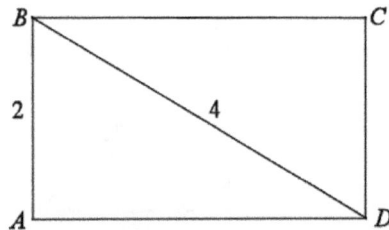

What is the area of rectangle $ABCD$ above?

(A) $2\sqrt{3}$
(B) $4\sqrt{3}$
(C) 6
(D) 8
(E) $4 + 4\sqrt{3}$

Answer 1: (A)

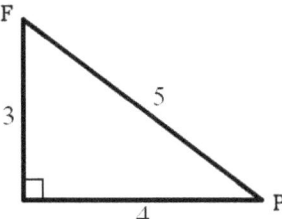

Phil's route to Frank's house is a right angle with legs of 4 and 3 miles, respectively. The straight line distance between the houses is therefore the hypotenuse of a right triangle.

Applying the Pythagorean Theorem ($c^2 = a^2 + b^2$), we get:
$c^2 = 4^2 + 3^2$
$c^2 = 16 + 9$
$c^2 = 25$
$c = 5$, or (A).

Tip:
Be on the lookout for 3-4-5 right triangles and their multiples (6-8-10, 9-12-15, 12-16-20, etc.). These integer-based lengths often appear in SAT right triangle questions.

Answer 2: (B)

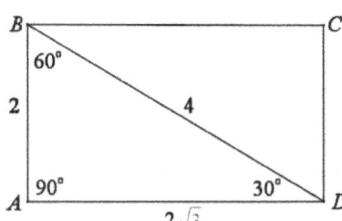

The angles of a rectangle are all right angles, so *ABD* is a right triangle with one side length of 2 and a hypotenuse of 4. Recognizing that the hypotenuse is twice the length of the one side (2*x* and *x*), we apply the special triangle formula for a 30-60-90 triangle to find that the other side is $2\sqrt{3}$ ($x\sqrt{3}$).

Since the area of a rectangle is length times width, the area of the rectangle is:
$2 \times 2\sqrt{3} = 4\sqrt{3}$, or (B).

Math: OSSG Right Triangles Questions

No.	Page	Q.	Diff.	Type	Test	Sect.	Answer
1	481	2	E	MC	2	8	
2	545	8	E	MC	3	8	
3	730	4	E	MC	6	8	
4	787	7	E	MC	7	7	
5	613	15	M	MC	4	9	
6	652	7	M	MC	5	4	
7	789	16	M	MC	7	7	
8	888	5	M	MC	9	2	
9	969	15	M	MC	10	5	
10	400	17	H	MC	1	3	
11	401	19	H	MC	1	3	
12	526	5	H	MC	3	5	
13	548	16	H	MC	3	8	
14	800	15	H	MC	7	9	
15	908	20	H	MC	9	5	
16	953	15	H	GI	10	2	

Math: OSSG Right Triangles Answers

1	2	3	4	5	6	7	8
D	D	E	C	C	E	C	A
9	10	11	12	13	14	15	16
A	C	A	A	D	D	B	192

Similar Triangles

Similar triangles have equal angles but not necessarily equal sides.

Where the corresponding ANGLES of two triangles are EQUAL, the SIDES are PROPORTIONAL.

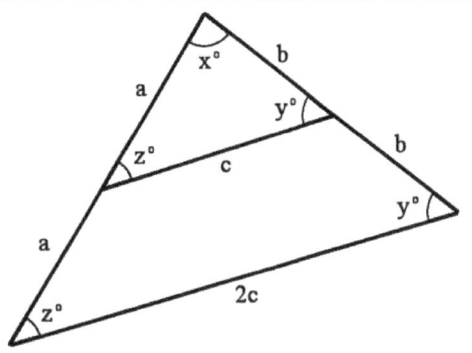

Example:

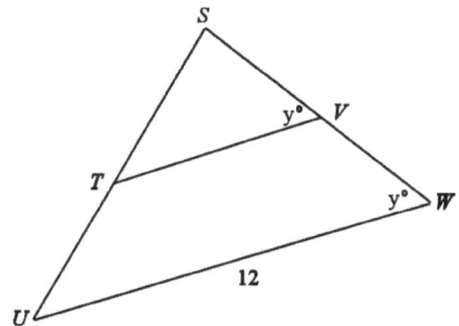

In the figure above, if $\overline{ST} = \overline{TU}$, what is the length of $\overline{TV}$?

(A) 4
(B) 6
(C) 8
(D) 10
(E) It cannot be determined from the information given.

Tip:
Be careful not to confuse 'SIMILAR' with 'CONGRUENT'.
Congruent triangles have both equal angles sides and equal sides.
Similar triangles have equal angles but not necessarily equal sides.

Answer: (B)

If $\angle SVT = \angle SWU$, the other corresponding angles of $\triangle SVT$ and $\triangle SUV$ must also be equal. ($\angle TSV$ and $\angle USW$ are equal because they are the same angle, and since two pairs of corresponding angles are equal, and triangle angles must always add up to 180 degrees, the third pair of corresponding angles must also be equal).

Since the corresponding angles of the two triangles are all equal, the triangles are SIMILAR. That means that the sides are PROPORTIONAL.

If $\overline{ST} = \overline{TU}$, then $\overline{SU}$ is two times the length of $\overline{ST}$. Since the sides of similar triangles $\triangle SVT$ and $\triangle SUV$ are proportional, and the length of one side is two times the length of its corresponding side, then the lengths of all sides of one triangle are two times the lengths of the corresponding sides of the other triangle.

So, if the length of $\overline{UW}$ is two times the length of $\overline{TV}$. Since the length of $\overline{UW} = 12$, then the length of $\overline{TV} = 6$, or (B).

Math: OSSG Similar Triangles Questions

No.	Page	Q.	Diff.	Type	Test	Sect.	Answer
1	966	5	E	MC	10	5	
2	455	10	M	MC	2	2	
3	832	7	M	MC	8	3	
4	860	12	M	MC	8	9	
5	970	18	H	MC	10	5	

Math: OSSG Similar Triangles Answers

1	2	3	4	5
B	E	B	E	A

Triangle Area

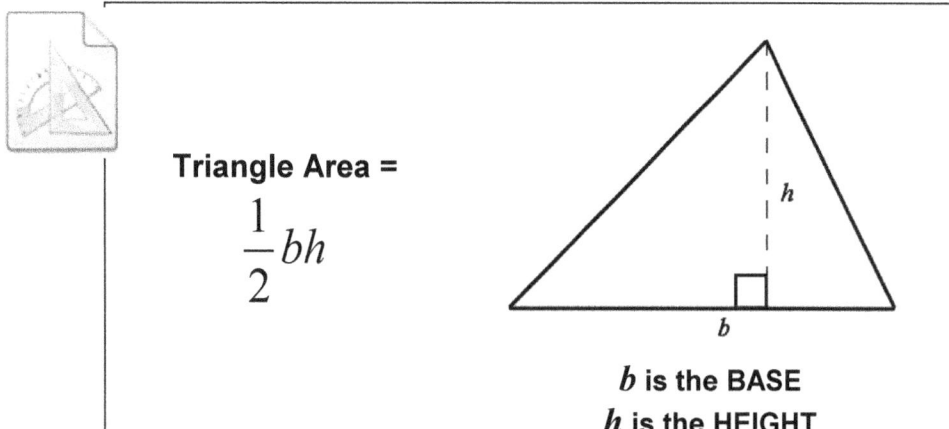

Triangle Area = $\frac{1}{2}bh$

b is the BASE
h is the HEIGHT

Example:

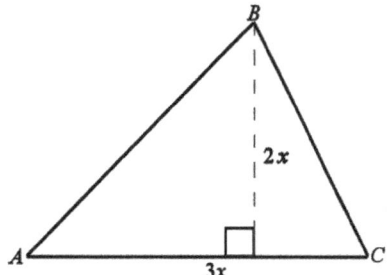

In the figure above, if the area of $\triangle ABC$ is 27, what is the value of x?

(A) $\sqrt{3}$
(B) $\sqrt{5}$
(C) 3
(D) 9
(E) 27

Answer: (C)

Applying the triangle area formula $A = \frac{1}{2}bh$, we get:

$27 = \frac{1}{2}(3x)(2x)$

$27 = \frac{1}{2}(6x^2)$

$27 = 3x^2$

$9 = x^2$

$3 = x$, or (C).

Math: OSSG Triangle Area Questions

No.	Page	Q.	Diff.	Type	Test	Sect.	Answer
1	597	15	M	GI	4	6	
2	651	5	M	MC	5	4	
3	714	7	M	MC	6	4	

Math: OSSG Triangle Area Answers

1	2	3
½ or .5	E	B

SAT Math

Circles

Circle Circumference & Area

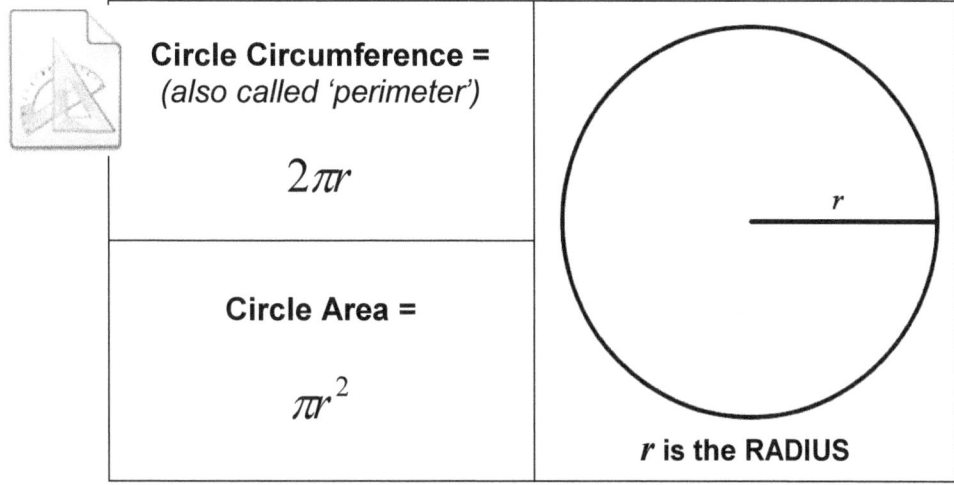

Circle Circumference = *(also called 'perimeter')* $2\pi r$	
Circle Area = πr^2	*r* is the RADIUS

Example:

If circle *B* is half the circumference of circle *A*, circle *A* is how many times the area of circle *B* ?

(A) 1
(B) $\sqrt{2}$
(C) 2
(D) 4
(E) 8

 Tip:
You never have to calculate π.
Where necessary, answer choices will always include the symbol.

Answer: (D)
If circle B is half the circumference of circle A, then the radius of circle A is two times the radius of circle B:

$$C_A = 2\pi r = (2r)\pi$$
$$C_B = \left(\frac{1}{2}\right)2\pi r = \pi r = (r)\pi$$

Since the radius of circle A is twice the radius of circle B, the area of circle A is four times the area of circle B:

$$A_A = \pi(2r)^2 = \pi(4r^2) = 4\pi r^2$$
$$A_B = \pi(r)^2 = \pi r^2$$

Remember!
Where one circle has **2 times the RADIUS** of another, the larger circle is <u>both</u>:

✓ **2 times the CIRCUMFERENCE, and**
✓ **4 times the AREA**

Example:

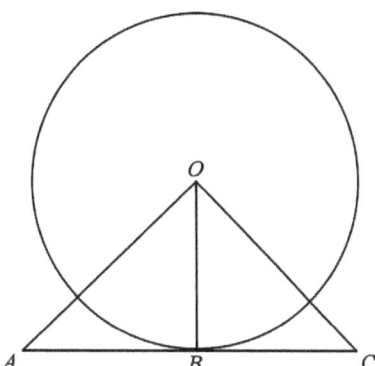

In the figure above, the circle with center O is tangent to line $\overline{AC}$ at point B. If $\overline{OB} = \overline{BC}$ and the length of $\overline{OC}$ is $2\sqrt{2}$, then the area of the circle is

(A) $\sqrt{2}\pi$
(B) $2\sqrt{2}\pi$
(C) 2π
(D) 4π
(E) 8π

Hint:
*A circle **TANGENT** to a line means the line and the circle touch at only one point.*

*At the point where a line and circle are tangent, the line is **PERPENDICULAR** (at a right angle) to the circle's radius.*

Answer: (D)

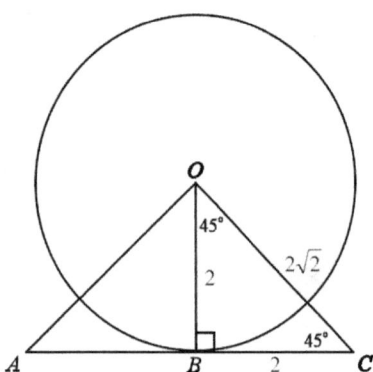

Since $\overline{AC}$ and the circle with center O are tangent at point B, we know that $\overline{AC}$ and $\overline{OB}$ are perpendicular (at a right angle of 90 degrees) to each other.

Since $\overline{OB} = \overline{BC}$, we know that $\triangle OBC$ is isosceles and that $\angle OCB = \angle BOC$, and since $\angle OBC$ is 90 degrees, $\angle OCB$ and $\angle BOC$ must then each be 45 degrees.

So, $\triangle OBC$ is a 45-45-90 triangle whose hypotenuse ($\overline{OC}$), the question tells us has a of length $2\sqrt{2}$. Applying the formula for a 45-45-90 triangle (x, x, $x\sqrt{2}$) we see that $\overline{OB}$, the circle's radius, = 2.

Applying the formula for the area of a circle ($A = \pi r^2$) with radius 2, we find that the area of circle O is:

$A = \pi 2^2$
$A = 4\pi$, or (D).

Math: OSSG Circle Circumference & Area Questions

No.	Page	Q.	Diff.	Type	Test	Sect.	Answer
1	398	8	E	MC	1	3	
2	463	2	E	MC	2	5	
3	528	10	E	GI	3	5	
4	949	3	E	MC	10	2	
5	641	11	M	MC	5	2	
6	703	16	M	MC	6	2	
7	789	17	M	MC	7	7	
8	906	11	M	MC	9	5	
9	518	17	H	MC	3	2	
10	643	19	H	MC	5	2	
11	773	16	H	GI	7	3	

Math: OSSG Circle Circumference & Area Answers

1	2	3	4	5	6	7	8	9	10	11
D	E	4	B	C	B	D	B	C	C	10

Circle Arc Length & Sector Area

'Arc Length' is a FRACTION of the circle's CIRCUMFERENCE:

$$\frac{x}{360} \times circumference$$

'Sector Area' is a FRACTION of the circle's AREA:

$$\frac{x}{360} \times area$$

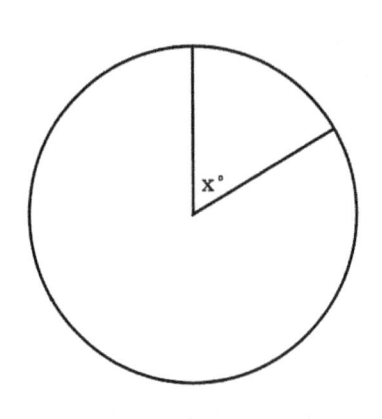

Example:

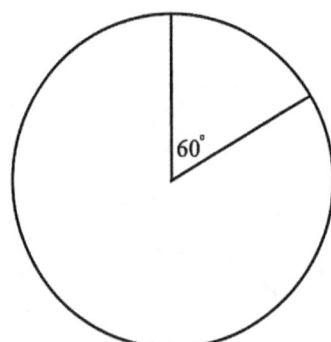

In the figure above, the circle has a circumference of 12π. If the angle at the center of the circle has a measurement of $60°$, what is the length of the arc created by the angle?

(A) π
(B) 2π
(C) 3π
(D) 4π
(E) 8π

Remember!

$\frac{x}{360}$ The **FRACTION** of the circle is the **ANGLE DIVIDED BY 360**.

Answer: (B)

The fraction of the circle created by the arc is the angle degrees divided by 360. So here, the fraction of the circle is $\frac{60}{360} = \frac{1}{6}$.

To find the arc length, multiply the fraction by the circle's circumference:

$\frac{1}{6} \times 12\pi = \frac{12\pi}{6} = 2\pi$, or (B).

 Math: OSSG Circle Arc Length & Sector Area Questions

No.	Page	Q.	Diff.	Type	Test	Sect.	Answer
1	516	7	E	MC	3	2	
2	414	5	M	MC	1	7	
3	597	13	M	GI	4	6	
4	834	14	M	GI	8	3	
5	979	8	M	MC	10	8	
6	586	19	H	MC	4	3	
7	852	20	H	MC	8	7	
8	907	18	H	MC	9	5	

Math: OSSG Circle Arc Length & Sector Area Answers

1	2	3	4	5	6	7	8
B	A	13,14,15,16,17	5/18, .277, .278	B	A	B	A

Rectangles & Squares

A rectangle is a 4-sided figure with all angles of 90 degrees.

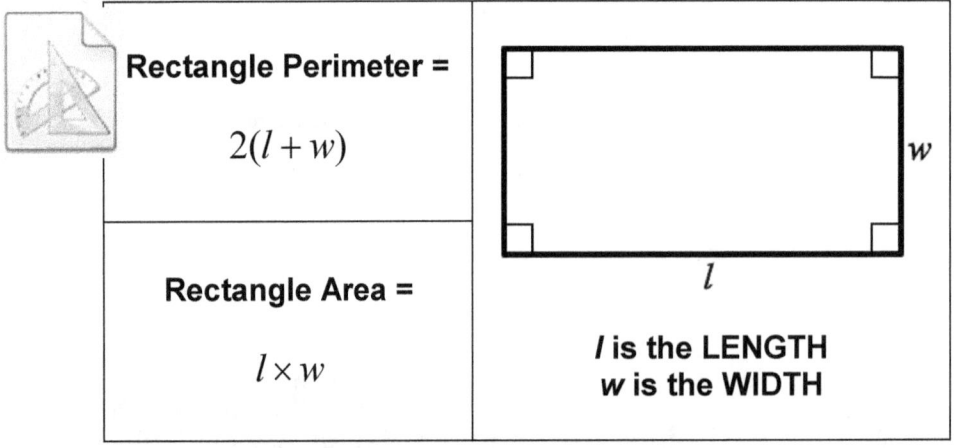

Rectangle Perimeter =

$2(l + w)$

Rectangle Area =

$l \times w$

l is the LENGTH
w is the WIDTH

A square is a rectangle with all sides of equal length.

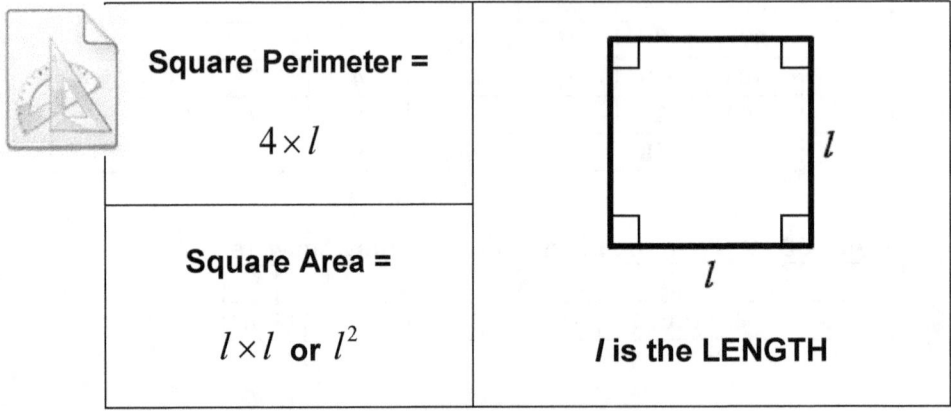

Square Perimeter =

$4 \times l$

Square Area =

$l \times l$ or l^2

l is the LENGTH

SAT Math

Example:

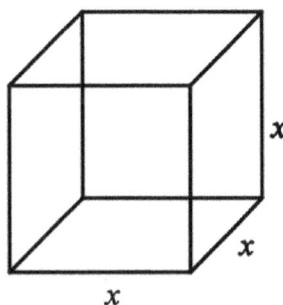

The figure above is a cube with all sides of length x.
If $x = 3$, what is the surface area of the cube?

(A) 3
(B) 9
(C) 18
(D) 27
(E) 54

 Hint:
'SURFACE AREA' is the total area of all of the sides of an object.

Answer: (E)
Each side of a cube is a square; here with each side with a length of 3. The area of each side of the cube is therefore:
3 x 3 = 9.

Since there are six sides to a cube, the total surface area is:
9 x 6 = 54, or (E).

Example:

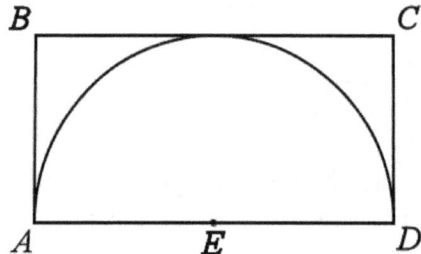

In the figure above, a semi-circle is inscribed in rectangle *ABCD*. If the length of the perimeter of the semi-circle is π, and points *A* and *D* are symmetric about point *E*, what is the perimeter of rectangle *ABCD*?

(A) π
(B) 6
(C) $\pi + 6$
(D) 12
(E) 4π

Tip:
'Symmetric about' means equal length on both sides.

Answer: (B)

Since points A and D are symmetric about point E (the same length on both sides), point E must be the center of the semicircle with $\overline{AE}$ and $\overline{ED}$ each a radius of the semi-circle.

If the perimeter (circumference) of the semi-circle with center E is π, then the perimeter of a full circle with center E is 2π.

The circumference of a circle is $C = 2\pi r$, so the length of the radius of the circle (which is also the radius of the semicircle) is:

$2\pi = 2\pi r$
$1 = r$

Since the radius = 1 and $\overline{AE}$ and $\overline{ED}$ are both radii, then $\overline{AD} = 2$, which means $\overline{BC} = 2$ also.

$\overline{AB}$ and $\overline{CD}$ are also equal to the radius of the semi-circle, so these segments each have lengths of 1. Adding up the lengths of all of the segments, we get 6, or (B).

Math: OSSG Rectangles & Squares Questions

No.	Page	Q.	Diff.	Type	Test	Sect.	Answer
1	454	8	E	MC	2	2	
2	786	4	E	MC	7	7	
3	848	6	E	MC	8	7	
4	890	12	E	GI	9	2	
5	904	5	E	MC	9	5	
6	612	12	M	MC	4	9	
7	716	12	M	GI	6	4	
8	732	12	M	MC	6	8	
9	835	16	M	GI	8	3	
10	424	15	H	MC	1	8	
11	468	18	H	GI	2	5	
12	671	16	H	MC	5	8	
13	861	16	H	MC	8	9	

Math: OSSG Rectangles & Squares Answers

1	2	3	4	5	6	7	8	9	10	11	12	13
B	C	C	2 or 3	B	B	3400	D	5	E	8/5 or 1.6	E	C

Volume

Volume is the space inside a three dimensional object, like a box or cylinder.

Box Volume

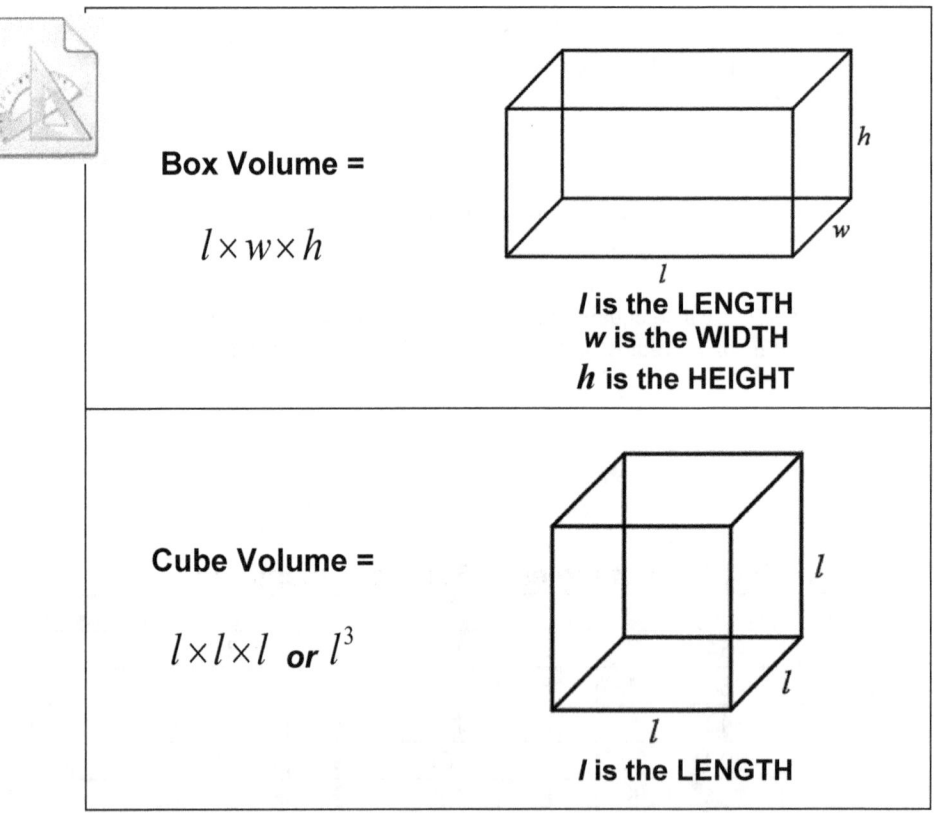

Box Volume =

$l \times w \times h$

l is the LENGTH
w is the WIDTH
h is the HEIGHT

Cube Volume =

$l \times l \times l$ **or** l^3

l is the LENGTH

Example:

What is the maximum number of cubes with sides of length 2 cm that can fit in a rectangular box with dimensions of 16 cm by 8cm by 4 cm?

(A) 8
(B) 16
(C) 32
(D) 64
(E) 256

Answer: (D)
The volume of a cube with sides of 2 is:
2 x 2 x 2 = 8.

The volume of a box with dimensions of 16 x 8 x 4 = 512.

The number of cubes that can fit in the box is the volume of the box (512) divided by the volume of the cube (8):

512/ 8 = 64, or (D).

Math: OSSG Box Volume Questions

No.	Page	Q.	Diff.	Type	Test	Sect.	Answer
1	467	11	E	GI	2	5	
2	423	11	M	MC	1	8	
3	702	12	M	MC	6	2	
4	979	10	M	MC	10	8	

Math: OSSG Box Volume Answers

1	2	3	4
32	A	D	C

Cylinder Volume

Cylinder Volume =

$$\pi r^2 \times h$$

(think: circle area x height)

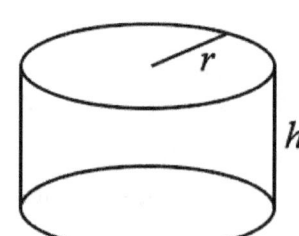

r is the RADIUS
h is the HEIGHT

Example:

Cylinder A has a volume of 24π and a height of 6. If cylinder B has the same radius as cylinder A and a height of 3, what is the volume of cylinder B?

(A) π
(B) 4π
(C) 6π
(D) 9π
(E) 12π

Tip:
Cylinder questions typically change the height of the cylinder and ask you to figure out the new volume. For cylinders with the same radius, when the height is halved, the volume is halved. When the height is doubled, the volume is doubled.

SAT Math

Answer: (E)

Applying the formula, $V = \pi r^2 \times h$ we find that the radius of cylinder *A* is:

$24\pi = \pi r^2 \times 6$
$4\pi = \pi r^2$
$4 = r^2$
$2 = r$

Since the radius of cylinder *A* (which is 2) is the same for cylinder *B*, we now apply the cylinder volume formula for cylinder *B* with radius of 2 and height of 3 to find the answer:

$V = \pi 2^2 \times 3$
$V = 4\pi \times 3$
$V = 12\pi$, or (E).

Math: OSSG Cylinder Volume Questions

No.	Page	Q.	Diff.	Type	Test	Sect.	Answer
1	669	10	M	MC	5	8	
2	457	18	H	MC	2	2	

Math: OSSG Cylinder Volume Answers

1	2
B	B

Internal Lines

The SAT will sometimes show you a two or three dimensional shape and ask you about the relationships of lengths passing from one corner (or 'vertex') of the shape to another.

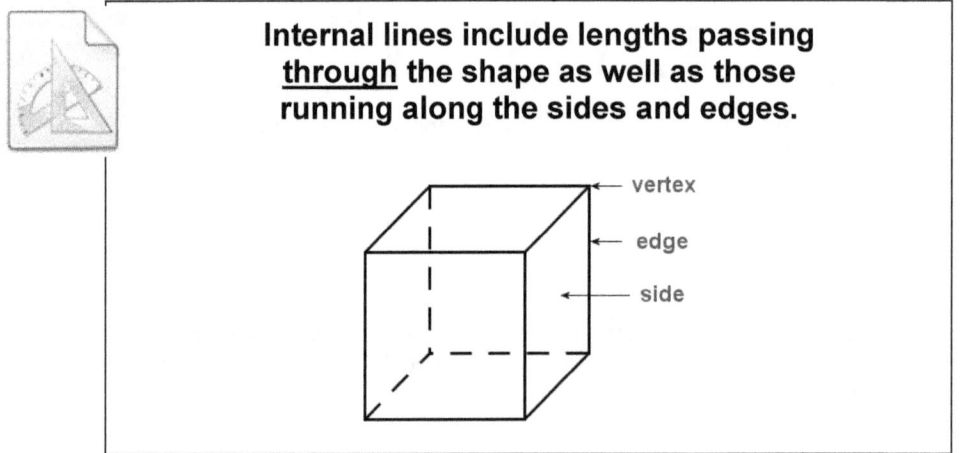

Internal lines include lengths passing through the shape as well as those running along the sides and edges.

Example:

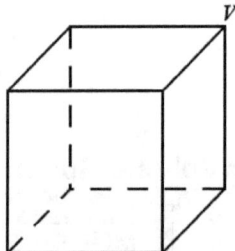

Line segments are to be drawn connecting vertex V with each of the other 7 vertices of the cube above. How many of the segments will <u>not</u> lie on an edge of the cube?

(A) 1
(B) 2
(C) 3
(D) 4
(E) 5

Hint:
An 'edge' of a shape is not the same as a 'side'.

Answer: (D)

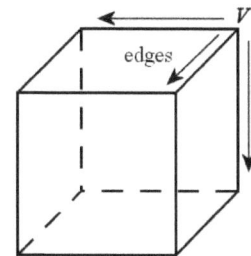

Out of 7 possible segments, 3 segments will lie on an edge, which means 4 segments will <u>not</u> lie on an edge, or (D).

 Math: OSSG Internal Lines Questions

No.	Page	Q.	Diff.	Type	Test	Sect.	Answer
1	419	2	E	MC	1	8	
2	650	2	E	MC	5	4	
3	851	15	M	MC	8	7	
4	919	15	M	MC	9	8	
5	485	12	H	MC	2	8	
6	527	7	H	MC	3	5	
7	717	17	H	GI	6	4	

Math: OSSG Internal Lines Answers

1	2	3	4	5	6	7
E	C	A	D	E	C	8

Coordinate Graphing

The SAT tests your knowledge of coordinate graphing concepts.

Coordinate Graphing (basic)

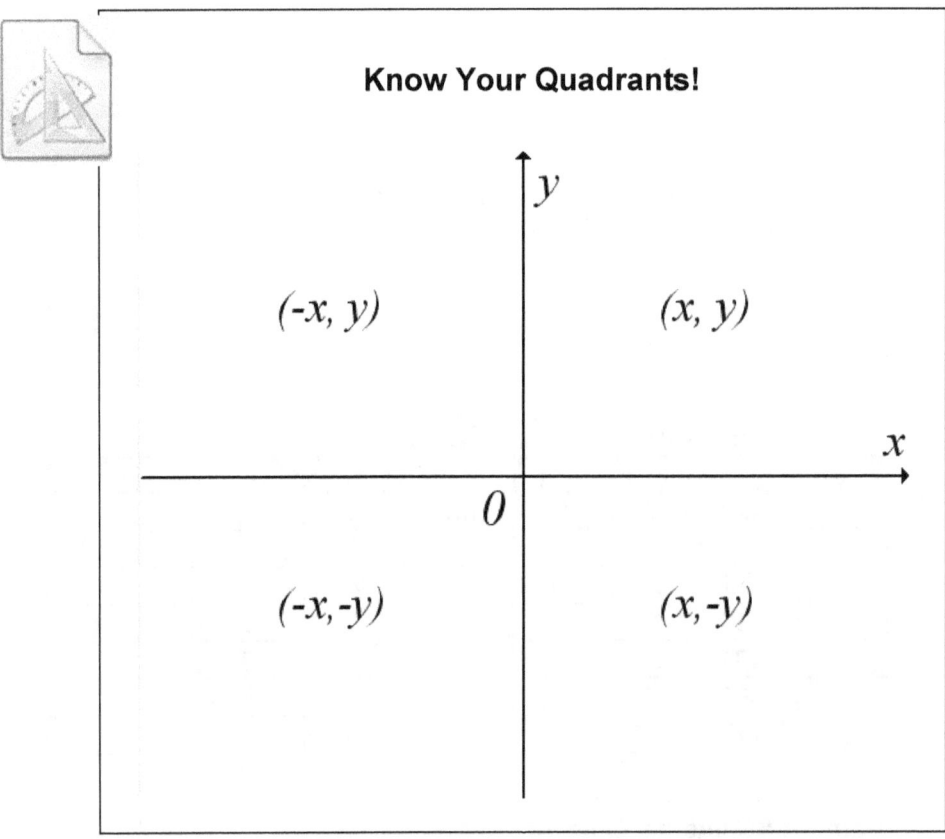

Basic SAT coordinate graphing questions focus primarily on testing whether you know where on the graph the x and y values are positive or negative.

Example:

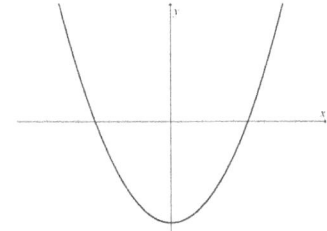

The equation of the graph above is $y = x^2 - 6$. Which of the following could be the graph of $y = |x^2 - 6|$?

(A)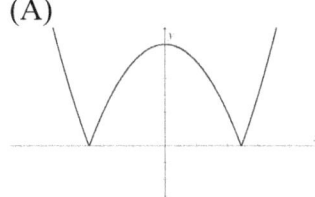

(B)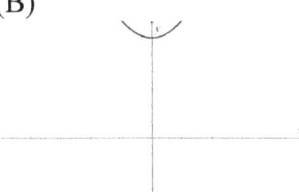

(C)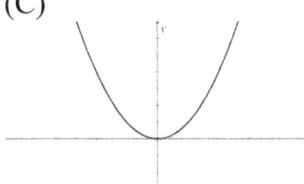

(D)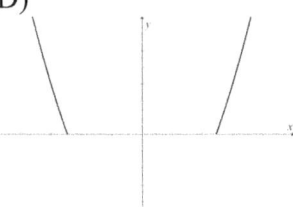

(E)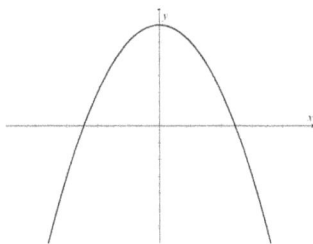

Answer: (A)
Adding the absolute value symbol simply means that wherever the *y* value in the original graph is negative that value becomes positive.

In other words, the part of the graph that was originally below the *x*-axis now flips above the *x*-axis.

Everything else about the graph stays the same. (A)

Math: OSSG Coordinate Graphing (basic) Questions

No.	Page	Q.	Diff.	Type	Test	Sect.	Answer
1	397	4	E	MC	1	3	
2	397	6	E	MC	1	3	
3	830	2	E	MC	8	3	
4	949	4	E	MC	10	2	
5	456	17	M	MC	2	2	
6	483	7	M	MC	2	8	
7	905	8	M	MC	9	5	

Math: OSSG Coordinate Graphing (basic) Answers

1	2	3	4	5	6	7
D	C	B	B	B	A	C

Coordinate Geometry

The SAT will also ask you to apply basic geometry formulas to a coordinate graphing system.

Where the question describes the graph of a triangle, circle or rectangle, use the given points to figure out your lengths and then apply the appropriate geometric formula(s).

Example:

In the *xy*-plane, a circle has a diameter with endpoints of (3, 3) and (3, -7). Which of the following are the coordinates of the center of the circle?

(A) (-7, 3)
(B) (0, -4)
(C) (0, 4)
(D) (3, -2)
(E) (3, 4)

Tip:
Draw 'quickie' graphs.
Where the question describes a geometric figure but does not provide a graph, drawing the graph can often help you better understand the question.

Answer: (D)

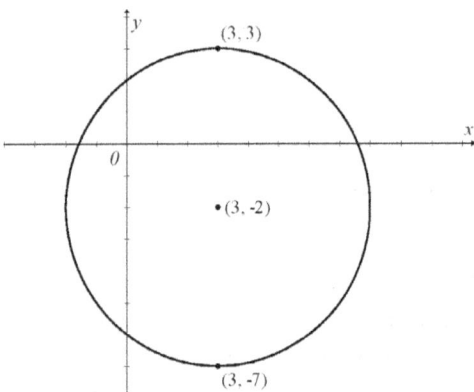

Because the shape is a circle, the center is located halfway between the two points of the diameter. Since the diameter of the circle has points at (3, 3) and (3, -7), the center of the circle is somewhere along the line $x = 3$.

The center's y coordinate is located halfway between 3 and -7, which is at -2. Thus (3, -2), or (D).

 Math: OSSG Coordinate Geometry Questions

No.	Page	Q.	Diff.	Type	Test	Sect.	Answer
1	420	4	E	MC	1	8	
2	525	2	E	MC	3	5	
3	611	8	M	MC	4	9	
4	669	8	M	MC	5	8	
5	702	8	M	MC	6	2	
6	717	15	M	GI	6	4	
7	769	4	M	MC	7	3	
8	655	18	H	GI	5	4	

Math: OSSG Coordinate Geometry Answers

1	2	3	4	5	6	7	8
C	B	C	E	A	12	C	2, 18

SAT Math

Coordinate Formulas

Where you are given a coordinate equation, plug coordinate values into the equation to solve for variables in other coordinate(s) and/or constants.

Example:

In the *xy*-coordinate system, $(3, t)$ is one of the points of intersection of the graphs $y = \frac{1}{3}x^2 - 1$ and $y = -\frac{1}{3}x^2 + h$ where h is a constant. What is the value of h?

Answer: (5)
To solve this problem, first plug in values of the point (3, *t*), where *x* = 3 and *y* = *t*, into the equation $y = \frac{1}{3}x^2 - 1$ to find *t*:

$t = \frac{1}{3}3^2 - 1$
$t = \frac{9}{3} - 1$
$t = 3 - 1 = 2$

Now that we know that *t* = 2, we plug the point (3, 2) into the equation $y = -\frac{1}{3}x^2 + h$ to find *h*:

$2 = -\frac{1}{3}3^2 + h$
$2 = -\frac{9}{3} + h$
$2 = -3 + h$

$5 = h$

Math: OSSG Coordinate Formula Questions

No.	Page	Q.	Diff.	Type	Test	Sect.	Answer
1	951	10	E	GI	10	2	
2	529	12	M	GI	3	5	
3	584	12	M	MC	4	3	
4	772	12	M	GI	7	3	
5	849	9	M	MC	8	7	
6	917	8	M	MC	9	8	
7	530	18	H	GI	3	5	
8	717	18	H	GI	6	4	

Math: OSSG Coordinate Formula Answers

1	2	3	4	5	6	7	8
10	13	D	3	A	A	½ or .5	16

Slope

Slope (basic)

SLOPE = $\dfrac{\text{RISE (how far the line travels UP or DOWN along the y-axis)}}{\text{RUN (how far the line travels LEFT or RIGHT along the x-axis)}}$

$y = \underline{m}x + \underline{b}$

m is the SLOPE

b is the *y*-INTERCEPT
(where line crosses the *y*-axis)

Example:

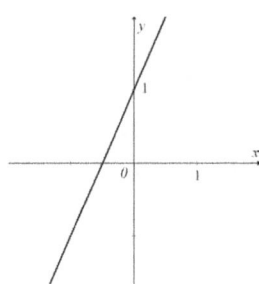

The figure above shows the graph of the line $y = ax + b$, where a and b are constants. Which of the following best represents the graph of the line $y = -ax - b$?

(A)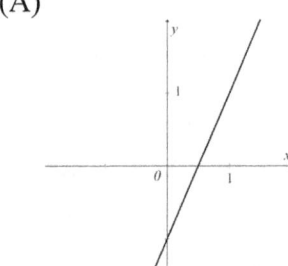

(B)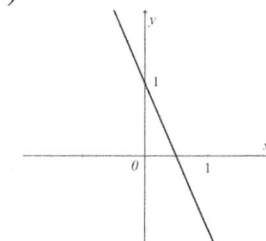

(C)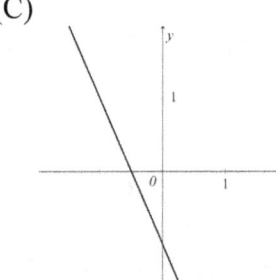

(D)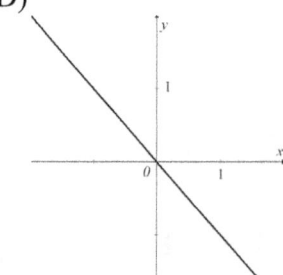

(E)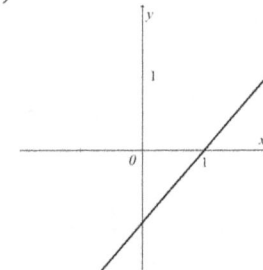

Tip:
Lines with POSITIVE slopes travel UP as they move right.
Lines with NEGATIVE slopes travel DOWN as they move right.

SAT Math

Answer: (C)

The graph of the original figure shows that the line $y = ax + b$ has a positive slope (moving upwards from left to right) and a y-intercept of 1.

The question asks what the figure would look like with a negative slope ($-a$) and a negative y-intercept ($-b$).

That means we are looking for a graph with a downward slope and a y-intercept of -1.

The only graph that satisfies both criteria is (C).

Math: OSSG Slope (basic) Questions

No.	Page	Q.	Diff.	Type	Test	Sect.	Answer
1	609	2	E	MC	4	9	
2	400	15	M	MC	1	3	
3	464	6	M	MC	2	5	
4	788	12	M	MC	7	7	
5	850	14	M	MC	8	7	
6	859	9	M	MC	8	9	
7	887	4	M	MC	9	2	
8	918	13	M	MC	9	8	
9	953	17	H	GI	10	2	

Math: OSSG Slope (basic) Answers

1	2	3	4	5	6	7	8	9
D	B	A	E	D	A	B	B	$0<x<3/8$

Slope: Perpendicular Lines and Reflections

**Slopes of PERPENDICULAR lines
(at right angles to each other)
are NEGATIVE RECIPROCALS.**

A line with slope of *m*, will *have* a perpendicular line with slope $-\dfrac{1}{m}$.

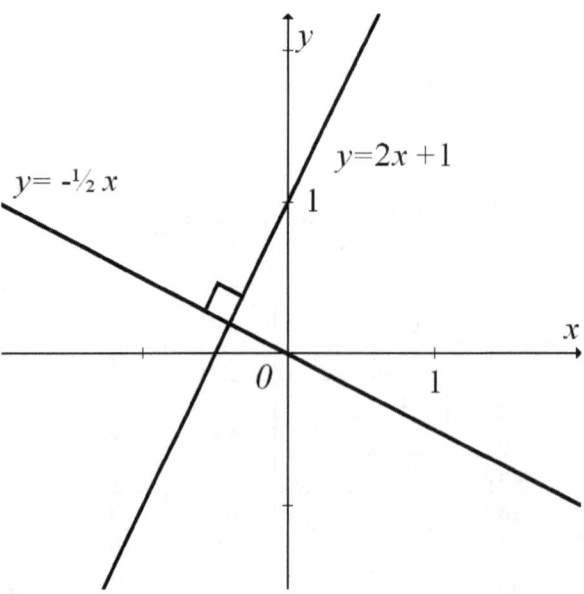

Perpendicular Lines

**_Tip:_
Perpendicular lines do not necessarily have related y-intercepts (b).** *Any line whose slope is the negative reciprocal of another is perpendicular to the other line regardless of where either line crosses the y-axis.*

SAT Math

A line REFLECTED about the x-axis has:

a NEGATIVE SLOPE
and
a NEGATIVE Y-INTERCEPT of the line it reflects

A line with slope of m and y-intercept of b ($y = mx + b$) will have a line reflected about the x-axis with a slope of $-m$ and a y-intercept of $-b$ ($y = -mx - b$).

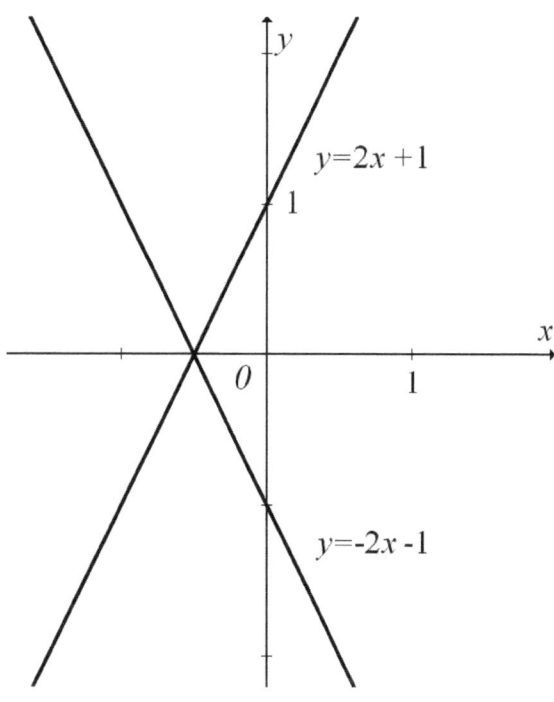

Reflected Lines
(about the x-axis)

Example 1:

The equation of line l is $3x + 2y = 8$. Which of the following is an equation of a line that is perpendicular to line l ?

(A) $y = \dfrac{2}{3}x + 1$

(B) $y = -\dfrac{2}{3}x - 1$

(C) $y = 3x + 4$

(D) $y = -\dfrac{3}{2}x + 4$

(E) $y = \dfrac{3}{2}x - 4$

Example 2:

The equation of line l is $3x + 2y = 8$. Which of the following is the equation of line l reflected about the x-axis ?

(A) $y = \dfrac{2}{3}x + 1$

(B) $y = -\dfrac{2}{3}x - 1$

(C) $y = 3x + 4$

(D) $y = -\dfrac{3}{2}x + 4$

(E) $y = \dfrac{3}{2}x - 4$

SAT Math

Answer 1: (A)
First, rewrite the equation $3x + 2y = 8$ in $y = mx + b$ form:

$2y = -3x + 8$
$y = -\frac{3}{2}x + 2$

So, now we know line l has a slope of $-\frac{3}{2}$.

A line *perpendicular* to line l will have a slope that is the negative reciprocal of $-\frac{3}{2}$, which is $\frac{2}{3}$.

The only equation with slope (m) of $\frac{2}{3}$ is (A).

Answer 2: (E)
Again, rewrite the equation $3x + 2y = 8$ in $y = mx + b$ form: $y = -\frac{3}{2}x + 2$

Line l has a slope of $-\frac{3}{2}$ and a y-intercept of 2.

A line *reflected* about the x-axis will have a negative slope and negative y-intercept of the other line, which means the reflected equation will be: $y = \frac{3}{2}x - 2$, or (E).

Math: OSSG Slope: Perpendicular Lines and Reflections Questions

No.	Page	Q.	Diff.	Type	Test	Sect.	Answer
1	484	9	E	MC	2	8	
2	415	6	M	MC	1	7	
3	546	10	M	MC	3	8	
4	585	16	M	MC	4	3	
5	731	7	M	MC	6	8	
6	798	11	M	MC	7	9	
7	457	20	H	MC	2	2	
8	642	17	H	MC	5	2	
9	888	8	H	MC	9	2	

Math: OSSG Slope: Perpendicular Lines and Reflections Answers

1	2	3	4	5	6	7	8	9
A	C	E	C	C	B	E	A	D

Algebra & Functions

Equations

Solving Equations

The SAT tests basic algebraic equation solving. These questions tend to be fairly easy but are worth practicing as a good way to rack up points.

Example:

If $5(x + 4) = 35$, then $x =$

(A) $\dfrac{31}{5}$

(B) $\dfrac{39}{5}$

(C) 3

(D) 11

(E) 31

Answer:
$5(x+4) = 35$

Divide by 5:
$x + 4 = 7$

Subtract 4:
$x = $ **3,** or (C).

Math: OSSG Solving Equations Questions

No.	Page	Q.	Diff.	Type	Test	Sect.	Answer
1	638	1	E	MC	5	2	
2	729	1	E	MC	6	8	
3	831	4	E	MC	8	3	
4	915	1	E	MC	9	8	
5	951	9	E	GI	10	2	
6	546	11	M	MC	3	8	
7	967	9	M	MC	10	5	

Math: OSSG Solving Equations Answers

1	2	3	4	5	6	7
D	D	C	C	13/2, 6.5	E	D

Writing Equations (basic)

One of the most important skills for solving many math questions on the SAT is the ability to write an equation based on textual information in the question.

SAT Equation Writing Terminology

Term	Symbol
increased by, added to, more than, plus, sum of, total	+
decreased by, fewer, less than, difference	-
multiplied by, product, times, of	X
divided by	/
is, equals, in terms of, is the same as	=
is less than	<
is greater than	>
percent	%
square	x^2
square root	$\sqrt{x}$

Example:

If 4 more than twice a number is equal to 13, what is 4 times the number?

(A) $4\frac{1}{2}$

(B) 9

(C) $13\frac{1}{2}$

(D) 18

(E) $22\frac{1}{2}$

Tip:
When writing equations, make 'a number' the variable 'x'.

Answer: (D)
"If 4 more than twice a number is equal to 13,"
$$4 + 2x = 13$$

or:
$4 + 2x = 13$

Subtract 4:
$2x = 9$

Divide by 2:
$x = 9/2$

"what is 4 times the number?"

$9/2 (4) = 36/2$ or 18, or (D).

Math: OSSG Writing Equations (basic) Questions

No.	Page	Q.	Diff.	Type	Test	Sect.	Answer
1	454	6	E	MC	2	2	
2	466	9	E	GI	2	5	
3	543	1	E	MC	3	8	
4	730	3	E	MC	6	8	
5	771	10	E	GI	7	3	
6	977	2	E	MC	10	8	
7	529	14	M	GI	3	5	
8	613	14	M	MC	4	9	
9	889	10	M	GI	9	2	
10	457	19	H	MC	2	2	

Math: OSSG Writing Equations (basic) Answers

1	2	3	4	5	6	7	8	9	10
D	9/2 or 4.5	C	B	128	E	5/4	E	10/3, 3.33	E

Writing Equations (Word Problems)

Another form of equation writing involves using real world examples instead of simple math terms.

Example:

A long distance phone call cost 50 cents for the first minute and 9 cents for each additional minute. If the phone call lasted 10 minutes, how much did the call cost in cents?

(A) 59
(B) 90
(C) 131
(D) 450
(E) 500

Tip:
When writing equations for word problems, make 'x' the value you are trying to find.

Answer: (C)

The equation for this question is:

cost = rate of 1st min. + (minutes of call - 1st min.) x (rate of additional min.)

or:

$x = 50 + (10-1)9$

$x = 50 + (9)9$

$x = 50 + 81$

$x = 131$, or (C).

Math: OSSG Writing Equations (Word) Questions

No.	Page	Q.	Diff.	Type	Test	Sect.	Answer
1	396	2	E	MC	1	3	
2	414	3	E	MC	1	7	
3	452	2	E	MC	2	2	
4	609	1	E	MC	4	9	
5	653	9	E	GI	5	4	
6	700	1	E	MC	6	2	
7	858	4	E	MC	8	9	
8	948	1	E	MC	10	2	
9	966	4	E	MC	10	5	
10	417	13	M	GI	1	7	
11	716	13	M	GI	6	4	
12	890	13	M	GI	9	2	
13	952	11	M	GI	10	2	
14	468	17	H	GI	2	5	

Math: OSSG Writing Equations (Word) Answers

1	2	3	4	5	6	7	8	9	10	11	12	13	14
E	E	A	C	7	C	C	C	E	D	6	450	36	45	40

Rate x Time = Distance (RT = D)

One type of word problem requires that you know the formula:

RT = D
(**R**ate x **T**ime = **D**istance)

Example:

A submerged submarine travels twice as fast as a surfaced submarine. If a submerged submarine travels 40 miles in 2 hours, how many minutes does it take a surfaced submarine to cover the same distance?

(A)   4
(B)   20
(C)   80
(D)   120
(E)   240

Tip:
Don't confuse minutes and hours.
A common SAT trick is to mix up the time scales for hours and minutes. Before answering, be sure to convert the time to the scale the question asks for.

Answer: (E)
'a submerged submarine travels 40 miles in 2 hours,'

```
R T  = D
R 2  = 40
R    = 20
```

(The submerged submarine travels **20 miles per hour**.)

'A submerged submarine travels twice as fast as a surfaced submarine.'

```
1/2   R (submerged)  = Rate (surfaced)
1/2      (20)        =      10
```

(If the submerged submarine travels 20 miles per hour, a surfaced submarine at half that rate travels **10 miles per hour**.)

"how many minutes does it take a surfaced submarine to cover the same distance?"

```
 R T = D
10 T = 40
   T = 4
```

(At 10 miles per hour, the surfaced submarine takes **4 hours** to travel 40 miles.)

4 hours = **240 minutes**, or (E).

Math: OSSG RT x D Questions

No.	Page	Q.	Diff.	Type	Test	Sect.	Answer
1	528	9	E	GI	3	5	
2	886	2	E	MC	9	2	
3	849	10	M	MC	8	7	
4	966	6	M	MC	10	5	

Math: OSSG RT x D Answers

1	2	3	4
93/2, 46.5	C	B	A

SAT Math

Exponents & Roots

Exponent Rules

$(x^a)^b = x^{ab}$	$(xy)^a = x^a y^a$	$x^a \times x^b = x^{a+b}$	$x^1 = x$
$x^{-a} = \dfrac{1}{x^a}$	$\left(\dfrac{x}{y}\right)^a = \dfrac{x^a}{y^a}$	$\dfrac{x^a}{x^b} = x^{a-b}$	$x^0 = 1$

Roots Rules

$\sqrt{x} \times \sqrt{y} = \sqrt{xy}$	$\sqrt[b]{x^a} = x^{\frac{a}{b}}$
$\sqrt{\dfrac{x}{y}} = \dfrac{\sqrt{x}}{\sqrt{y}}$	$\sqrt{x} + \sqrt{y} \neq \sqrt{x+y}$

Simplifying Exponents & Roots

Simplify roots by squaring BOTH sides.

Example:

If $\sqrt{x} = y^4$, what is x in terms of y?

(A) $\sqrt{y}$
(B) y
(C) y^2
(D) y^4
(E) y^8

Tip:
'what is x in terms of y?' simply means 'solve for x'.

Answer: (E)

$$\sqrt{x} = y^4$$

To solve for x, square both sides:
$$(\sqrt{x})^2 = (y^4)^2$$

which solves as:
$x = y^8$, or (E).

Where both sides of the equation are squares or cubes, take the root of BOTH sides.

Example 1:

If $x^2 = y^4$, what is x in terms of y?

(A) $\sqrt{y}$
(B) y
(C) y^2
(D) y^3
(E) y^8

Example 2:

If $(x+4)^3 = 27$, what is the value of x?

(A) -7
(B) -1
(C) 5
(D) 23
(E) 31

SAT Math

Answer 1: (C)

$x^2 = y^4$

To solve for x, take the square root of both sides:

$\sqrt{x^2} = \sqrt{y^4}$

which solves as:

$x = y^2$ or (C).

Answer 2: (B)

$(x+4)^3 = 27$

To solve for x, first take the cube root of both sides:

$\sqrt[3]{(x+4)^3} = \sqrt[3]{27}$

which solves as:

$x + 4 = 3$
$x = 3 - 4$
$x = -1$, or (B).

Simplify NEGATIVE exponents by raising both sides to a power of '–1'.

Example:

If $x^{-2} = y^4$, what is x in terms of y?

(A) y^{-8}
(B) y^{-4}
(C) y^{-2}
(D) y^6
(E) y^8

Remember!
When <u>raising</u> an exponent by another exponent, <u>multiply</u> the exponents.

Answer: (C)

$x^{-2} = y^4$

To solve for x, first 'raise both sides by a power of -1:

$(x^{-2})^{-1} = (y^4)^{-1}$

which solves as:

$x^2 = y^{-4}$

Next, take the square root of both sides:

$\sqrt{x^2} = \sqrt{y^{-4}}$

which solves as:

$x = y^{-2}$, or (C).

Simplify values of square roots by factoring out squares from underneath the root sign.

Example:

If $12\sqrt{12} = h\sqrt{k}$, where h & k are positive integers and $h > k$, which of the following could be the value of $h + k$?

(A) 12
(B) 24
(C) 27
(D) 51
(E) 144

Answer: (C)

$12\sqrt{12} = h\sqrt{k}$

To solve, first simplify the root by factoring out any squares:
$12\sqrt{4 \times 3} = 12\sqrt{4}\sqrt{3} = 12(2)\sqrt{3} = 24\sqrt{3}$

If:
$24\sqrt{3} = h\sqrt{k}$

Then:
$h = 24$ and $k = 3$

So:
$h + k = 24 + 3 = 27$, or (C).

You can NOT take the square root of a negative number!

Example:

If $y = \sqrt{x+2}$, and x and y are real numbers, which of the following can NOT be the value of x ?

(A) -3
(B) -2
(C) -1
(D)   1
(E)   2

Remember!
Whenever a question asks 'which of the following' or 'what is the value', plug the answer choices into the question.

Answer: (A)

$y = \sqrt{x+2}$

Plugging in each answer for *x* in the equation, we see that for (A)

$y = \sqrt{-3+2}$

$y = \sqrt{-1}$

Because the square root of a number cannot be negative, the correct answer is (A).

(All other answers produce non-negative values under the root sign.)

Math: OSSG Simplifying Exponents Questions

No.	Page	Q.	Diff.	Type	Test	Sect.	Answer
1	416	9	E	GI	1	7	
2	454	9	E	MC	2	2	
3	544	5	E	MC	3	8	
4	667	2	E	MC	5	8	
5	456	14	M	MC	2	2	
6	484	10	M	MC	2	8	
7	788	11	M	MC	7	7	
8	788	14	M	MC	7	7	
9	595	7	H	MC	4	6	
10	652	6	H	MC	5	4	
11	790	19	H	MC	7	7	

Math: OSSG Simplifying Exponents Answers

1	2	3	4	5	6	7	8	9	10	11
9	D	C	B	E	C	C	C	C	D	A

Equalizing Exponent Bases

The SAT also tests your ability to set the exponent bases equal to each other.

To set exponent bases equal to one another, FACTOR the larger number so that the BASE of this number is EQUAL TO the smaller.

Once the bases of the numbers are the same, you can solve for variable(s) in the exponents.

Example:

If and x and y are positive integers and $2^x \times 2^y = 64$, what is the value of $x + y$?

(A) $\dfrac{1}{6}$

(B) $\dfrac{1}{2}$

(C) 6

(D) 32

(E) 64

 Remember!
When <u>multiplying</u> numbers with the same base, <u>add</u> the exponents.

Answer: (C)

$2^x \times 2^y = 64$

Factoring 64 in terms of base 2, we get 2^6.

Substituting 2^6 for 64 in our original equation we get:
$2^x \times 2^y = 2^6$

Since:
$2^x \times 2^y = 2^{x+y}$

Then:
$2^{x+y} = 2^6$

Thus:
$x + y = 6$, or (C).

Math: OSSG Equalizing Exponent Bases Questions

No.	Page	Q.	Diff.	Type	Test	Sect.	Answer
1	529	11	E	GI	3	5	
2	581	2	E	MC	4	3	
3	422	8	M	MC	1	8	
4	611	7	M	MC	4	9	
5	669	7	M	MC	5	8	
6	831	5	M	MC	8	3	
7	891	15	M	GI	9	2	
8	980	11	M	MC	10	8	
9	714	8	H	MC	6	4	

Math: OSSG Equalizing Exponent Bases Answers

1	2	3	4	5	6	7	8	9
1,2,4	A	B	D	A	D	5	A	B

Inequalities

Questions testing your knowledge of inequalities (< 'less than', > 'greater than') also appear on the SAT.

**For inequalities:
watch out for negative numbers and
positive fractions less than 1**

Remember that larger negative numbers are <u>less</u> than smaller ones. For example: -8 < -2.

Also remember that positive fractions less than 1 behave differently than integers.

For example: $\left(\frac{1}{2}\right)^2 < \frac{1}{2}$

Example:

If $x - y = 28$ and $x < 9$, which of the following must be true?

(A) $y > 0$
(B) $y < -19$
(C) $y = 19$
(D) $y > -19$
(E) $x > 0$

Tip:
Change the < or > to = and solve.
Instead of trying to substitute numbers less than or greater than x, simply substitute the number as <u>equal to</u> x and solve to find the value of y. Then figure out whether the final answer needs to be greater or less than that value.

Answer: (B)

$x - y = 28$ and $x < 9$

First set $x = 9$ and substitute:
$9 - y = 28$
$-y = 19$
$y = -19$

Now that we have the value of y (-19), we need to figure out whether y needs to be greater or less than that value.

Since $x < 9$ and we are subtracting a negative y value (which is the same as adding a positive y), y needs to be a negative value <u>less</u> than -19 in order for the equation $x - y$ to equal 28.

Thus (B).

Math: OSSG Inequalities Questions

No.	Page	Q.	Diff.	Type	Test	Sect.	Answer
1	464	5	E	MC	2	5	
2	581	1	E	MC	4	3	
3	581	3	E	MC	4	3	
4	712	2	E	MC	6	4	
5	769	3	E	MC	7	3	
6	640	10	M	MC	5	2	
7	703	13	M	MC	6	2	
8	906	13	M	MC	9	5	
9	732	14	H	MC	6	8	

Math: OSSG Inequalities Answers

1	2	3	4	5	6	7	8	9
E	E	E	A	B	B	E	D	E

SAT Math

Absolute Value

The absolute value | x | is ALWAYS the POSITIVE value of x.

For instance, the absolute value of -2 is 2, written as | -2 | = 2.

Example:

$$|x-2|=1$$

What is the least value of x that satisfies the equation above?

Remember!
Whether the value inside the | | is positive or negative, the value always comes outside as <u>positive</u>.

Answer:
The two possible values of x that satisfy the equation are 3 and 1:

$|3-2|=1$

$|1-2|=|-1|=1$

Since $1 < 3$, the *least* value that satisfies the equation is **1**.

Absolute Value and Inequalities

Absolute value questions can also include an inequality ($<$, $>$) in place of the equal ($=$) sign.

Example:

If $4 < |x-2| < 5$ and $x < 0$, what is one possible value of $|x|$?

SAT Math

Answer: 2 < x < 3

The key here is that the question says that *x* must be <u>less than</u> zero (or negative).

Thus, negative values for *x* that satisfy the equation are those between -2 and -3, or -2 < *x* < -3

For example, if *x* = -2.5, then | -2.5 – 2 | = |-4.5| = 4.5

Usually a negative value is not permitted for grid-in answers, but notice that the question asks for the <u>absolute value of *x*</u>.

The absolute value of -2 < *x* < -3 is the same as **2 < x < 3**, which is the final answer.

Math: OSSG Absolute Value Questions

No.	Page	Q.	Diff.	Type	Test	Sect.	Answer
1	545	7	E	MC	3	8	
2	653	10	E	GI	5	4	
3	418	15	M	GI	1	7	
4	669	9	M	MC	5	8	
5	860	10	M	MC	8	9	
6	917	9	M	MC	9	8	

Math: OSSG Absolute Value Answers

1	2	3	4	5	6
A	13	2.5 or 5/2	D	E	A

Substitution

Substituting Numbers

Solve for one equation and
plug the numerical answer into another equation.

Example:

If $x = y + 4$ and $4x + 8x = 12$, what is the value of y?

(A)   -5
(B)   -3
(C)   0
(D)   7
(E)   12

Answer: (B)

$4x + 8x = 12$
$12x = 12$
$x = 1$

Now, plug 1 into the first equation for x and solve for y:
$x = y + 4$
$1 = y + 4$
$-3 = y$, or (B).

Math: OSSG Substituting Numbers Questions

No.	Page	Q.	Diff.	Type	Test	Sect.	Answer
1	414	4	E	MC	1	7	
2	463	1	E	MC	2	5	
3	514	1	E	MC	3	2	
4	701	7	E	MC	6	2	
5	712	1	E	MC	6	4	
6	771	9	E	GI	7	3	
7	857	2	E	MC	8	9	
8	772	13	M	GI	7	3	

Math: OSSG Substituting Numbers Answers

1	2	3	4	5	6	7	8
D	B	A	B	E	2/5 or .4	D	8/3, 2.66, 2.67

Substituting Variables

Find or solve for one variable and plug the variable into another equation.

Example:

If $4x = 3y$ and $3y = 8z$, what does x equal in terms of z?

(A) $\dfrac{32}{9}z$

(B) $\dfrac{8}{3}z$

(C) $2z$

(D) $6z$

(E) $24z$

Answer: (C)
$3y = 8z$
$4x = 8z$
$x = 2z$

Math: OSSG Substituting Variables Questions

No.	Page	Q.	Diff.	Type	Test	Sect.	Answer
1	887	3	E	MC	9	2	
2	422	10	M	MC	1	8	
3	594	5	M	MC	4	6	
4	640	7	M	MC	5	2	

Math: OSSG Substituting Variables Answers

1	2	3	4
C	B	D	C

Substituting Combinations

Find the value of a variable COMBINATION (rather than a single variable),

then plug the value of the COMBINATION into the other equation.

Example:

If $x^3 = 127$, what is the value of $5x^3$?

Answer: 635

$x^3 = 127$

$5x^3 = 5(127) = 635$

Math: OSSG Substituting Combinations Questions

No.	Page	Q.	Diff.	Type	Test	Sect.	Answer
1	398	7	E	MC	1	3	
2	516	6	E	MC	3	2	
3	596	9	E	GI	4	6	
4	650	1	E	MC	5	4	
5	768	2	E	MC	7	3	
6	833	9	E	GI	8	3	
7	950	8	H	MC	10	2	

Math: OSSG Substituting Combinations Answers

1	2	3	4	5	6	7
D	B	1404	A	E	120	A

Substituting Combinations and Factoring

Sometimes you may need to FACTOR an equation before plugging in the value of the variable combination.

Example:

If $x^2y + xy^2 = 21$ and $x + y = 3$, what is the value of xy?

Tip:
When the question asks for the value of a <u>combination</u> of variables, **solve for the combination**. Do NOT try to solve for variables individually.

Answer: 7

Factor:

$$x^2y + xy^2 = 21$$

$$xy(x+y) = 21$$

$$xy(3) = 21$$

$$xy = 7$$

Math: OSSG Substituting Combinations & Factoring Questions

No.	Page	Q.	Diff.	Type	Test	Sect.	Answer
1	700	3	E	MC	6	2	
2	847	2	E	MC	8	7	
3	903	2	E	MC	9	5	
4	400	16	M	MC	1	3	
5	716	14	M	GI	6	4	
6	919	16	H	MC	9	8	

Math: OSSG Substituting Combinations & Factoring Answers

1	2	3	4	5	6
C	B	E	A	½ or .5	D

Substituting Difference of Two Squares

If an SAT math question includes the difference of two squares, factoring the expression will almost always be the key to figuring out the correct answer.

ALWAYS FACTOR the difference of two squares:

$$a^2 - b^2 = (a+b)(a-b)$$

Example:

If $5(x^2 - y^2) = 80$ and $x + y = 8$, what is the value of $x - y$?

Answer: 2

$5(x^2 - y^2) = 80$ and $x + y = 8$

$5(x + y)(x - y) = 80$
$5(8)(x - y) = 80$
$40(x - y) = 80$
$x - y = 2$

Math: OSSG Substituting Difference of Two Squares Questions

No.	Page	Q.	Diff.	Type	Test	Sect.	Answer
1	399	14	M	MC	1	3	
2	597	12	M	GI	4	6	
3	797	7	M	MC	7	9	
4	835	15	H	GI	8	3	

Math: OSSG Substituting Difference of Two Squares Answers

1	2	3	4
E	9	B	2

Functions

One of the most important skills you need for the SAT Math section is the ability to understand and solve questions about functions.

Function Tables

For function table questions, plug the value of x into each answer to find the value of $f(x)$.

The correct answer will be the equation that works for EVERY pair of values in the table.

Think of a function like a math machine. For every value x you plug into an equation, $f(x)$ is the value you get out.

Example:

x	0	1	2	3
$f(x)$	5	4	3	2

The table above gives values of the linear function f for selected values of x. Which of the following defines f ?

(A) $f(x) = x + 3$
(B) $f(x) = 3x - 2$
(C) $f(x) = x - 5$
(D) $f(x) = -x + 3$
(E) $f(x) = -x + 5$

Tip:
If a table includes 0 (which it usually will), <u>plug in 0 first</u> to quickly eliminate incorrect answer choices.

SAT Math

Answer: (E)

Here we see that that one of the pairs includes 0 for x. Plugging 0 into each equation for x, we can quickly see that $-x+5$ is the only equation that produces the corresponding value of 5 for $f(x)$.

Math: OSSG Function Tables Questions

No.	Page	Q.	Diff.	Type	Test	Sect.	Answer
1	482	3	E	MC	2	8	
2	948	2	E	MC	10	2	
3	702	9	M	MC	6	2	
4	849	11	M	MC	8	7	
5	400	18	H	MC	1	3	

Math: OSSG Function Tables Answers

1	2	3	4	5
C	E	A	E	D

Values of Functions

Functions Values questions most often include TWO function equations:

1. The first equation tells you the function FORMULA.

2. The second function tells you which VALUES to plug into the formula to find the answer.

Steps to solve:

Step 1: Where the function symbol in the second equation is multiplied a number, simplify the second equation by DIVIDING both sides by that number.

Step 2: If the second equation function symbol equals a value, set the formula EQUAL TO that value.

Step 3: Plug any value and/or variable(s) INSIDE THE PARENTHESES of the second function symbol into formula for x.

Example:

If $f(x) = 2x + 1$ and $2f(2p) = 6$, solve for p.

SAT Math

Answer: $\frac{1}{2}$

Step 1: Where the function symbol in the second equation is multiplied a number, simplify the second equation by <u>dividing</u> both sides by that number.

Dividing both sides of $2f(2p) = 6$ by 2, we get $f(2p) = 3$.

Step 2: If the second function symbol equals a value, set the formula <u>equal to</u> that value.

Now that we know that the function $f(2p) = 3$, we need to set the first function formula *equal to* 3. So $f(x) = 2x + 1$ becomes $3 = 2x + 1$.

Step 3: Plug any value and/or variable(s) *inside* the parentheses of the second function symbol into the first function formula for *x*.

Plugging the value in the parentheses of the second equation ($2p$) into the formula $2x + 1$, we get $3 = 2(2p) + 1$.

Step 4: Solve the first equation.

$$3 = 2(2p) + 1, \quad 3 = 4p + 1, \quad 2 = 4p, \quad p = \frac{2}{4} = \frac{1}{2}$$

Math: OSSG Values of Functions Questions

No.	Page	Q.	Diff.	Type	Test	Sect.	Answer
1	639	4	E	MC	5	2	
2	467	14	M	GI	2	5	
3	583	10	M	MC	4	3	
4	654	13	M	GI	5	4	
5	861	13	M	MC	8	9	
6	906	14	M	MC	9	5	
7	970	19	M	MC	10	5	
8	518	16	H	MC	3	2	
9	519	19	H	MC	3	2	
10	597	16	H	GI	4	6	
11	861	14	H	MC	8	9	
12	891	18	H	GI	9	2	

Math: OSSG Values of Functions Answers

1	2	3	4	5	6	7	8	9	10	11	12
D	4.25<x<8.5 or 17/4<x<17/2	D	28	D	B	E	A	C	2,7	A	3

Function Word Problems

For function word problems, simply plug in values for variables the same way you would for any other function problem (see above).

Example:

For Alex's dog walking business, the net profit P, in dollars, of money made by walking d dogs is given by the function $P(d) = 20d - 20$. If Alex walked 5 dogs, what is her net profit?

(A) $10
(B) $20
(C) $40
(D) $60
(E) $80

Answer: (E)

Plugging in 5 for *d* into the equation:

$$P(d) = 20d - 20$$

we get:

$$P(5) = 20(5) - 20 = 100 - 20 = 80,$$

or (E).

Math: OSSG Function Word Problems Questions

No.	Page	Q.	Diff.	Type	Test	Sect.	Answer
1	594	4	E	MC	4	6	
2	517	10	M	MC	3	2	
3	641	13	M	MC	5	2	
4	731	8	M	MC	6	8	
5	980	13	M	MC	10	8	
6	424	16	H	MC	1	8	
7	773	18	H	GI	7	3	
8	851	17	H	MC	8	7	
9	908	19	H	MC	9	5	

Math: OSSG Function Word Problems Answers

1	2	3	4	5	6	7	8	9
E	D	B	E	D	B	70	B	C

Symbol Functions

Don't be confused by strange symbols; they are simply function questions in disguise.

The values next to or within a symbol function tell you which values to plug in for which variables in the formula.

Example:

For all integers x and y, let the operation ◊ be defined by $x \diamond y = 2x - y$. If $2 \diamond 1 = 3 \diamond a$, what is the value of a?

(A) 0
(B) 1
(C) 2
(D) 3
(E) 4

Answer: (D)

$x \diamond y = 2x - y$

Whatever value appears on the left side of the $\diamond$ symbol is what we plug into the formula $2x - y$ for x and whatever value appears on the right side of the $\diamond$ symbol is what we plug into the formula $2x - y$ for y.

So, for the values:
$2 \diamond 1 = 3 \diamond a$

On the left side of the equation we plug in 2 for x and 1 for y into the formula $2x - y$.

$\quad 2 \diamond 1 = 3 \diamond a$
$\quad 2x - y = 3 \diamond a$
$2(2) - 1 = 3 \diamond a$
$\quad\quad 3 = 3 \diamond a$

Now on the right side of the equation we plug in 3 for x and a for y into the formula $2x - y$ and then solve for a.

$\quad 3 = 3 \diamond a$
$\quad 3 = 2x - y$
$\quad 3 = 2(3) - a$
$\quad 3 = 6 - a$
$-3 = -a$
$\quad 3 = a$, or (D).

Math: OSSG Symbol Functions Questions

No.	Page	Q.	Diff.	Type	Test	Sect.	Answer
1	420	3	E	MC	1	8	
2	543	2	E	MC	3	8	
3	593	1	E	MC	4	6	
4	890	11	E	GI	9	2	
5	585	17	M	MC	4	3	
6	670	11	M	MC	5	8	
7	967	10	M	MC	10	5	
8	456	15	H	MC	2	2	
9	705	20	H	MC	6	2	
10	800	16	H	MC	7	9	
11	835	17	H	GI	8	3	

Math: OSSG Symbol Functions Answers

1	2	3	4	5	6	7	8	9	10	11
A	B	D	875	A	A	E	B	E	C	11

Graphing Functions

**A value EQUAL TO $f(x)$ is the y value on the graph.
Use this y value to find the x coordinate.**

Example:

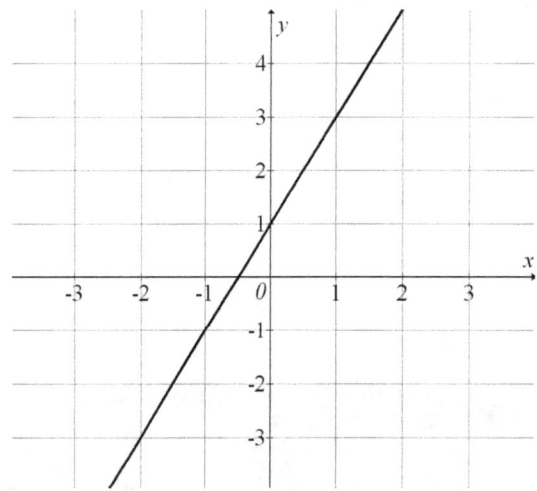

The figure above shows the graph of the function f.
If $f(x) = 1$, which of the following could be a value of x?

(A) 0
(B) 1
(C) 2
(D) 3
(E) 4

SAT Math

Answer: (A)

Here, 1 is the y value because it is set equal to the function $f(x)$.
The x value is located at the point on the line where $y = 1$, which is $x = 0$, or (A).

**A value INSIDE THE PARENTHESES (x)
is the x value on the graph.
Use this x value to find the y coordinate.**

Example:

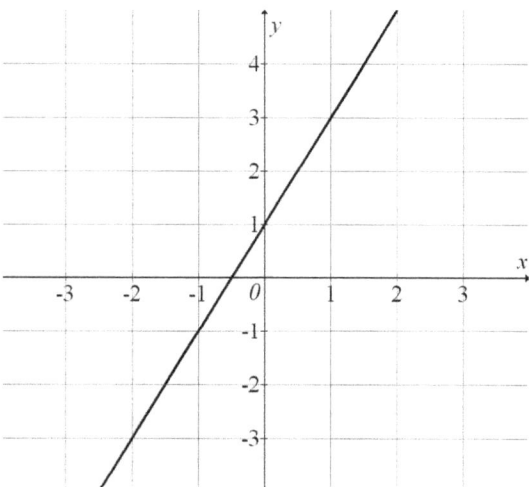

The figure above shows the graph of the function f.
Find the value of $f(1)$.

(A) 0
(B) 1
(C) 2
(D) 3
(E) 4

Remember:
*If a question asks for 'the value of $f(x)$' or 'value of the function f',
it is simply asking for the y value.*

Answer: (D)
1 is the *x* value because it is inside the parentheses of the function. The *y* value of $f(1)$ is located at the point on the line where $x = 1$, which is $y = 3$, or (D).

Example:

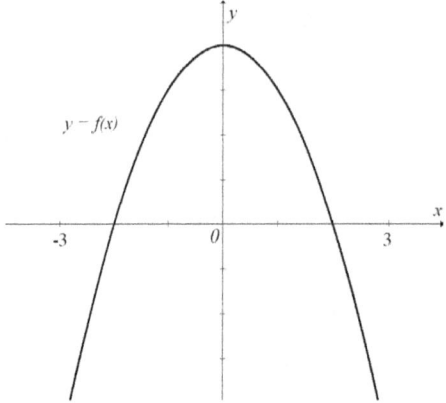

The figure above shows the graph of the function $y = f(x)$ from $x = -3$ to $x = 3$. For what value of x in this interval does the function f attain its maximum value?

(A) -3
(B) 0
(C) 2
(D) 3
(E) 4

<u>Tip:</u>
Every SAT function graphing question can be answered without knowing components like focus, vertex, etc. You do not need to know how to graph quadratic or polynomial equations to answer even the hardest SAT function graphing questions.

Answer: (E)
The "maximum value" of a function is the place on the graph where the *y* value is greatest. Here the greatest *y* value is located at *y* = 4 or (E).

Note: "the graph of the function *f(x)* from *x* = -3 to *x* = -3" simply means the graph is limited to a range where the *x* value is between -3 and 3.

 Math: OSSG Function Graphing Questions

No.	Page	Q.	Diff.	Type	Test	Sect.	Answer
1	610	5	E	MC	4	9	
2	422	9	M	MC	1	8	
3	612	11	M	MC	4	9	
4	669	6	M	MC	5	8	
5	732	13	M	MC	6	8	
6	799	14	M	MC	7	9	
7	969	16	M	MC	10	5	
8	979	9	M	MC	10	8	
9	652	8	H	MC	5	4	

Math: OSSG Function Graphing Answers

1	2	3	4	5	6	7	8	9
C	B	A	B	B	E	A	B	C

Graphing Function Shifts

ADDING or SUBTRACTING $y = f(x)$ shifts the entire graph.	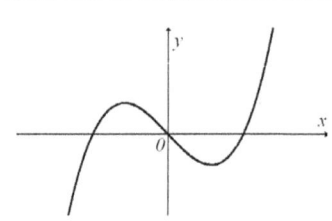
ADDING OUTSIDE the parentheses $y = f(x) + a$ shifts the graph UP ↑	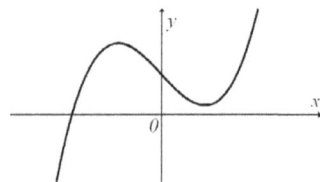
SUBTRACTING OUTSIDE the parentheses $y = f(x) - a$ shifts the graph DOWN ↓	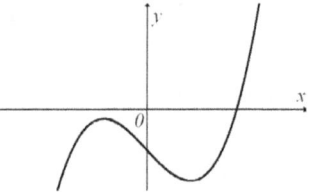
ADDDING INSIDE the parentheses $y = f(x + a)$ shifts the graph LEFT ←	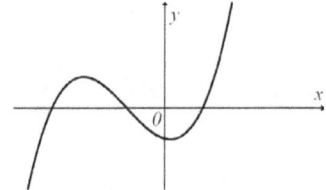
SUBTRACTING INSIDE the parentheses $y = f(x - a)$ shifts the graph RIGHT →	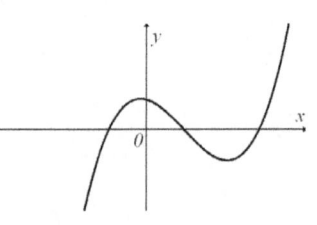

Example:

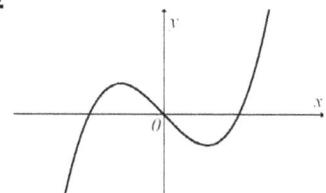

The graph of $y = f(x)$ is shown above. Which of the following could be the graph of $y = f(x - 1)$?

(A)

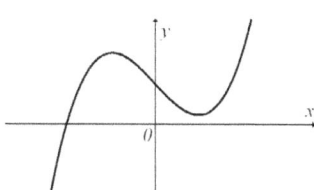

(B)

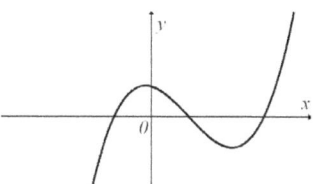

(C)

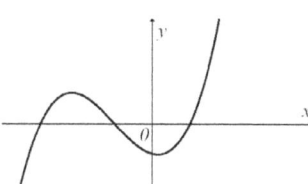

(D)

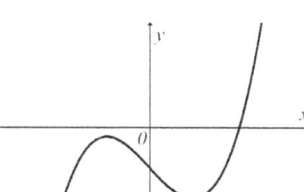

(E)

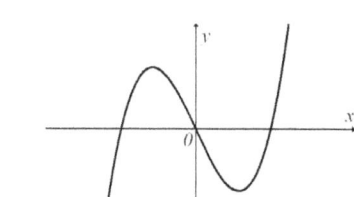

Careful!
When adding or subtracting <u>inside</u> the parentheses, remember that the graph shifts left and right in the <u>opposite</u> direction.

Answer: (B)
The question for the graph of $y = f(x - 1)$,
which means we shift the graph one unit to the right.

(A) Shifts the graph upwards: $y = f(x) + 1$
(B) Shifts the graph to the right: $y = f(x - 1)$
(C) Shifts the graph to the left: $y = f(x + 1)$
(D) Shifts the graph downwards: $y = f(x) - 1$
(E) Makes the graph narrower: $y = 2f(x)$ (see below for explanation)

Graphing Function Shapes

MULTIPLYING the function changes the shape of the graph.	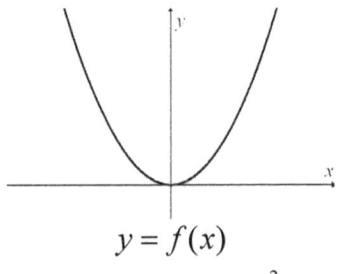 $y = f(x)$ (similar to: $y = ax^2$)
MULTIPLYING OUTSIDE the function makes the graph NARROWER.	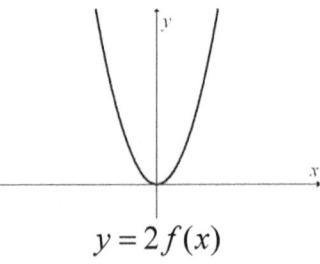 $y = 2f(x)$ (similar to: $y = 2ax^2$)
MULTIPLYING INSIDE the function makes the graph WIDER.	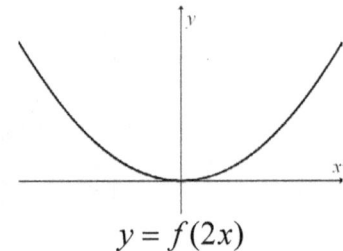 $y = f(2x)$ (similar to: $y = \dfrac{a}{2}x^2$)

Example:

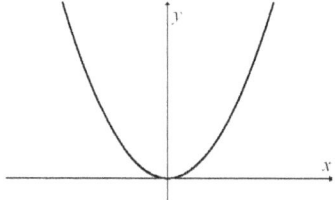

The graph of $y = f(x)$ is shown above. Which of the following could be the graph of $y = 2f(x)$?

(A)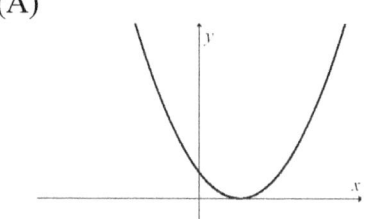

(B)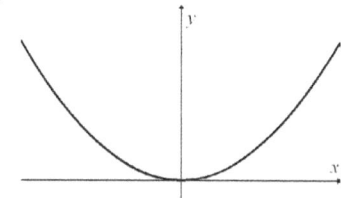

(C)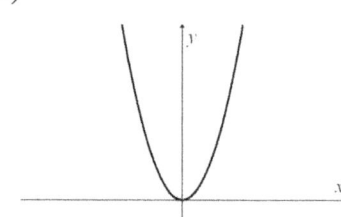

(D)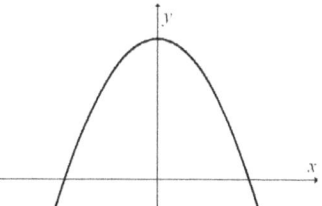

(E)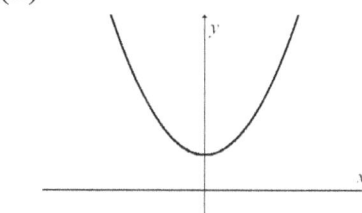

Answer: (C)
The question for the graph of $y = 2f(x)$.
Multiplying outside the function makes the graph narrower.

(A) Shifts the graph to the right.
(B) Makes the graph wider.
(C) Makes the graph narrower.
(D) Flips the graph downwards.
(E) Shifts the graph upwards.

Math: OSSG Function Shifts & Shapes Questions

No.	Page	Q.	Diff.	Type	Test	Sect.	Answer
1	465	7	M	MC	2	5	
2	547	14	M	MC	3	8	
3	704	17	M	MC	6	2	
4	418	18	H	GI	1	7	
5	790	20	H	MC	7	7	

Math: OSSG Function Shifts & Shapes Answers

1	2	3	4	5
B	D	C	4.2 OR 21/5	E

Data & Statistics

Average (Arithmetic Mean)

AVERAGE (arithmetic mean): $\dfrac{\text{SUM TOTAL}}{\text{NUMBER (of terms)}}$

SUM TOTAL (when you know the AVERAGE): NUMBER x AVERAGE

Example:

If the average (arithmetic mean) of 5, j and k is 6, what is the value of $j + k$?

(A) 1
(B) 11
(C) 12
(D) 13
(E) 30

Tip:
Most medium to hard SAT average questions tell you the average and want you to figure out the TOTAL amount.

Answer: (D)

If the average of the 3 terms (5, j and k) is 6, then the sum total of all three terms added together = number of terms (3) x average (6) = 18.

Therefore:
$j + k + 5 = 18$
$j + k = 18 - 5$
$j + k = 13$, or (D).

Math: OSSG Average Questions

No.	Page	Q.	Diff.	Type	Test	Sect.	Answer
1	397	3	E	MC	1	3	
2	464	3	E	MC	2	5	
3	525	1	E	MC	3	5	
4	610	3	E	MC	4	9	
5	610	4	E	MC	4	9	
6	701	5	E	MC	6	2	
7	713	3	E	MC	6	4	
8	786	6	E	MC	7	7	
9	421	7	M	MC	1	8	
10	467	13	M	GI	2	5	
11	517	11	M	MC	3	2	
12	732	11	M	MC	6	8	
13	859	7	M	MC	8	9	
14	891	16	M	GI	9	2	
15	967	7	M	MC	10	5	
16	642	18	H	MC	5	2	
17	835	18	H	GI	8	3	

Math: OSSG Average Answers

1	2	3	4	5	6	7	8	9
B	D	A	B	B	C	B	D	A
10	11	12	13	14	15	16	17	
1750	E	D	E	71	C	A	3/8 or .375	

SAT Math

Median & Mode

MEDIAN: MIDDLE number

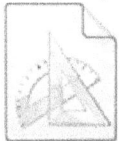
MODE: number that appears MOST OFTEN

Example:

$$14, 6, 1, 11, 3, 9, 12, x$$

For the set of numbers above, the median is equal to the mode. Which of the following could be the value of x?

(A)   6
(B)   7
(C)   8
(D)   9
(E)   10

Tip:
Where numbers are jumbled up, rewrite them in numerical order.

Answer: (D)
Rewriting the set in numerical order we get:

1, 3, 6, 9, 11, 12, 14, and x.

Without x, the median (middle number) is 9. If x equals 9, then the median will remain the same (9) and the mode (the number that appears most often) will also equal 9, or (D).

Math: OSSG Median & Mode Questions

No.	Page	Q.	Diff.	Type	Test	Sect.	Answer
1	423	13	M	MC	1	8	
2	455	12	M	MC	2	2	
3	584	13	M	MC	4	3	
4	611	10	M	MC	4	9	
5	703	14	M	MC	6	2	
6	888	6	M	MC	9	2	
7	770	8	H	MC	7	3	
8	852	19	H	MC	8	7	
9	953	18	H	GI	10	2	

Math: OSSG Median & Mode Answers

1	2	3	4	5	6	7	8	9
D	A	E	B	C	C	A	E	1350

Data Analysis

Data analysis questions show you a table, chart, or graph and ask you to figure something out about the numbers.

Tables

Fill in the missing values in the table. Then answer the question.

Example:

	Website Hits	Unique Visitors
Monday	450	100
Tuesday	300	50
Wednesday	900	250
Thursday	750	150
Friday		
Total	3000	

In the table above, the number of website hits on Friday was three times the number of unique visitors for that day. What was the total number of unique visitors for the week?

(A) 200
(B) 600
(C) 750
(D) 900
(E) 3000

Answer: (C)
Adding up the number of website hits for Monday through Thursday, we get 2400.

The number of website hits for Friday is therefore 3000 − 2400 = 600.

Since the number of website hits on Friday is three times the number of unique visitors, we divide 600 by 3 to get 200 unique visitors for Friday.

Then, adding up the total of unique visitors for the week we get 750, or (C).

Math: OSSG Tables Questions

No.	Page	Q.	Diff.	Type	Test	Sect.	Answer
1	594	3	E	MC	4	6	
2	772	11	E	GI	7	3	
3	965	2	E	MC	10	5	
4	545	9	M	MC	3	8	
5	717	16	M	GI	6	4	
6	860	11	M	MC	8	9	
7	598	17	H	GI	4	6	

Math: OSSG Tables Answers

1	2	3	4	5	6	7
A	2400	E	C	5/11, .454, .455	C	149

SAT Math

Bar Graphs

Bar graphs represent data by the height of vertical bars.

Example:

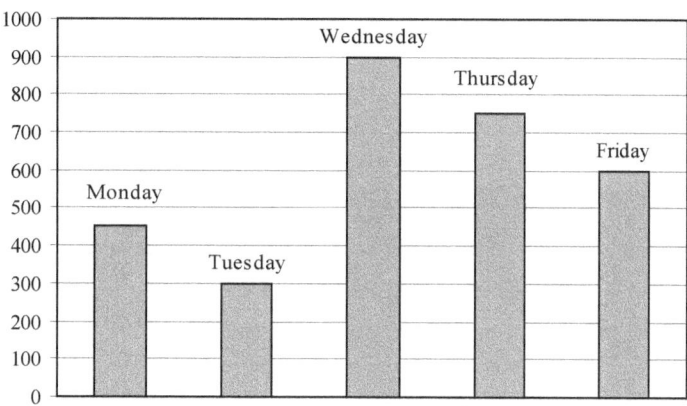

According to the graph above, which day saw greatest the change in website hits from the previous day?

(A) Monday
(B) Tuesday
(C) Wednesday
(D) Thursday
(E) Friday

Tip:
To find the answer to most bar graph questions, look for the two bars that have the greatest difference in height.

Answer (C):
The greatest change in website hits from one day to the next was Tuesday to Wednesday (300 to 900), or (C).

Math: OSSG Bar Graphs Questions

No.	Page	Q.	Diff.	Type	Test	Sect.	Answer
1	419	1	E	MC	1	8	
2	668	5	E	MC	5	8	
3	786	5	E	MC	7	7	
4	978	5	E	MC	10	8	

Math: OSSG Bar Graphs Questions

1	2	3	4
D	D	B	C

SAT Math

Line Graphs

Line Graphs are similar to Bar Graphs except the data is represented by points on a line instead of vertical bars.

Example:

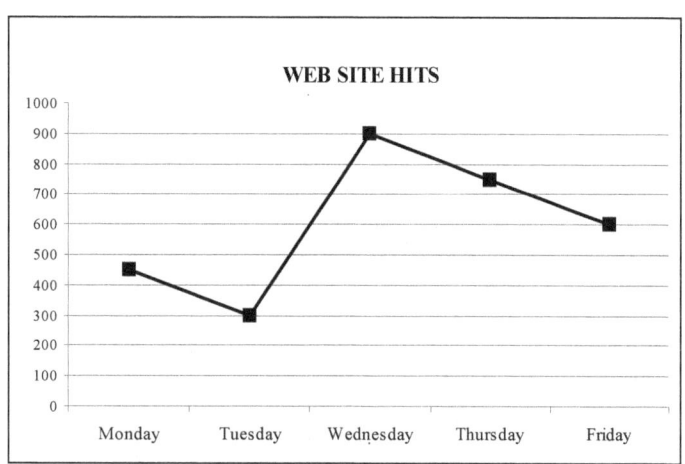

According to the graph above, by what percentage did website hits decrease between Wednesday and Friday?

(A) 10%
(B) 33%
(C) 66%
(D) 100%
(E) 300%

Answer: (B)
The change in website hits from Wednesday to Friday was 900 - 600 = 300.

To figure out the percent of this change, divide the difference (300) by the number for the *first* of the two days (900):

$$\frac{300}{900} = .333 = 33\%$$, or (B).

Math: OSSG Line Graphs Questions

No.	Page	Q.	Diff.	Type	Test	Sect.	Answer
1	453	3	E	MC	2	2	
2	544	3	E	MC	3	8	
3	399	12	M	MC	1	3	
4	831	6	M	MC	8	3	
5	917	7	M	MC	9	8	

Math: OSSG Line Graphs Answers

1	2	3	4	5
A	D	D	C	E

Circle Graphs (Pie Charts)

Circle Graphs (commonly known as 'Pie Charts') show data as sections of a circle.

Example:

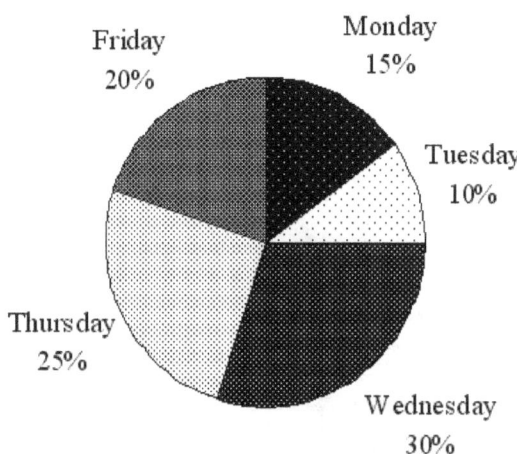

WEB SITE HITS

The circle graph above represents the portion of website hits on each day from Monday through Friday. If the website had 750 hits on Thursday, how many total website hits for the five days together?

(A) 600
(B) 750
(C) 900
(D) 3000
(E) 4500

Tip:
On the SAT, slices of data within a circle graph are often shown as <u>percentages</u> of the whole.

Answer: (D)
If 25% of all website hits occurred on Thursday, and the number on Thursday was 750, then the total for the week is represented by the ratio:

$$\frac{25}{100} = \frac{750}{x}$$

Cross multiplying the ratios and solving for x, we get

$25x = 75000$

$x = 3000$, or (D).

Math: OSSG Circle Graphs (Pie Charts) Questions

No.	Page	Q.	Diff.	Type	Test	Sect.	Answer
1	515	4	E	MC	3	2	
2	651	3	E	MC	5	4	
3	848	5	E	MC	8	7	
4	453	4	M	MC	2	2	
5	949	5	M	MC	10	2	
6	486	15	H	MC	2	8	

Math: OSSG Circle Graphs (Pie Charts) Answers

1	2	3	4	5	6
D	D	E	C	D	D

Scatter Plots

Scatter Plots compare TWO SETS OF DATA at the same time, with each set charted on a separate axis.

Example:

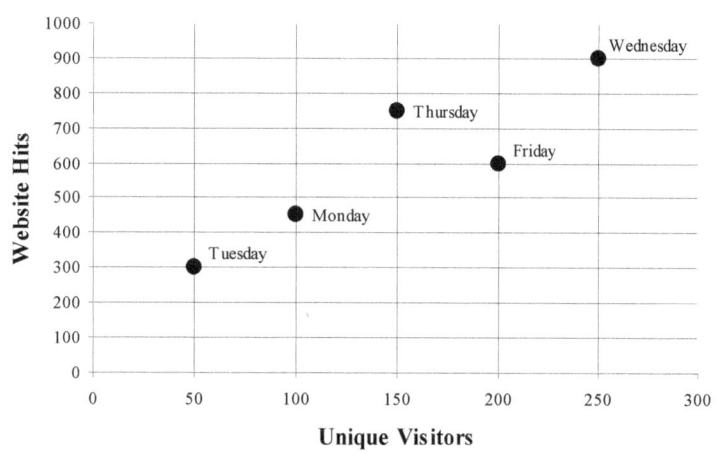

On which day was the ratio of website hits to unique visitors the greatest?

(A) Monday
(B) Tuesday
(C) Wednesday
(D) Thursday
(E) Friday

Answer: (B)

Comparing the ratio of website hits to unique visitors for each day we get the following:

(A) Monday $= \dfrac{450}{100} = 4.5$

(B) Tuesday $= \dfrac{300}{50} = 6$

(C) Wednesday $= \dfrac{900}{250} = 3.6$

(D) Thursday $= \dfrac{750}{150} = 5$

(E) Friday $= \dfrac{600}{200} = 3$

The largest ratio is on Tuesday, or (B).

Math: OSSG Scatter Plots Questions

No.	Page	Q.	Diff.	Type	Test	Sect.	Answer
1	455	11	E	MC	2	2	
2	529	13	E	GI	3	5	
3	701	4	E	MC	6	2	
4	850	12	M	MC	8	7	
5	671	15	H	MC	5	8	

Math: OSSG Scatter Plots Answers

1	2	3	4	5
D	1992	A	C	A

SAT Math

Pictographs

Pictographs represent data as a repeating series of pictures.

Example:

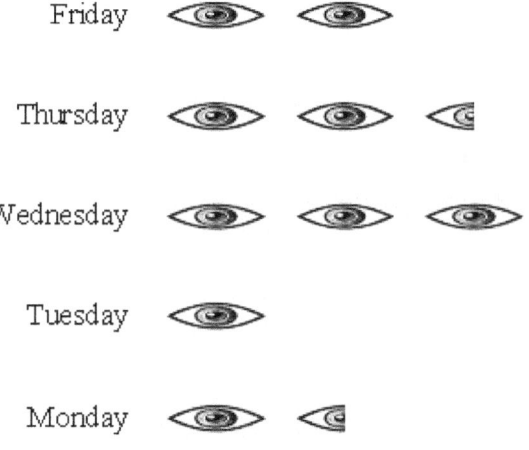

If the legend of the pictograph above shows that 👁 = 300 website hits, on which day of the week did the website have 450 hits?

(A) Monday
(B) Tuesday
(C) Wednesday
(D) Thursday
(E) Friday

Answer: (A)
If each picture represents 300 website hits, then 450 website hits is represented by 1 1/2 pictures. Thus Monday is the correct answer, or (A).

Math: OSSG Pictographs Questions

No.	Page	Q.	Diff.	Type	Test	Sect.	Answer
1	413	1	E	MC	1	7	
2	796	6	M	MC	7	9	

Math: OSSG Pictographs Answers

1	2
E	D

Combinations

Easy combination questions ask you to find the total number of ways to combine two or more groups of different things.

To find the number of combinations between members of two distinct groups:

MULTIPLY the number of one group by the number of the other.

Example:

If there are four girls and three boys, how many different combinations of one girl and one boy are possible?

Answer: 12
4 (girls) x 3 (boys) = 12 possible combinations of one girl and one boy.

Harder combination questions limit the position in which individuals appear.

Where individuals can only appear in certain positions:

1) **Start with the first position and figure out how many individuals can appear there.**

2) **Next figure out how many individuals can appear in the second position, and subtract one for the individual placed in the first position.**

3) **Then figure out how many individuals can appear in the third position, and subtract two for the individuals placed in the first and second positions.**

4) **Repeat for all positions, subtracting the number of previously placed individuals.**

5) **Multiply the numbers together.**

Example:
At the movies, five people sit in a row of five consecutive seats, if only one person can sit in each seat at a time, how many different ways can these five people sit in the five seats?

SAT Math

Answer: 120
Where individuals can only appear in certain positions:

Start with the first position and figure out how many individuals can appear there.
= **5**

Next figure out how many individuals can appear in the second position, and subtract <u>one</u> for the individual placed in the first position. = **4**

Then figure out how many individuals can appear in the third position, and subtract <u>two</u> for the individuals placed in the first and second positions. = **3**

Repeat for all positions, subtracting the number of previously placed individuals. = 2 and 1

Multiply the numbers together. = 5 x 4 x 3 x 2 x 1 = **120**.

NOTE:
The multiplication of numbers that decrease by one each time is called a FACTORIAL, signified by (!).
For example: 5 x 4 x 3 x 2 x 1 = 5! or 'five factorial'.

Math: OSSG Combinations Questions

No.	Page	Q.	Diff.	Type	Test	Sect.	Answer
1	639	3	E	MC	5	2	
2	729	2	E	MC	6	8	
3	904	4	E	MC	9	5	
4	977	1	E	MC	10	8	
5	890	14	M	GI	9	2	
6	424	14	H	MC	1	8	
7	465	8	H	MC	2	5	
8	519	18	H	MC	3	2	
9	547	13	H	MC	3	8	
10	598	18	H	GI	4	6	
11	773	15	H	GI	7	3	

Math: OSSG Combinations Answers

1	2	3	4	5	6	7	8	9	10	11
B	D	C	A	12	B	B	A	E	72	24

Probability

Probability simply means the odds that an event will occur.

PROBABILTY: $\dfrac{\text{TOTAL of the EVENT (what you want to happen)}}{\text{TOTAL of ALL EVENTS}}$

Example:

One marble is to be randomly chosen from a bag containing only red marbles, green marbles, and blue marbles. The number of green marbles is two times the number of red marbles. The number of blue marbles is three times the number of green marbles. If there are 36 marbles in the bag, what is the probability that a green marble will be chosen?

(A) $\dfrac{1}{36}$

(B) $\dfrac{1}{18}$

(C) $\dfrac{2}{9}$

(D) $\dfrac{1}{6}$

(E) $\dfrac{1}{4}$

Answer: (C)

Red = x
Green = $2x$
Blue = $3(2x) = 6x$

Total Marbles:
$x + 2x + 6x = 36$
$9x = 36$
$x = 4$ Red

Number of Green Marbles = $2x = 8$

Probability of Green = $\frac{8}{36} = \frac{2}{9}$, or (C).

Math: OSSG Probability Questions

No.	Page	Q.	Diff.	Type	Test	Sect.	Answer
1	417	11	E	GI	1	7	
2	514	2	E	MC	3	2	
3	795	1	E	MC	7	9	
4	858	5	E	MC	8	9	
5	916	4	E	MC	9	8	
6	978	3	E	MC	10	8	
7	483	8	M	MC	2	8	
8	583	7	M	MC	4	3	
9	641	12	M	MC	5	2	
10	731	10	M	MC	6	8	

Math: OSSG Probability Answers

1	2	3	4	5	6	7	8	9	10
15	C	B	B	C	C	A	E	C	B

SAT Unlocked II

SAT Math Quick Review

SAT Math

General
- Qs in order of difficulty (easy to hard).
- Concentrate on first 2/3 of Qs.
- If stuck, skip Q and come back.
- Grid-Ins:
  - <u>Grid-Ins FIRST!</u>
  - Always Answer! (no guessing penalty)
  - Start in the far left column.
  - Last resort: write in number of Q.
  - Answers never negative.
  - Can have multiple answers or range (0<x<1).
  - Improper fractions are proper (reduce!).
  - Decimals: carry repeaters to end.

Important terms
- Integer: whole number.
- Prime: div only by 1 & itself (1 NOT prime).
- Remainder: amount left over when dividing.
- Fraction 'of' a value = multiply frac by value
- Percentage 'of' a value:
  - Convert percentage to decimal.
  - Then multiply decimal by value.
- '*x* in terms of *y*': solve for *x*.

Numbers & Operations
- Plug in Answers: "which of the following" or "what is the value".
- Plug in Numbers: Q or A contains <u>variables</u>
  - Pick easy numbers
  - Check <u>all</u> answers!
- Number lines: estimate values of points.
- Sequences: write out the missing values.
- Word problems: make 'x' thing to find.
- Combinations: Use factorials for specific places (4! = 4x3x2x1).
- Ratios (parts): "the ratio of x to y", add x and y to find <u>total</u> number of parts.
- Direct and Inverse Proportions:
  - "x is <u>di</u>rectly proportional to y" = $\frac{x}{y}$
    (di: think division)
  - "x is inversely proportional to y" = xy

Data/Stats
- Average (Arithmetic Mean) find <u>total</u> = avg. times # of terms.
- Median = middle number.
- Mode = number most often.
- Combinations: easy: multiply terms
  hard: factorial! (4x3x2x1)
- Probability= what you want / total.

Geometry
- Formulas on first page.
- Write down everything you know.
- Assume enough information to answer.
- Assume figure drawn to scale.
- If figure says NOT to scale, don't trust.
- Irregular figures: draw lines to create triangle and/or rectangle.
- Triangles:
  - Know formulas.
  - Isosceles : If two sides =, opp angles =.
  - Equilateral: If three sides =, angles = 60°.
  - The sum of two sides greater than third.
  - Right Triangles:
    - Pythagorean Theorem $c^2 = a^2 + b^2$.
    - Know 'special' formulas.
    - Look for 3-4-5 (6-8-10, etc.).
  - Similar Triangles: If angles =, sides proportional.
- Circles
  - 2x radius = 2x circumference but 4x area.
  - Circle Arc Length and Sector Area: divide angle by 360 to find fraction.
- Graphing
  - Slope = $\frac{rise}{run}$.
  - y = mx + b: *m* = slope, *b* = y intercept.
  - Perpendicular slope = negative reciprocal.

Algebra & Functions
- Exponents & Roots:
  - Simplify roots by squaring both sides.
  - Square roots positive <u>or</u> negative.
  - If both sides squares or cubes, take roots of BOTH sides.
  - Simplify negative exponents: 'flip' exponent.
  - Factor out squares from within square roots.
  - To set exp bases =, factor larger number.
- Absolute Value: |x| always <u>positive.</u>
- Where combination of variables = value, plug in combination.
- Always factor difference of two squares: $a^2 - b^2 = (a+b)(a-b)$
- Functions $f(x) = y$
  - Whatever inside parens, plug into equation.
  - Whatever function =, set = to equation.
  - If multiplied by function, divide out first.
- Function Graphing:
  - Value *equal to* function $f(x) = y$ value.
  - Value *inside the parentheses* = *x* value.
- Symbol Functions: Q will tell you what values go where.

SAT Writing Introduction

SAT Writing includes one essay question and two sections of multiple choice questions.

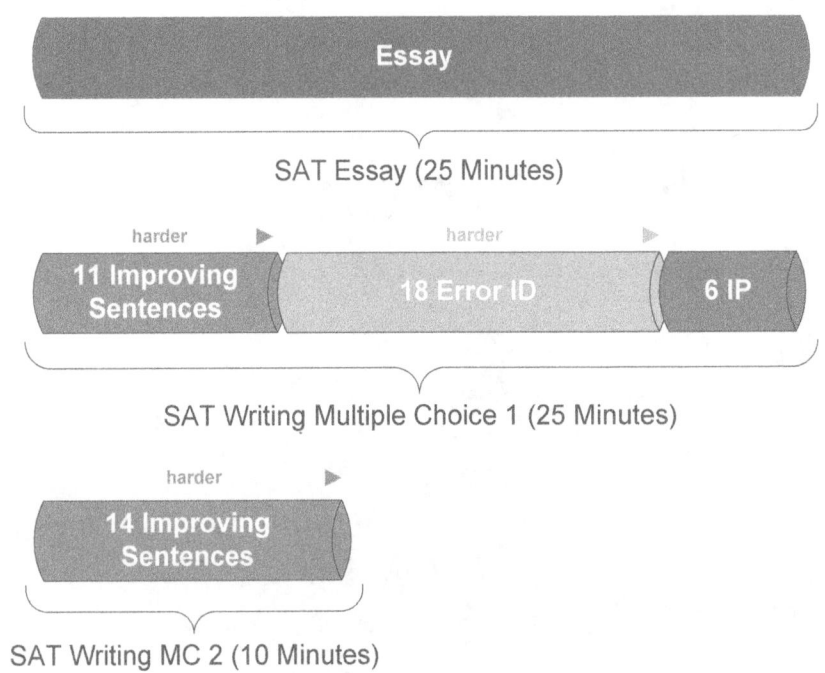

Note:
This section primarily covers Writing Multiple Choice questions.
For more on the SAT Essay, see the later chapter in this book.

SAT Writing

SAT Writing Multiple Choice (non-Essay) includes three types of questions:

✓ Improving Sentences (IS)
✓ Error Identification (EI)
✓ Improving Paragraphs (IP)

The Essay (Writing 1) is always the FIRST section on the SAT.

The bulk of multiple choice questions come in one big, 25 minute section of 35 questions, and which appears somewhere between Sections 2-7.

Additionally, a short, ten minute section of 14 Improving Sentences questions is always the *last* section of the SAT (Section 10).

Improving Sentences (25 questions) and Error IDs (18 Questions) make up the vast majority of SAT Writing MC questions, while Improving Paragraphs account for 6 out of the 49 total questions.

PSAT Writing is one Multiple Choice section and does NOT include an Essay.

harder ▶	harder ▶	
20 Improving Sentences	14 Error ID	5 IP

PSAT Writing (30 Minutes)

Like on the SAT, Improving Sentences (20 questions) and Error IDs (14 Questions) make up the vast majority of PSAT Writing MC questions, while Improving Paragraphs account for five out of the 39 total questions.

SAT Unlocked II

**Answer Improving Paragraphs questions FIRST.
Then go back to the beginning and finish the section.**

After slogging through 11 Sentence Improvements and 18 Error IDs, test fatigue and time pressure combine to make the Improving Paragraph questions far more difficult at the end of the long Writing section than they would be if they were positioned earlier.

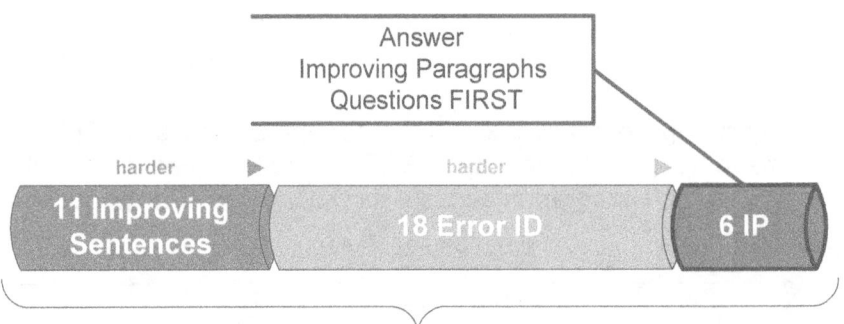

By moving to the back of the long Writing section and answering Improving Paragraphs questions first, you can pick up easy points other students miss.

Using this strategy also helps you better manage your time because the final questions will then be short Error IDs instead of the longer Paragraph Improvements.

SAT Writing

WARNING: Don't go hunting for rules not tested!

The grammar rules we will learn here are the ONLY rules tested on the SAT

Even though you may think you notice a different grammar issue, unless it involves a rule that has been specifically discussed in this section, it is most likely <u>not</u> a rule tested on the SAT.

In this section, we will discuss:

1. **Rules tested primarily on Improving Sentences**

2. **Rules tested primarily on Error IDs**

3. **Rules tested on BOTH types of questions**

4. **Special strategies for Paragraph Improvements**

Note:
The College Board identifies 19 specific grammar rules they say they test on the SAT. In actuality there are about 30. All of these rules will be discussed below.

Improving Sentences

Each Improving Sentence question provides a sentence and asks to you to change the underlined portion if necessary.

Once in awhile, the underlined portion may include the whole sentence, but usually only a part of the sentence is underlined.

Questions appear in order of difficulty.

The easiest questions Improving Sentence questions appear at the beginning and become progressively more difficult.

Answer choice (A) is always 'no error'.

Answer choice (A) simply repeats the underlined portion of the sentence as it appears in the question prompt. If there is no error in the sentence, (A) is the correct answer.

Tip:
Don't be afraid to pick (A).
Statistically, each answer choice appears approximately the same number of times (one out of five), so there will always be at least a few Sentence Improvement questions in each section where (A) is the correct answer.

SAT Writing

Improving Sentences Strategies

**Trust your gut.
The best sounding answer is usually the right one.**

Especially among the easier questions at the beginning of the section, choose the answer that you would most likely use if you were writing the sentence.

Shorter is usually better.

The SAT likes concise, simply written sentences, so shorter answers are usually preferred over longer ones. It's also a lot easier to include grammatical mistakes by adding words to an answer than by subtracting them.

<u>Tip:</u>
*Especially on questions with longer answers, it's often helpful to **start with the shortest answer first.***

**Read the sentence carefully and
try to spot the issue is before looking at the answers.**

Rewrite the sentence in your head the way you think it should appear and then look for your rewrite in the answers. When you know what improvement to look for, you can often eliminate incorrect answers with just a single word.

<u>Tip:</u>
When practicing, read the question out loud.
Your ears are often better than your eyes at recognizing errors.

Improving Sentences Grammar Rules & Questions

These rules are tested primarily on Sentence Improvement questions.

Wordy Sentences

As a general rule when answering Sentence Improvement questions, the <u>most concise</u> answer is usually best. Overly wordy answers tend to be incorrect. The best way to spot these wordy sentences is to look for extra pronouns and strange uses of the verb 'to be'.

Extra pronouns and strange uses of the verb 'to be' are almost always signs of an INCORRECT answer.

extra pronouns	strange uses of 'to be'
it, they, that, this, etc.	being, had been, were being, are being, etc.

Incorrect: Payment in advance, <u>it is being required</u> by the campsite.

Problem: extra pronoun ('it') and strange use of 'to be' ('is being').

Correct: The campsite <u>requires</u> payment in advance.

<u>*Note:*</u>
For more on verbs and pronouns, see below.

Writing: OSSG Wordy Sentences Questions

No.	Page	Q.	Diff.	Type	Test	Sect.	Answer
1	407	2	E	IS	1	6	
2	429	2	E	IS	1	10	
3	469	1	E	IS	2	6	
4	469	4	E	IS	2	6	
5	470	8	E	IS	2	6	
6	491	2	E	IS	2	10	
7	491	3	E	IS	2	10	
8	492	5	E	IS	2	10	
9	531	1	E	IS	3	6	
10	553	4	E	IS	3	10	
11	614	4	E	IS	4	10	
12	615	6	E	IS	4	10	
13	656	1	E	IS	5	6	
14	719	6	E	IS	6	6	
15	719	11	E	IS	6	6	
16	738	1	E	IS	6	10	

17	774	1	E	IS	7	4	
18	801	2	E	IS	7	10	
19	836	3	E	IS	8	4	
20	862	2	E	IS	8	10	
21	892	2	E	IS	9	3	
22	893	5	E	IS	9	3	
23	954	1	E	IS	10	3	
24	955	7	E	IS	10	3	
25	955	8	E	IS	10	3	
26	986	1	E	IS	10	10	
27	408	10	M	IS	1	6	
28	430	6	M	IS	1	10	
29	554	8	M	IS	3	10	
30	600	10	M	IS	4	7	
31	615	8	M	IS	4	10	
32	615	9	M	IS	4	10	
33	616	11	M	IS	4	10	
34	657	8	M	IS	5	6	
35	657	10	M	IS	5	6	
36	677	9	M	IS	5	10	
37	677	11	M	IS	5	10	
38	719	7	M	IS	6	6	
39	739	9	M	IS	6	10	
40	775	7	M	IS	7	4	
41	775	10	M	IS	7	4	
42	801	4	M	IS	7	10	
43	802	9	M	IS	7	10	
44	803	12	M	IS	7	10	
45	803	14	M	IS	7	10	
46	893	10	M	IS	9	3	
47	924	4	M	IS	9	10	
48	925	8	M	IS	9	10	
49	986	4	M	IS	10	10	
50	987	5	M	IS	10	10	
51	987	12	M	IS	10	10	
52	470	10	H	IS	2	6	
53	555	13	H	IS	3	10	
54	616	14	H	IS	4	10	

Writing: OSSG Wordy Sentences Answers

1	2	3	4	5	6	7	8	9	10	11	12	13	14	15	16
C	C	D	C	A	C	C	E	B	D	B	E	C	D	A	E
17	18	19	20	21	22	23	24	25	26	27	28	29	30	31	32
B	B	D	D	B	E	C	B	C	B	C	E	C	C	A	D
33	34	35	36	37	38	39	40	41	42	43	44	45	46	47	48
C	C	D	D	C	D	B	C	A	D	B	A	E	A	D	C
49	50	51	52	53	54										
A	E	D	A	E	D										

Using 'Because'

The SAT likes the word 'because', and it is often included in the correct Sentence Improvement answer.

> **Use 'because' to show cause and effect or to make a wordy sentence less awkward.**

Incorrect: <u>Being that</u> her car was in the shop, <u>is the reason why</u> Jesse took the bus to work.

Problem: *'being that' is awkward;*
also 'because' is better than 'is the reason why'.

Correct: <u>Because</u> her car was in the shop, Jesse took the bus to work.

Writing: OSSG 'Because' Questions

No.	Page	Q.	Diff.	Type	Test	Sect.	Answer
1	430	7	E	IS	1	10	
2	554	7	E	IS	3	10	
3	658	17	E	EI	5	6	
4	739	11	E	IS	6	10	
5	924	1	E	IS	9	10	
6	955	6	E	IS	10	3	
7	431	11	M	IS	1	10	
8	492	10	M	IS	2	10	
9	554	10	M	IS	3	10	
10	657	9	M	IS	5	6	
11	739	12	M	IS	6	10	
12	775	6	M	IS	7	4	
13	802	7	M	IS	7	10	
14	893	9	M	IS	9	3	

Writing: OSSG 'Because' Answers

1	2	3	4	5	6	7	8	9	10	11	12	13	14	15
D	B	D	E	B	D	D	B	B	E	D	C	A	B	E

Sentence Fragments

About two times per test, an SAT Writing question will include a 'Sentence Fragment' – in other words, a sentence that is not complete.

Complete sentences always contain both:

SUBJECT
and
MAIN VERB
(or "predicate")

Incorrect: Jesse Owens, the first man to win four gold medals in a single Olympiad, <u>and setting</u> world records in three of four events at the 1936 games in Berlin.

Problem: The sentence lacks a main verb.

Correct: Jesse Owens, the first man to win four gold medals in a single Olympiad, <u>set</u> world records in three of four events at the 1936 games in Berlin.

Writing: OSSG Sentence Fragments Questions

No.	Page	Q.	Diff.	Type	Test	Sect.	Answer
1	407	3	E	IS	1	6	
2	469	2	E	IS	2	6	
3	470	6	E	IS	2	6	
4	553	2	E	IS	3	10	
5	614	1	E	IS	4	10	
6	614	2	E	IS	4	10	
7	738	3	E	IS	6	10	
8	836	1	E	IS	8	4	
9	862	3	E	IS	8	10	
10	892	3	E	IS	9	3	
11	924	3	E	IS	9	10	
12	954	2	E	IS	10	3	
13	532	9	M	IS	3	6	
14	656	4	M	IS	5	6	
15	657	5	M	IS	5	6	
16	677	5	M	IS	5	10	
17	775	8	M	IS	7	4	
18	863	7	M	IS	8	10	
19	863	10	M	IS	8	10	

Writing: OSSG Sentence Fragments Answers

1	2	3	4	5	6	7	8	9	10
B	E	C	B	B	B	D	D	E	D

11	12	13	14	15	16	17	18	19
D	D	D	E	D	E	E	E	D

Combining Sentences

The SAT tests your knowledge of how to combine two clauses that can each be a sentence by itself.

Example: **Sentence 1:** Sam studied hard.

Sentence 2: The test was not difficult.

Follow the 'Goldilocks Rule':

	Just Right (CORRECT)
comma + conjunction	Sam studied hard**,** **so** the test was not difficult.
semi-colon (or colon)	Sam studied hard**;** the test was not difficult.

	Too Weak (INCORRECT)
comma	Sam studied hard**,** the test was not difficult.
conjunction	Sam studied hard **so** the test was not difficult.

	Too Strong (INCORRECT)
conjunction + semi-colon (or colon)	Sam studied hard**; so** the test was not difficult.

Did you know?
Combining Sentences is the ONLY punctuation rule tested on the SAT.

To remember the seven (7) conjunctions, use the acronym 'FANBOYS'.

For
And
Nor
But
Or
Yet
So

Writing: OSSG Combining Sentences Questions

No.	Page	Q.	Diff.	Type	Test	Sect.	Answer
1	531	3	E	IS	3	6	
2	532	5	E	IS	3	6	
3	554	6	E	IS	3	10	
4	776	18	E	EI	7	4	
5	863	9	E	IS	8	10	
6	986	3	E	IS	10	10	
7	554	11	M	IS	3	10	
8	602	24	M	EI	4	7	
9	614	3	M	IS	4	10	
10	657	6	M	IS	5	6	
11	719	8	M	IS	6	6	
12	775	9	M	IS	7	4	
13	802	6	M	IS	7	10	
14	987	10	M	IS	10	10	
15	864	14	H	IS	8	10	
16	893	11	H	IS	9	3	

Writing: OSSG Combining Sentences Answers

1	2	3	4	5	6	7	8
A	D	D	C	B	B	A	A
9	10	11	12	13	14	15	16
A	D	E	C	B	A	C	E

SAT Writing

Rewriting Sentences

Instead of combining two independent clauses using conjunctions and punctuation, you can also rewrite the sentence so that one of the clauses is no longer a sentence on its own.

Correct: Sam studied hard for the test, <u>which</u> was not difficult.

 Tip:
A dash (-) works the same way a comma does.

 Writing: OSSG Rewriting Sentences Questions

No.	Page	Q.	Diff.	Type	Test	Sect.	Answer
1	407	1	E	IS	1	6	
2	470	5	E	IS	2	6	
3	491	4	E	IS	2	10	
4	599	2	E	IS	4	7	
5	599	4	E	IS	4	7	
6	615	5	E	IS	4	10	
7	676	2	E	IS	5	10	
8	738	4	E	IS	6	10	
9	492	12	M	IS	2	10	
10	532	6	M	IS	3	6	
11	739	10	M	IS	6	10	
12	740	13	M	IS	6	10	
13	802	8	M	IS	7	10	
14	925	6	M	IS	9	10	
15	555	12	H	IS	3	10	
16	555	14	H	IS	3	10	

Writing: OSSG Rewriting Sentences Answers

1	2	3	4	5	6	7	8	9	10	11	12	13	14	15	16
C	B	B	C	E	D	C	B	E	C	C	D	D	C	E	A

Introductory Phrases

> **Whenever a phrase ending with a comma INTRODUCES a sentence:**
>
> **whatever IMMEDIATELY FOLLOWS the comma must be EXACTLY who or what the phrase describes.**

Incorrect: After throwing for hours, <u>Jake's dog</u> finally learned to catch a Frisbee.

Problem: *'Jake's dog' did not throw for hours. 'Jake' did.*

Correct: After throwing for hours, <u>Jake</u> finally taught his dog to catch a Frisbee.

<u>Tip:</u>
Watch out for possessives ('Jake's dog') that look like the person or thing the phrase describes.

SAT Writing

 Writing: OSSG Introductory Phrases Questions

No.	Page	Q.	Diff.	Type	Test	Sect.	Answer
1	408	7	E	IS	1	6	
2	469	3	E	IS	2	6	
3	492	6	E	IS	2	10	
4	531	2	E	IS	3	6	
5	532	8	E	IS	3	6	
6	600	8	E	IS	4	7	
7	774	3	E	IS	7	4	
8	801	1	E	IS	7	10	
9	836	2	E	IS	8	4	
10	892	1	E	IS	9	3	
11	954	3	E	IS	10	3	
12	955	5	E	IS	10	3	
13	430	5	M	IS	1	10	
14	430	8	M	IS	1	10	
15	430	9	M	IS	1	10	
16	470	7	M	IS	2	6	
17	470	9	M	IS	2	6	
18	493	13	M	IS	2	10	
19	599	5	M	IS	4	7	
20	616	10	M	IS	4	10	
21	616	12	M	IS	4	10	
22	677	12	M	IS	5	10	
23	719	10	M	IS	6	6	
24	740	14	M	IS	6	10	
25	837	10	M	IS	8	4	
26	863	11	M	IS	8	10	
27	893	7	M	IS	9	3	
28	925	7	M	IS	9	10	
29	925	10	M	IS	9	10	
30	987	6	M	IS	10	10	
31	955	11	H	IS	10	3	

Writing: OSSG Introductory Phrases Answers

1	2	3	4	5	6	7	8	9	10	11	12	13	14	15	16
D	C	E	B	D	E	C	B	C	B	A	E	C	E	E	C
17	18	19	20	21	22	23	24	25	26	27	28	29	30	31	
D	A	D	B	D	B	D	E	A	A	A	B	D	E	D	

Spotting Contrasts

Sentence Improvement questions occasionally test whether you can spot that the sentence is talking about two opposing things.

When a sentence talks about two opposing things, change the connector to show a contrast between them.

Incorrect: Many are called, <u>and</u> few are chosen.

Problem: 'and' does not show the contrast between 'many' and 'few'.

Correct: Many are called, <u>yet</u> few are chosen.

Tip:
Other connector words include: 'although', 'however', etc.

Writing: OSSG Spotting Contrasts Questions

No.	Page	Q.	Diff.	Type	Test	Sect.	Answer
1	407	5	E	IS	1	6	
2	553	3	E	IS	3	10	
3	774	4	E	IS	7	4	
4	862	5	E	IS	8	10	
5	863	6	E	IS	8	10	
6	676	4	M	IS	5	10	
7	864	13	M	IS	8	10	
8	925	12	M	IS	9	10	
9	987	9	M	IS	10	10	
10	408	11	H	IS	1	6	

Writing: OSSG Spotting Contrasts Answers

1	2	3	4	5	6	7	8	9	10
E	C	B	A	C	E	A	A	C	E

Error IDs

Each Error ID sentence includes four possible errors.

It is up to you to spot which, if any, of the underlined choices contains a grammatical error.

Tip:
Read the sentence completely before trying to spot the error.
Many times, the error is most easily spotted simply by reading the full sentence in context. By contrast, when you try to pick apart each answer choice without this context, you can sometimes become confused.

Questions appear in order of difficulty.

Like sentence improvements, the easiest Error ID questions appear at the beginning and become progressively harder as the section moves along.

Answer choice (E) is always 'no error'

Like Sentence Improvements, 'no error' appears approximately the same number of times as any other correct answer choice.

Error ID Strategies

Many students shy away from answering (E) and inevitably lose points because they skip questions that actually have 'No error'.

Embrace the (E)!

Stay consistent. Remember that about one out of every five Error ID questions has '(E) No error' as its answer, so while you may lose a ¼ point here and there for not spotting an error where there is one, you can always be certain of gaining the full point on each question that actually has 'No error'.

Remember!
Answering (E) whenever you do not see an error is the best way to ensure you earn the most points on the Error ID part of the Writing section.

Skipping an Error ID question
       A
because you do <u>not see an error</u> is a
                   B
<u>poor strategy</u> that almost always
       C
results in <u>lost points</u>. No error
            D   (E)

Do not skip Error ID questions.

If you can not spot an error, ALWAYS answer 'E'.

If you do not see an error, <u>always</u> answer (E). DON'T SKIP!

Tip:
Circle your (E)'s and check them at the end if you have time.
Don't waste time pondering whether or not there is an error. If you do not see one, simply answer (E) and move on. If you have time at the end, go back to see whether or not you missed anything.

Error ID Grammar Rules & Questions

These grammar rules are tested primarily on Error ID questions.

Adverbs

About once per test, an SAT Error ID question will leave the 'ly' off the end of an adverb.

> **An adverb is a word, ending in 'ly'**
> **(like 'clearly', 'mostly' or faithfully'),**
> **that helps describe (or 'modify')**
> **an adjective, a verb, or another adverb.**

Incorrect: Researchers examined the <u>constant changing</u> river bed for signs of invasive species.

Problem: The adverb 'constant' is missing 'ly'. (A river bed cannot be both 'constant' and 'changing' at the same time.)

Correct: Researchers examined the <u>constantly changing</u> river bed for signs of invasive species.

Writing: OSSG Adverbs Questions

No.	Page	Q.	Diff.	Type	Test	Sect.	Answer
1	409	14	E	EI	1	6	
2	776	13	E	EI	7	4	
3	838	12	E	EI	8	4	
4	838	15	E	EI	8	4	
5	956	15	E	EI	10	3	
6	409	17	M	EI	1	6	
7	721	22	M	EI	6	6	
8	602	29	H	EI	4	7	
9	839	28	H	EI	8	4	

Writing: OSSG Adverbs Answers

1	2	3	4	5	6	7	8	9
A	D	C	D	D	C	B	B	E

Word Choice

The SAT tests common words and phrases students tend to use improperly.

Dual Phrases

Dual Phrases	
Correct	Incorrect
either ... or ...	either ... and ...
neither ... nor ...	neither ... or ...
not only ... but also ...	not only ... and also ...
between... and (me)	between... or (I)
as... as...	as... than...
... and ...	... as well as ..., ...with...

Incorrect: Neither Chris or Lara arrived at the party on time.

Problem: The proper phrase is 'neither ... nor ...'

Correct: Neither Chris nor Lara arrived at the party on time.

 ### Writing: OSSG Dual Phrases Questions

No.	Page	Q.	Diff.	Type	Test	Sect.	Answer
1	533	17	E	EI	3	6	
2	601	14	E	EI	4	7	
3	720	12	E	EI	6	6	
4	777	22	E	EI	7	4	
5	956	18	E	EI	10	3	
6	409	18	M	EI	1	6	
7	471	15	M	EI	2	6	
8	721	28	M	EI	6	6	
9	839	29	H	EI	8	4	

Writing: OSSG Dual Phrases Answers

1	2	3	4	5	6	7	8	9
C	B	D	C	D	A	B	D	D

'Verby' Words with Prepositions

Any time a preposition is underlined, check to make sure it is the correct word, especially when associated with 'verby' word.

Common SAT Prepositions			
about	below	in	outside
above	beneath	including	over
according to	beside	inside	since
across	between	instead of	through
after	beyond	into	throughout
against	by	less	to
ahead of	concerning	like	toward
along	considering	near	under
among	despite	next to	underneath
around	down	of	unlike
as	due to	off	until
at	during	on	up
because of	except	onto	upon
before	for	opposite	while
behind	from	out	with

Incorrect: Josh's <u>preoccupation in</u> video games has hurt his grades.

Problem: The phrase 'preoccupation in' should be 'preoccupation with'.

Correct: Josh's <u>preoccupation with</u> video games has hurt his grades.

Writing: OSSG 'Verby' Words with Prepositions Questions

No.	Page	Q.	Diff.	Type	Test	Sect.	Answer
1	720	17	E	EI	6	6	
2	957	25	E	EI	10	3	
3	472	23	M	EI	2	6	
4	533	16	M	EI	3	6	
5	602	25	M	EI	4	7	
6	721	21	M	EI	6	6	
7	721	25	M	EI	6	6	
8	777	26	M	EI	7	4	
9	839	23	M	EI	8	4	
10	895	24	M	EI	9	3	
11	957	21	M	EI	10	3	
12	472	26	H	EI	2	6	
13	896	26	H	EI	9	3	

Writing: OSSG 'Verby' Words with Prepositions Answers

No.	A	Proper Idiom
1	C	necessary for
2	A	listening to
3	A	arrived in / from
4	D	(while) wandering
5	A	preoccupation with
6	C	threat to
7	C	results when
8	A	regarded as
9	C	protested
10	A	far from
11	A	world where
12	D	offers of
13	C	inconsistent with

SAT Writing

Other Phrases

> The SAT sometimes includes phrases that sound strange but are often actually correct.

Correct: Archeologists continue to dig up evidence of an ancient Mayan civilization <u>long since gone</u>.

Remember!
Don't go hunting for errors that are not there!
The SAT likes to include strange sounding yet correct phrases near the end of Error ID sets to trick you into NOT picking 'No error'.

Writing: OSSG Other Phrases Questions

No.	Page	Q.	Diff.	Type	Test	Sect.	Answer
1	471	19	E	EI	2	6	
2	601	16	E	EI	4	7	
3	410	22	M	EI	1	6	
4	472	24	M	EI	2	6	
5	896	29	M	EI	9	3	
6	957	23	M	EI	10	3	
7	410	27	H	EI	1	6	
8	535	28	H	EI	3	6	
9	777	29	H	EI	7	4	

Writing: OSSG Other Phrases Answers

No.	A	Proper Idiom
1	E	long been regarded; as a means of
2	**D**	**one of its kind**
3	E	contrary to what
4	E	so painstakingly
5	E	had long been
6	E	something of a phenomenon
7	E	long since forgotten
8	E	because by
9	E	long since gone

SAT Unlocked II

Grammar Rules for Both Improving Sentences & Error IDs
These grammar rules are tested on both Sentence Improvements and Error IDs.

Parallelism

> Similar phrases within a sentence must be written in the SAME (or 'parallel') grammatical form.

Parallelism & Lists
Parallelism questions can include a list of things or activities in which one of the items on the list is not like the other.

> Whenever you see a LIST, look for problems with parallelism.

Incorrect: A talented basketball player, Sarah can run quickly, pass crisply, and <u>is an accurate shooter</u>.

Problem: 'is an accurate shooter' is not in parallel form with the other talents listed.

Correct: A talented basketball player, Sarah can run quickly, pass crisply, and <u>shoot accurately</u>.

Writing: OSSG Parallelism & Lists Questions

No.	Page	Q.	Diff.	Type	Test	Sect.	Answer
1	532	7	E	IS	3	6	
2	533	12	E	EI	3	6	
3	718	2	E	IS	6	6	
4	776	17	E	EI	7	4	
5	837	6	E	IS	8	4	
6	862	4	E	IS	8	10	
7	471	14	M	EI	2	6	
8	472	21	M	EI	2	6	
9	600	9	M	IS	4	7	
10	895	22	M	EI	9	3	
11	924	5	M	IS	9	10	
12	431	12	H	IS	1	10	

SAT Writing

Writing: OSSG Parallelism & Lists Answers

1	2	3	4	5	6	7	8	9	10	11	12
E	D	C	E	B	E	C	C	E	C	D	D

Parallelism & Dual Phrases

Look for parallelism problems within DUAL PHRASES such as:

… but …
… or …
… than …
both … and …
either … or …
neither … nor …
not only … but also …

Incorrect: The last few years have seen a sharp decline not only in crop production but also <u>textiles that are manufactured</u>.

Problem: 'textiles that are manufactured' is not in parallel form with 'in crop production'.

Correct: The last few years have seen a sharp decline not only in crop production but also <u>in textile manufacturing</u>.

Tip:
When checking for parallelism, make sure that prepositions (like 'in') are also parallel.

Writing: OSSG Parallelism & Dual Phrases Questions

No.	Page	Q.	Diff.	Type	Test	Sect.	Answer
1	408	6	E	IS	1	6	
2	492	9	E	IS	2	10	
3	554	5	E	IS	3	10	
4	599	1	E	IS	4	7	
5	600	6	E	IS	4	7	
6	600	7	E	IS	4	7	
7	615	7	E	IS	4	10	
8	658	13	E	EI	5	6	
9	720	18	E	EI	6	6	
10	739	5	E	IS	6	10	
11	739	6	E	IS	6	10	
12	776	15	E	EI	7	4	
13	837	4	E	IS	8	4	
14	862	1	E	IS	8	10	
15	955	9	E	IS	10	3	
16	408	9	M	IS	1	6	
17	492	8	M	IS	2	10	
18	493	14	M	IS	2	10	
19	554	9	M	IS	3	10	
20	600	11	M	IS	4	7	
21	602	20	M	EI	4	7	
22	602	22	M	EI	4	7	
23	616	13	M	IS	4	10	
24	659	25	M	EI	5	6	
25	676	3	M	IS	5	10	
26	677	8	M	IS	5	10	
27	678	13	M	IS	5	10	
28	678	14	M	IS	5	10	
29	739	8	M	IS	6	10	
30	802	10	M	IS	7	10	
31	803	11	M	IS	7	10	
32	837	9	M	IS	8	4	
33	893	8	M	IS	9	3	
34	926	13	M	IS	9	10	
35	988	13	M	IS	10	10	
36	431	14	H	IS	1	10	
37	470	11	H	IS	2	6	
38	775	11	H	IS	7	4	
39	863	12	H	IS	8	10	

SAT Writing

Writing: OSSG Parallelism & Dual Phrases Answers

1	2	3	4	5	6	7	8	9	10	11	12	13	14	15	16
A	A	C	E	C	A	E	B	B	D	D	D	B	B	C	E
17	18	19	20	21	22	23	24	25	26	27	28	29	30	31	32
D	C	E	C	D	B	C	C	E	A	A	E	E	E	E	E
33	34	35	36	37	38	39
D	B	E	E	A	E	E

Verbs

Verb Agreement and Verb Tense are tested extensively on both Sentence Improvement and Error ID questions.

Verb Agreement

> If the verb is singular, its subject must also be singular.
> If a verb is plural, the subject must also be plural.

A verb and its subject must agree in NUMBER.

Incorrect: *'Great Expectations'* <u>were written</u> by Charles Dickens.

Problem: The singular book takes a singular verb.

Correct: *'Great Expectations'* <u>was written</u> by Charles Dickens.

 Tip:
Whenever you see a verb underlined in a question, find its subject.

Writing: OSSG Verb Agreement (basic) Questions

No.	Page	Q.	Diff.	Type	Test	Sect.	Answer
1	472	20	M	EI	2	6	
2	721	26	M	EI	6	6	

Writing: OSSG Verb Agreement (basic) Answers

1	2
B	C

Verb Agreement & Prepositional Phrases

A common SAT trick is to insert a prepositional phrase between the subject and the verb, which makes it difficult to find the real subject of the sentence.

**A prepositional phrase includes both:
a PREPOSITION
and
its OBJECT
(what the preposition is talking about).**

Examples: about the book
under the bridge
according to the newspaper

**A word within a PREPOSITIONAL PHRASE
is NEVER the SUBJECT of a sentence.**

Incorrect: The management of the apartments <u>have installed</u> air conditioning.

Problem: *The prepositional phrase 'of the apartments' is placed between the singular subject 'management' and the plural verb 'have installed' to confuse you into thinking the subject is plural.*

Correct: The management ~~of the apartments~~ <u>has installed</u> air conditioning.

Tip:
Simplify the question by drawing lines through prepositional phrases. This way, you eliminate extra words that are designed to keep you from seeing the proper subject.

Tip:
'Collective nouns' are singular.
For words like 'management', 'school board', 'agency', 'flock', etc., each describes a group of people or things, but each is a <u>singular</u> group that takes a <u>singular</u> verb.

SAT Writing

'EACH', 'ONE' and 'EVERY' are always SINGULAR.

Incorrect: Each of the dogs <u>bark</u> louder than the cat meows.

Problem: The prepositional phrase 'of the dogs' is placed between the singular subject 'each' and the plural verb 'bark'.

Correct: Each ~~of the dogs~~ <u>barks</u> louder than the cat meows.

Writing: OSSG Verb Agreement & Prep Phrases Questions

No.	Page	Q.	Diff.	Type	Test	Sect.	Answer
1	659	19	E	EI	5	6	
2	718	1	E	IS	6	6	
3	892	4	E	IS	9	3	
4	956	16	E	EI	10	3	
5	986	2	E	IS	10	10	
6	410	20	M	EI	1	6	
7	472	22	M	EI	2	6	
8	533	15	M	EI	3	6	
9	656	3	M	IS	5	6	
10	660	26	M	EI	5	6	
11	777	27	M	EI	7	4	
12	839	20	M	EI	8	4	
13	839	27	M	EI	8	4	
14	895	23	M	EI	9	3	
15	957	29	M	EI	10	3	
16	987	7	M	IS	10	10	
17	410	28	H	EI	1	6	

Writing: OSSG Verb Agreement & Prep Phrases Answers

1	2	3	4	5	6	7	8	9
B	D	D	A	A	E	D	A	C

10	11	12	13	14	15	16	17
B	B	C	A	A	E	D	D

Verb Agreement & Parenthetical Expressions

Like it does with prepositional phrases, the SAT will also insert parenthetical expressions between the subject and the verb to confuse you.

A parenthetical expression is a phrase, SET BETWEEN COMMAS, that provides extra information NOT NEEDED for the overall structure of the sentence.

A word within a PARENTHETICAL EXPRESSION is NEVER the SUBJECT of the sentence.

Incorrect: The artifacts, including a stone tablet and a bronze cup, <u>was discovered</u> in the attic of a collector.

Problem: The parenthetical expression 'including a stone tablet and a bronze cup' is placed between the plural subject 'artifacts' and the singular verb 'was discovered' to confuse you into thinking the subject is also singular.

Correct: The artifacts, ~~including a stone tablet and a bronze cup~~, <u>were discovered</u> in the attic of a collector.

Tip:
Simplify the question by drawing lines through parenthetical expressions. Just like with prepositional phrases, eliminate extra words that are designed to keep you from seeing the proper subject.

Writing: OSSG Verb Agreement & Parentheticals Questions

No.	Page	Q.	Diff.	Type	Test	Sect.	Answer
1	837	8	E	IS	8	4	
2	410	23	M	EI	1	6	
3	430	10	M	IS	1	10	
4	534	19	M	EI	3	6	
5	721	24	M	EI	6	6	
6	895	21	M	EI	9	3	
7	957	24	M	EI	10	3	
8	472	25	H	EI	2	6	

Writing: OSSG Verb Agreement & Parentheticals Answers

1	2	3	4	5	6	7	8
B	C	A	B	A	B	D	C

SAT Writing

Verb Agreement & Compound Subjects

A compound subject occurs when two or more things are BOTH SUBJECTS of the SAME VERB.

When a sentence contains a compound subject, the VERB is PLURAL.

Incorrect: The bass guitarist and the drummer <u>plays</u> the rhythm.

Problem: 'bass guitarist' and 'drummer' are both subjects of the singular verb 'plays', so we need to make 'plays' plural.

Correct: The bass guitarist and the drummer <u>play</u> the rhythm.

Writing: OSSG Verb Agreement & Compound Subject Questions

No.	Page	Q.	Diff.	Type	Test	Sect.	Answer
1	956	14	E	EI	10	3	
2	657	7	M	IS	5	6	
3	410	24	H	EI	1	6	
4	431	13	H	IS	1	10	
5	534	23	H	EI	3	6	
6	988	14	H	IS	10	10	

Writing: OSSG Verb Agreement & Compound Subject Answers

1	2	3	4	5	6
E	A	E	C	B	A

Verb Agreement & Inverted Subjects

Another trick the SAT uses to confuse you is to place the subject *after* the verb in the sentence. This is known as an 'Inverted Subject'.

Watch out for SUBJECT(S) placed AFTER the VERB.

Incorrect: Along the highway across from the airport is a flashing light and roadside signs warning of the construction zone.

Problem: *The plural, compound subject 'a flashing light and roadside signs' is placed after the singular verb 'is'.*

Correct: Along the highway across from the airport are a flashing light and roadside signs warning of the construction zone.

Tip:
Watch out for compound subjects that are also inverted.

Writing: OSSG Verb Agreement & Inverted Subjects Questions

No.	Page	Q.	Diff.	Type	Test	Sect.	Answer
1	429	1	E	IS	1	10	
2	776	19	E	EI	7	4	
3	894	14	E	EI	9	3	
4	895	18	E	EI	9	3	
5	956	12	E	EI	10	3	
6	602	27	M	EI	4	7	
7	721	29	M	EI	6	6	

Writing: OSSG Verb Agreement & Inverted Subjects Answers

1	2	3	4	5	6	7
D	A	B	B	B	B	A

Verb Tense

Another form of SAT verb question asks you to identify proper tense of a verb.

**NON-UNDERLINED VERBS
often tell you the tense of the underlined verb.**

For instance, if you notice that all of the other verbs in the sentence are past tense, this is a good indication that the underlined verb should also be past tense.

Incorrect: King Arthur <u>had continued</u> his search for the Holy Grail once he found knights to join him on his quest.

Problem: *The verb 'had continued' should be the same tense as the non-underlined verb 'found'.*

Correct: King Arthur <u>continued</u> his search for the Holy Grail once he found knights to join him on his quest.

**For harder verb tense questions,
SIGNALLING WORDS like 'since', 'after' and 'before'
are clues to the tense of the underlined verb.**

Incorrect: Ever since the tennis player won the championship, advertisers <u>showered</u> him with endorsements.

Problem: *The connector words 'ever since' tell us that the tennis player won the championship <u>prior to</u> the advertisers showering him with endorsements. The tense of 'showered' must show it has been ongoing <u>since</u> the win.*

Correct: Ever since the tennis player won the championship, advertisers <u>have showered</u> him with endorsements.

Writing: OSSG Verb Tense Questions

No.	Page	Q.	Diff.	Type	Test	Sect.	Answer
1	407	4	E	IS	1	6	
2	409	15	E	EI	1	6	
3	534	18	E	EI	3	6	
4	601	13	E	EI	4	7	
5	601	18	E	EI	4	7	
6	676	1	E	IS	5	10	
7	720	19	E	EI	6	6	
8	776	16	E	EI	7	4	
9	777	21	E	EI	7	4	
10	838	13	E	EI	8	4	
11	838	16	E	EI	8	4	
12	894	17	E	EI	9	3	
13	924	2	E	IS	9	10	
14	956	17	E	EI	10	3	
15	957	20	E	EI	10	3	
16	535	26	M	EI	3	6	
17	601	17	M	EI	4	7	
18	602	23	M	EI	4	7	
19	659	22	M	EI	5	6	
20	719	9	M	IS	6	6	
21	777	24	M	EI	7	4	
22	895	25	M	EI	9	3	
23	987	8	M	IS	10	10	

Writing: OSSG Verb Tense Answers

1	2	3	4	5	6	7	8	9	10	11	12
C	C	E	E	A	B	A	E	C	A	C	E

13	14	15	16	17	18	19	20	21	22	23
A	D	A	B	E	E	B	A	E	B	A

SAT Writing

Verb Tense & Dates

**Anytime you see a reference to a date,
(day, month, year, century, etc.)
use the time to figure out the tense.**

Incorrect: In 1890, the Census Bureau <u>declares</u> the frontier of the western United States officially closed.

Problem: The date 1890 is in the past, so the verb 'declares' must be past tense.

Correct: In 1890, the Census Bureau <u>declared</u> the frontier of the western United States officially closed.

Tip:
Questions that include dates are usually past tense.

Writing: OSSG Verb Tense & Dates Questions

No.	Page	Q.	Diff.	Type	Test	Sect.	Answer
1	409	13	E	EI	1	6	
2	471	13	E	EI	2	6	
3	471	16	E	EI	2	6	
4	601	12	E	EI	4	7	
5	718	5	E	IS	6	6	
6	720	13	E	EI	6	6	
7	777	20	E	EI	7	4	
8	894	12	E	EI	9	3	
9	408	8	M	IS	1	6	
10	492	7	M	IS	2	10	
11	534	24	M	EI	3	6	
12	718	3	M	IS	6	6	
13	839	21	M	EI	8	4	

Writing: OSSG Verb Tense & Dates Answers

1	2	3	4	5	6	7	8	9	10	11	12	13
E	D	C	C	C	E	C	C	A	A	A	B	C

Verb Tense & '-ing'

> Underlined verbs ending in 'ing' are often errors.

Incorrect: Rachel knew a lot about how <u>fixing</u> old cars.

Problem: 'fixing' is not proper when used with 'how'.

Correct: Rachel knew a lot about how <u>to fix</u> old cars.

Writing: OSSG Verb Tense & '-ing' Questions

No.	Page	Q.	Diff.	Type	Test	Sect.	Answer
1	491	1	E	IS	2	10	
2	533	14	E	EI	3	6	
3	656	2	E	IS	5	6	
4	658	12	E	EI	5	6	
5	658	15	E	EI	5	6	
6	658	16	E	EI	5	6	
7	956	13	E	EI	10	3	
8	409	16	M	EI	1	6	
9	410	25	M	EI	1	6	
10	534	21	M	EI	3	6	
11	659	21	M	EI	5	6	
12	863	8	M	IS	8	10	
13	895	20	M	EI	9	3	

Writing: OSSG Verb Tense & '-ing' Answers

1	2	3	4	5	6	7	8	9	10	11	12	13
B	A	D	A	D	A	B	D	C	D	B	D	A

SAT Writing

Pronouns

Pronouns are tested on both Sentence Improvement and Error ID questions.

**A pronoun is a small word
(I, me, he, us, her, who which, that, etc.)
that refers to a person, place, or thing.**

Pronouns		
Subjects	Objects	Possessives
I	me	mine
you	you	yours
she	her	her
he	him	his
it	it	its
we	us	our / ours
they	them	their / theirs
who	whom	whose

Tip:
Whenever you see a pronoun underlined in a question, find the person, place or thing to whom or to which it refers.

Ambiguous Pronouns

A pronoun must always refer to a specific person, place or thing in the sentence.

> **If you CANNOT TELL to whom or to what an underlined pronoun refers,**
> *or*
> **if the pronoun could possibly refer to MORE THAN ONE person, place, or thing, the pronoun is INCORRECT.**

Incorrect: Harry, Chuck, and Dick all met at the coffee shop, where <u>he</u> ordered a mocha.

Problem: 'he' can refer to any of the three people listed.

Correct: Harry, Chuck, and Dick all met at the coffee shop, where <u>Harry</u> ordered a mocha.

> **Watch out for the undefined 'they'.**

Incorrect: The clown was so funny that <u>they</u> laughed out loud at his antics.

Problem: 'they' does not refer to anything in the sentence.

Correct: The clown was so funny that <u>the audience</u> laughed out loud at his antics.

Writing: OSSG Ambiguous Pronouns Questions

No.	Page	Q.	Diff.	Type	Test	Sect.	Answer
1	429	4	E	IS	1	10	
2	774	2	E	IS	7	4	
3	954	4	E	IS	10	3	
4	955	10	E	IS	10	3	
5	677	6	M	IS	5	10	
6	802	5	M	IS	7	10	
7	839	26	M	EI	8	4	
8	925	11	M	IS	9	10	
9	957	26	M	EI	10	3	
10	472	28	H	EI	2	6	
11	657	11	H	IS	5	6	

Writing: OSSG Ambiguous Pronouns Answers

1	2	3	4	5	6	7	8	9	10	11
E	E	D	B	C	B	D	C	C	C	B

Pronoun Number Agreement

**A pronoun must AGREE
with its person, place or thing in NUMBER.**

If the person, place or thing is singular, the pronoun must also be singular.
If the person, place or thing is plural, the pronoun must also be plural.

Incorrect: Although the country had a long history of peaceful relations with other nations, their leaders nevertheless voted to go to war.

Problem: 'country' is singular, while 'their' is plural.

Correct: Although the country had a long history of peaceful relations with other nations, its leaders nevertheless voted to go to war.

Remember!
Any single group of people or things, like 'country', 'agency', etc., is always singular.

Writing: OSSG Pronoun Number Agreement Questions

No.	Page	Q.	Diff.	Type	Test	Sect.	Answer
1	553	1	E	IS	3	10	
2	601	15	E	EI	4	7	
3	659	20	E	EI	5	6	
4	720	16	E	EI	6	6	
5	721	20	E	EI	6	6	
6	721	23	E	EI	6	6	
7	895	19	E	EI	9	3	
8	409	19	M	EI	1	6	
9	471	18	M	EI	2	6	
10	534	20	M	EI	3	6	
11	659	23	M	EI	5	6	
12	677	10	M	IS	5	10	
13	720	15	M	EI	6	6	
14	775	5	M	IS	7	4	
15	801	3	M	IS	7	10	
16	837	5	M	IS	8	4	
17	837	11	M	IS	8	4	
18	957	19	M	EI	10	3	
19	410	26	H	EI	1	6	
20	472	29	H	EI	2	6	
21	532	10	H	IS	3	6	
22	534	22	H	EI	3	6	
23	535	27	H	EI	3	6	
24	602	28	H	EI	4	7	
25	660	28	H	EI	5	6	

Writing: OSSG Pronoun Number Agreement Answers

1	2	3	4	5	6	7	8	9	10	11	12	13
A	D	C	E	B	E	B	C	C	C	E	D	C

14	15	16	17	18	19	20	21	22	23	24	25
C	C	B	E	C	D	E	A	A	C	C	A

Pronoun Consistency

> Pronouns 'you' and 'one' must be used consistently.

Incorrect: <u>One</u> can never be a great musician unless <u>you</u> practice daily.

Problem: The sentence mixes 'one' and 'you'.

Correct: <u>You</u> can never be a great musician unless <u>you</u> practice daily.

Tip:
'You' is proper as long as it is used consistently.

Writing: OSSG Pronoun Consistency Questions

No.	Page	Q.	Diff.	Type	Test	Sect.	Answer
1	838	19	E	EI	8	4	
2	677	7	M	IS	5	10	
3	739	7	M	IS	6	10	
4	777	23	M	EI	7	4	
5	777	25	M	EI	7	4	
6	925	9	M	IS	9	10	

Writing: OSSG Pronoun Consistency Answers

1	2	3	4	5	6
D	E	B	C	B	D

Who vs. Which

> 'Who' refers to people.
> 'Which' refers to animals and things.

Incorrect: The best baseball players are those <u>which</u> can not only hit and catch but also run and throw.

Problem: 'which' refers to people ('baseball players').

Correct: The best baseball players are those <u>who</u> can not only hit and catch but also run and throw.

Tip:
On a few rare SAT questions, the pronoun 'whose' is used for both people and animals and things.

Writing: OSSG Who vs. Which Questions

No.	Page	Q.	Diff.	Type	Test	Sect.	Answer
1	601	19	E	EI	4	7	
2	658	14	E	EI	5	6	
3	838	14	E	EI	8	4	
4	838	17	E	EI	8	4	
5	894	15	E	EI	9	3	
6	894	16	E	EI	9	3	
7	839	22	M	EI	8	4	

Writing: OSSG Who vs. Which Answers

1	2	3	4	5	6	7
E	A	E	A	B	E	E

Pronoun Case

Use of a pronoun sometimes depends on whether it is a subject or an object.

**For SAT purposes,
if a pronoun is NOT the SUBJECT of a verb,
it is ALWAYS an OBJECT.**

Pronoun Case	
Subjects	Objects
I	me
she	her
he	him
we	us
they	them
who	whom

Pronouns listed under 'Subjects' are only used as the subject of some verb, while those listed under 'Objects' are used for most everything else.

Incorrect: Alice drove to the store with Sandra and I.

Problem: *'I' is not the subject of the verb 'drove' ('Alice' is).*
'I' should therefore be replaced with objective case 'me'.

Also, crossing out 'Sandra and', makes it easier to see that 'me' is the proper sounding pronoun.

Correct: Alice drove to the store with ~~Sandra and~~ me.

SAT Writing

Tip:
Cross out any other people or things included with the pronoun to better hear the correct usage.

Tip:
Pronouns within prepositional phrases are always <u>objects</u>.

Tip:
The correct SAT answer is usually the <u>objective</u> case pronoun.

Writing: OSSG Pronoun Case Questions

No.	Page	Q.	Diff.	Type	Test	Sect.	Answer
1	471	12	E	EI	2	6	
2	721	27	E	EI	6	6	
3	776	14	E	EI	7	4	
4	602	21	M	EI	4	7	
5	602	26	M	EI	4	7	
6	839	24	M	EI	8	4	
7	896	28	M	EI	9	3	
8	957	22	M	EI	10	3	

Writing: OSSG Pronoun Case Answers

1	2	3	4	5	6	7	8
B	A	A	B	B	A	A	A

Noun Agreement

Like pronouns, nouns that refer to other nouns must agree in NUMBER.

Incorrect: Alma and Christie both found jobs as <u>a lifeguard</u> for the summer.

Problem: 'lifeguard' is singular but 'jobs' is plural.
(Alma and Christie can not both be the same lifeguard.)

Correct: Alma and Christie both found jobs as <u>lifeguards</u> for the summer.

Tip:
Whenever a question mentions some kind of a job or occupation, look for Noun Agreement problems.

Writing: OSSG Noun Agreement Questions

No.	Page	Q.	Diff.	Type	Test	Sect.	Answer
1	409	12	E	EI	1	6	
2	531	4	E	IS	3	6	
3	776	12	E	EI	7	4	
4	429	3	M	IS	1	10	
5	471	17	M	EI	2	6	
6	839	25	M	EI	8	4	
7	957	28	M	EI	10	3	

Writing: OSSG Noun Agreement Answers

1	2	3	4	5	6	7
C	B	B	B	D	A	A

Comparisons

Comparison questions test different ways to describe the relationship between two or more people or things.

Faulty Comparisons

Watch out for sentences that compare things that are not the same TYPE.

Incorrect: The novels of Patrick O'Brian, which take place during the Napoleonic era, are more detailed than <u>CS Forester</u>.

Problem: *The sentence compares novels to an author.*

Correct: The novels of Patrick O'Brian, which take place during the Napoleonic era, are more detailed than <u>the novels of CS Forester</u>.

Correct: The novels of Patrick O'Brian, which take place during the Napoleonic era, are more detailed than <u>those of CS Forester</u>.

Correct: The novels of Patrick O'Brian, which take place during the Napoleonic era, are more detailed than <u>CS Forester's novels</u>.

Writing: OSSG Faulty Comparisons Questions

No.	Page	Q.	Diff.	Type	Test	Sect.	Answer
1	533	13	E	EI	3	6	
2	599	3	E	IS	4	7	
3	720	14	E	EI	6	6	
4	738	2	E	IS	6	10	
5	837	7	E	IS	8	4	
6	410	21	M	EI	1	6	
7	660	27	M	EI	5	6	
8	803	13	M	IS	7	10	
9	893	6	M	IS	9	3	
10	896	27	M	EI	9	3	
11	410	29	H	EI	1	6	
12	492	11	H	IS	2	10	
13	532	11	H	IS	3	6	
14	534	25	H	EI	3	6	
15	777	28	H	EI	7	4	
16	926	14	H	IS	9	10	

Writing: OSSG Faulty Comparisons Answers

1	2	3	4	5	6	7	8
D	B	D	B	A	B	D	E
9	10	11	12	13	14	15	16
E	D	D	D	B	D	D	D

SAT Writing

Comparing Two vs. Three or More Things

When Comparing:	
Two things use:	Three or more things use:
-er	**-est**
at the end of the comparing word	

Incorrect: Of the two instruments, the bass violin is <u>largest</u>, but the trumpet is <u>loudest</u>.

Problem: '<u>two</u> instruments' uses -er.

Correct: Of the two instruments, the bass violin is <u>larger</u>, but the trumpet is <u>louder</u>.

Incorrect: Curly is the <u>funnier</u> of the Three Stooges.

Problem: '<u>Three</u> Stooges' uses -est.

Correct: Curly is the <u>funniest</u> of the Three Stooges.

Writing: OSSG Two vs. Three or More Things Questions

No.	Page	Q.	Diff.	Type	Test	Sect.	Answer
1	659	24	M	EI	5	6	
2	472	27	H	EI	2	6	
3	660	29	H	EI	5	6	
4	957	27	H	EI	10	3	

Writing: OSSG Two vs. Three or More Things Answers

1	2	3	4
D	E	E	E

Redundancies

> Watch out for sentences that use
> extra words where they are not needed.

Incorrect: The windows are <u>more cleaner</u> than they were before.

Problem: 'more' is redundant when used with 'clean<u>er</u>'.

Correct: The windows are <u>cleaner</u> than they were before.

Writing: OSSG Redundancies Questions

No.	Page	Q.	Diff.	Type	Test	Sect.	Answer
1	659	18	E	EI	5	6	
2	838	18	E	EI	8	4	
3	894	13	E	EI	9	3	
4	718	4	M	IS	6	6	
5	535	29	H	EI	3	6	

Writing: OSSG Redundancies Answers

1	2	3	4	5
D	B	C	B	D

SAT Writing

Improving Paragraphs

Improving Paragraph questions ask you to improve certain parts of a student written passage.

Think of yourself as the editor of the school newspaper and the passage is an article submitted by another student.

Tip:
*Many questions are like Improving Sentence questions. Questions are 'faux' Improving Sentence questions where answer (A) says: **(as it is now)**.*

Improving Paragraphs questions do NOT appear in order difficulty.

Questions are randomly sorted.

Improving Paragraphs Strategies

Answer Improving Paragraphs questions FIRST. Then go back to the beginning and complete the Writing section.

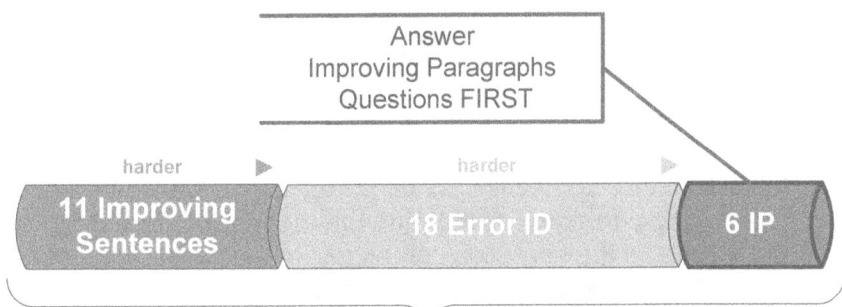

SAT Writing Multiple Choice 1 (25 Minutes)

**Scan the questions and
circle sentence numbers in the passage.**

This helps you know where to focus your attention within the passage.

Read the passage quickly.

It's not important to read Improving Paragraphs Passages too carefully. Simply try to understand the context for the sentences being asked about, and get a feel for the author's point of view.

Tip:
Don't get hung up on the passage.
The passage is poorly written on purpose. If it seems confusing at times, that's because it's supposed to be.

**When answering the questions, quickly scan the
paragraph to understand how the sentence fits.**

Remember, we are trying to improve *paragraphs* here.

CONTEXT is the key.

If the sentence comes first in the paragraph, it should introduce the topic of the paragraph and/or provide a transition from the previous paragraph. If the sentence comes last in the paragraph, it should conclude the paragraph and sum up the key point.

Improving Paragraphs Question Sets

Test	Section	Pages	Questions	Answers Page
1	6	411-12	30-35	432
2	6	473-74	30-35	494
3	6	535-36	30-35	556
4	6	603-04	30-35	618
5	6	660-61	30-35	680
6	6	722-23	30-35	742
7	4	778-79	30-35	804
8	4	840-41	30-35	866
9	3	896-97	30-35	928
10	3	958-59	30-35	990

SAT Writing Multiple Choice Quick Review

SAT Writing Multiple Choice

Improving Paragraphs (Answer First!)
- Qs do NOT appear in order difficulty.
- Scan Qs for sentence numbers, and circle in passage.
- Read passage quickly.
- Many Qs are like Improving Sentences.
- <u>Context</u> is key for others.

Improving Sentences
- Q's appear in order of difficulty.
- Trust your gut.
- Try to spot issue before looking at answers.
- When practicing, read the question out loud.
- Start with shortest answer first.
- Answer choice (A) is always 'no error'. Don't be afraid to pick (A).

Error IDs
- Qs appear in order of difficulty.
- Read the sentence completely answering.
- Answer choice (E) is always 'no error'.
- Expect 3 to 4 E's.
- Don't skip Error IDs! Just answer (E).
- Check E's at the end if you have time.

Note:
For a complete list of Writing MC rules, see the SAT Quick Review section at the end of this book.

Frequently Asked Questions

First, let's address some basic questions and dispel a few of the more prevalent myths about the SAT essay.

"Oh my God, do I really have to write an essay?"

This is often the first reaction of many students when they learn that the SAT includes an essay section.

Relax. As we will see, the SAT essay is actually one of the easiest sections to do well on. Far from hurting your score, the essay will usually improve your overall score on the Writing section.

Where does the essay appear on the test?

The essay always comes FIRST (Section 1).

How much time do I have to write the essay?

The SAT essay section is 25 MINUTES.

While this may not seem like a lot of time in which to write an essay, once you know how to approach it, you should have little problem writing a complete essay in the required time.

SAT Essay

How much do I have to write?

> The SAT provides a TWO PAGE answer sheet with 46 LINES in which to write your essay.

Tip:
More is better.
The more you are able to fill up both pages, the better your score is likely to be.

How is the essay scored?

> The TWO ESSAY GRADERS each score your essay on a 6-POINT SCALE, with 6 the top score and 1 the lowest.
>
> These two scores are then added together for a total of 12 POSSIBLE POINTS.

Who grades the essay?

> The SAT essay is graded primarily by high school and college writing teachers.

Can I get a zero on the essay?

> Essays that fail to address the topic are scored as zero.

Always make sure you write about the topic suggested by the essay prompt.

How does the essay affect my SAT score?

The essay makes up approximately 30% of your Writing score.

Your essay score adds to or subtracts from your Writing Multiple Choice score to determine your final overall Writing score.

Example SAT Writing Composite Score Conversion Table														
Writing MC Score			Writing Score Combined With Essay (Final Score)											
Raw	Scaled	Equiv	12	11	10	9	8	7	6	5	4	3	2	0
49	80	800	800	800	800	790	770	750	740	720	710	700	680	670
48	78	780	800	800	780	760	740	720	710	690	680	670	650	640
47	75	750	790	770	760	740	720	700	690	670	660	640	630	620
46	73	730	770	750	740	720	700	680	670	650	640	630	610	600
45	71	710	760	740	720	710	690	670	650	640	630	610	590	580
44	70	700	740	730	710	700	670	660	640	620	610	600	580	570
43	68	680	730	720	700	680	660	640	630	610	600	590	570	560
42	67	670	720	700	690	670	650	630	620	600	590	570	560	550
41	66	660	710	690	680	660	640	620	610	590	580	560	550	540
40	64	640	700	680	670	650	630	610	600	580	570	550	540	530
39	63	630	690	680	660	640	620	600	590	570	560	550	530	520
38	62	620	680	670	650	630	610	600	580	560	550	540	520	510
37	61	610	670	660	640	630	610	590	570	550	540	530	510	500
36	60	600	660	650	630	620	600	580	560	550	530	520	500	490
35	59	590	660	640	620	610	590	570	550	540	530	510	490	480
34	58	580	650	630	620	600	580	560	550	530	520	500	490	480
33	57	570	640	620	610	590	570	550	540	520	510	490	480	470
32	56	560	630	620	600	580	560	540	530	510	500	490	470	460
31	55	550	620	610	590	580	550	540	520	500	490	480	460	450
30	54	540	610	600	580	570	550	530	510	500	480	470	450	440
29	53	530	610	590	570	560	540	520	500	490	480	460	440	430
28	52	520	600	580	570	550	530	510	490	480	470	450	440	430
27	51	510	590	570	560	540	520	500	490	470	460	440	430	420
26	50	500	580	570	550	530	510	490	480	460	450	440	420	410
25	49	490	570	560	540	530	500	490	470	450	440	430	410	400
24	48	480	560	550	530	520	500	480	460	450	430	420	400	390
23	47	470	560	540	520	510	490	470	450	440	430	410	390	380
22	46	460	550	530	520	500	480	460	450	430	420	400	390	380
21	45	450	540	520	510	490	470	450	440	420	410	390	380	370
20	44	440	530	520	500	480	460	440	430	410	400	390	370	360
19	43	430	520	510	490	480	460	440	420	410	390	380	360	350
18	42	420	520	500	480	470	450	430	410	400	390	370	350	340
17	41	410	510	490	480	460	440	420	410	390	380	360	350	340
16	40	400	500	490	470	450	430	410	400	380	370	360	340	330

Source: College Board

Did you know?
You can get an overall score of 800 on the SAT writing section with an essay score of only 10.

SAT Essay

> **A score of 9 will almost never hurt your writing score, while a 10 or above almost always helps.**

Depending on how well you do on the multiple choice portion, an essay in the 9-10 range will typically improve your overall writing score by between 10 and 50 points, while an 11 or 12 can improve your score by as much as 100 points.

Example SAT Writing Composite Score Difference Table													
Writing MC Score			Writing Essay Score Difference										
Raw	Scaled	Equiv	12	11	10	9	8	7	6	5	4	3	2	0
49	80	800	0	0	0	-10	-30	-50	-60	-80	-90	-100	-120	-130
48	78	780	20	20	0	-20	-40	-60	-70	-90	-100	-110	-130	-140
47	75	750	40	20	10	-10	-30	-50	-60	-80	-90	-110	-120	-130
46	73	730	40	20	10	-10	-30	-50	-60	-80	-90	-100	-120	-130
45	71	710	50	30	10	0	-20	-40	-60	-70	-80	-100	-120	-130
44	70	700	40	30	10	0	-30	-40	-60	-80	-90	-100	-120	-130
43	68	680	50	40	20	0	-20	-40	-50	-70	-80	-90	-110	-120
42	67	670	50	30	20	0	-20	-40	-50	-70	-80	-100	-110	-120
41	66	660	50	30	20	0	-20	-40	-50	-70	-80	-100	-110	-120
40	64	640	60	40	30	10	-10	-30	-40	-60	-70	-90	-100	-110
39	63	630	60	50	30	10	-10	-30	-40	-60	-70	-80	-100	-110
38	62	620	60	50	30	10	-10	-20	-40	-60	-70	-80	-100	-110
37	61	610	60	50	30	20	0	-20	-40	-60	-70	-80	-100	-110
36	60	600	60	50	30	20	0	-20	-40	-50	-70	-80	-100	-110
35	59	590	70	50	30	20	0	-20	-40	-50	-60	-80	-100	-110
34	58	580	70	50	40	20	0	-20	-30	-50	-60	-80	-90	-100
33	57	570	70	50	40	20	0	-20	-30	-50	-60	-80	-90	-100
32	56	560	70	60	40	20	0	-20	-30	-50	-60	-70	-90	-100
31	55	550	70	60	40	30	0	-10	-30	-50	-60	-70	-90	-100
30	54	540	70	60	40	30	10	-10	-30	-40	-60	-70	-90	-100
29	53	530	80	60	40	30	10	-10	-30	-40	-50	-70	-90	-100
28	52	520	80	60	50	30	10	-10	-30	-40	-50	-70	-80	-90
27	51	510	80	60	50	30	10	-10	-20	-40	-50	-70	-80	-90
26	50	500	80	70	50	30	10	-10	-20	-40	-50	-60	-80	-90
25	49	490	80	70	50	40	10	0	-20	-40	-50	-60	-80	-90
24	48	480	80	70	50	40	20	0	-20	-30	-50	-60	-80	-90
23	47	470	90	70	50	40	20	0	-20	-30	-40	-60	-80	-90
22	46	460	90	70	60	40	20	0	-10	-30	-40	-60	-70	-80
21	45	450	90	70	60	40	20	0	-10	-30	-40	-60	-70	-80
20	44	440	90	80	60	40	20	0	-10	-30	-40	-50	-70	-80
19	43	430	90	80	60	50	30	10	-10	-20	-40	-50	-70	-80
18	42	420	100	80	60	50	30	10	-10	-20	-30	-50	-70	-80
17	41	410	100	80	70	50	30	10	0	-20	-30	-50	-60	-70
16	40	400	100	90	70	50	30	10	0	-20	-30	-40	-60	-70

What am I graded on?

SAT essay graders look for five things:

1. **A clear opinion supported with <u>detailed</u> examples***
2. **Good overall organization and smooth transitions***
3. **Skillful use of language (vocabulary)**
4. **Variety in sentence structure**
5. **Proper grammar, usage, and mechanics**

The chart on page 105 of the OSSG describes in detail the differences between various essay scores, with each of the score descriptions falling generally into one of the five categories above.

Tip:
*Of these five categories, the first two are by far the most important. While skillful use of language, sentence structure variety, and proper grammar will help improve your score, the bulk of your points are earned from the first two categories.

What about spelling mistakes?

You can still do very well on the SAT essay even with a few spelling or grammar mistakes.

While you always want to spell as accurately as you can, the SAT understands that you are writing a first draft in a very short period of time, and tells its graders not to nitpick spelling and/or other grammar mistakes too closely.

What can I write about?

You can write about practically ANYTHING.

The SAT is not particularly interested in what you write about, only that you write well *about* it.

Ideas can come from anywhere, so do not feel constricted to academic or literary examples. Friends, family, current events, extracurricular activities, even your favorite TV show are all fair game to write about.

Can I write about personal experiences?

You CAN write about personal experiences.

In fact, personal experiences are many times the best examples to use because they are the ones about which you have the most detailed knowledge.

What <u>should</u> I write about?

Write about what you KNOW.

You should always write about topics with which you are the most familiar – topics about which, if you are not expert in, you at least know more about than most people.

When you write about what you know, your writing flows more freely because you are able to focus on simply telling a story rather than struggling to remember facts and events.

What if I can't remember a specific name or date?

Factual accuracy is not important.

Factual accuracy is not one of the criteria for grading essays. Still, if you are having trouble remembering a lot of basic facts, you may want to rethink using that specific example, since you probably don't know enough about the topic to write a strong essay.

Believe it or not:
SAT Essay graders are specifically told NOT to fact check.

Can I just make something up?

**There is nothing stopping you
from making up an example.**

The graders do not fact check, and, especially with personal experiences, there is really no way for them to know whether or not the event actually happened.

Careful:
Unless you are a budding fiction writer, it is usually preferable to use actual events and experiences, since these are the ones you will know most about and can describe in the most detail.

SAT Essay

Analyzing the Question

Essay Tutorial 1:
Turn to OSSG page 699.
Read everything up to the box halfway down the page

Here we see a typical essay question. At the top of the page you are told that you have 25 minutes to write the essay. Below that are various rules for writing the essay, most of which we have already discussed.

In the box you see another box with a short quote which is meant to address the essay topic. The quote in the box is an example of someone else's opinion of the question in the prompt.

> **Ignore the quote in the center box.**

You do not need to talk about the quote (the text in the center box) in your essay, and it is usually a good idea simply to ignore it altogether to avoid reading something that might distract you from developing your own answer to the Assignment.

Tip:
If you would like to mention the quote in your essay, do it in your conclusion (see below), but be sure to read the quote only after you read the "Assignment:".

Finally, you are given an Assignment and told to write an essay developing a point of view and supporting your position with reasoning and examples.

> **Read the essay prompt FIRST!**
> **(the first sentence after the word 'Assignment:')**

The essay prompt is the question you need to write your essay about and basically the only thing on the whole page that has any real effect on your score.

Tip:
Underline the essay prompt.
Underlining the prompt helps you focus squarely on the issue.

SAT Unlocked II

Brainstorming Exercises

Coming up with ideas is the most important part of writing a good essay. With only twenty five minutes to write, you need to think up examples quickly.

Practice thinking up various ideas from different categories, so that whatever question you get on the test, you have a number of ready-made examples to choose from.

 Essay Tutorial 2:

Using any of the categories below, write down two or three possible essay notes for the prompt on OSSG page 699.

Essay Topics				
Social Studies	Arts & Literature	Science	Popular Culture	Personal Experiences
Business Government History News Politics	Books Movies Music Poetry Theater	Computers Experiments Environment History People	Celebrities Magazines Sports TV Websites	Athletics Family Friends Hobbies School

 Tip:
If you can't think of examples, Martin Luther King Jr. and/or Mohandas Gandhi are usually good fallbacks because they work with almost every SAT prompt.

Essay Tutorial 3:

Using any of the categories below, write down two or three possible essay notes for the prompt on OSSG page 761.

Essay Topics				
Social Studies	Arts & Literature	Science	Popular Culture	Personal Experiences
Business Government History News Politics	Books Movies Music Poetry Theater	Computers Experiments Environment History People	Celebrities Magazines Sports TV Websites	Athletics Family Friends Hobbies School

Writing Your Essay

Before you write your essay, a few considerations:

Pick ONE side.

The SAT wants you to make a clear point, and will penalize you if you waffle back and forth.

Use one or two examples in your essay.

You won't have time to write about more than two examples with any of the detail the SAT requires.

Tip:
Come up with your examples FIRST; THEN pick the side they best support. Otherwise, you run the risk of taking a side and realizing only later that your examples actually support the other side better.

Keep your examples balanced.

Your two examples should both be about the same length. If you find yourself writing so much about the first example that you don't have time to write enough about the second to maintain this balance, skip the second example and write a one example essay.

Keep it simple.

State your point simply and back it up with one or two detailed examples. Stick to the topic and avoid sidetracks.

Don't try to sound smarter than you are.

Write the way you would normally. Let it flow.

SAT Essay

Organizing Your Essay
Follow the four-paragraph essay outline below.

Paragraph 1: <u>Short</u> Introduction.
Your introduction should be <u>short</u>, only about two or three sentences. Save the important writing for your examples.

> **Sentence 1: Rewrite the prompt as a statement.**

The SAT awards points for taking a clearly defined stand or 'thesis'. The easiest way to show the reader up front that you taking a stand is to simply rewrite the prompt as a one-sided statement rather than a question.

Tip:
For more advanced students: come up with a 'hook' - a creative way to write your thesis that restates the prompt but doesn't parrot it.

> **Sentence 2: Throw the other side a bone.**

Your second sentence should begin with 'while' or 'although' and briefly say why the other side's argument has some merit. Then end the sentence by telling why your side is still better.

> **Sentence 3: Introduce your examples.**

In the last sentence of your introduction, broadly mention your examples and show how they fit with the prompt.

Paragraph 2: Your BETTER example.
Your first example should be the one that will make the greatest impression on the reader.

For your first example, choose the one that you can write about more descriptively and that better supports your thesis.

Tip:
Detail. Detail. Detail.
The more detail you use to describe your examples, the better your score will be. When writing examples, write as descriptively as you can. Try to paint a word picture for your reader using as many facts as possible.

Conclude your example by referring back to the prompt.

Finish up your paragraph by reminding the reader how your example supports your thesis.

Paragraph 3: Transition, then your second example.

> **Start your second example
> with a transition sentence that links
> your first and second examples together.**

After transitioning, describe your second example in detail.

Tip:
Detail. Detail. Detail.
This cannot be stressed enough.
Always describe examples with as much detail as you can.

> **Conclude your example
> by referring back to the prompt.**

Again, remind the reader why you are using this example by stating how it supports your thesis.

Paragraph 4: Conclusion.
Conclude your essay with a general, philosophical statement about your position. Be sure to mention your examples again and how they generally support this broader concept.

> **ALWAYS conclude your essay.**

One of the skills tested on the Essay section of the SAT is how well you can manage your time. Even if your conclusion is only one sentence, always write something down to show the grader that you were able to finish.

Tip:
Conclude using the quote in the box.
Although not necessary, if you notice something interesting in the text of the quote, you can include it to round out your conclusion.

Essay Example

The student-written essay below received a score of 12 on the SAT.

Essay question:

> People generally put more trust in what they have learned for themselves than in what they learn from others. Few people, however, are really motivated to learn anything on their own. They are much more apt to learn when others are willing to teach them. Even though learning from others means occasionally learning things that are not useful or important, people are still better off when they learn from others.

Read the quote in the box only AFTER you've read the 'ASSIGNMENT:'.

Underline the sentence after 'ASSIGNMENT:'.

ASSIGNMENT: Is it better for people to learn from others than to learn on their own? Plan and write an essay in which you develop your point of view on this issue. Support your position with reasoning and examples taken from your reading, studies, experience, or observations.

This 'prompt' is what you need to write about.

Student essay:

Begin your essay on this page. If you need more space, continue on the next page.

Intro sentence 1: Re-write the prompt as a statement.

It is better for people to learn from others. Although some might say that you learn at your own pace, so therefore it is better to learn by yourself, it is only through the intervention of others that one learns best. This idea of learning from others manifested itself both in the life of Martin Luther King Jr. and myself.

Intro sentence 2: Throw the other side a bone. Start with 'Although' or 'While'.

Intro sentence 3: Introduce your example(s).

First example: Your BETTER example.

Martin Luther King Jr. learned his method of peaceful protest from Gandhi, and that is what made him successful. Gandhi had led a hunger strike in India so that the Hindus and Muslims would stop fighting and talk. This form of protest lasted seventy days and was successful in getting both sides to lay down their arms and have a conference on the porch of Gandhi's house. It is this success that Martin Luther King Jr. studied, and his own peaceful protest would not have been as successful had it not been for his imitation of Gandhi. Martin Luther King Jr. was a pioneer and central figure in the Civil Rights movement in the 1950s. The difference between this movement and others throughout history is that King proposed non-violence as a solution to the problem as he had learned from Gandhi. Martin Luther King Jr. organized sit-ins, where African-Americans would just sit in typically

Include as much DETAIL as you can in your examples. Be specific.

318

SAT Essay

Continuation of ESSAY Section 1 from previous page. Write below only if you need more space.
IMPORTANT: DO NOT START on this page — If you do, your essay may appear blank and your score may be affected.

Second body paragraph: Start with a TRANSITION.

segregated areas and say nothing and never fight back against the whites who would harm them. Another strategy that King learned from Gandhi was the peaceful march. Much like Gandhi led marches through India in the early 1910's, King led marches through Washington D.C. in the 1950's and 1960's. The purpose of these marches was not to promote violence, but simply to show others their message of equality without violence. Martin Luther King also took one of Gandhi's ideas for nonviolence and used it to his success: speeches. Gandhi was celebrated for his speeches that united the Muslims and Hindus of the early 20th century India. King also learned this technique, and used it to inspire whites and African Americans to live together peacefully, like in his "I Have a Dream" speech of 1963. It was a combination of every form of non-violent protest that made Martin Luther King Jr. an icon of America and a voice of freedom, yet everything he did was based off of Gandhi's work, so

Conclude example by referring back to the prompt.

→ King's success came from his ability to learn from others.

As it was once said, "people are still better off when they learn from others", and it is this idea that aided the success of such icons as Martin Luther King Jr. Had it not been for his ability to learn from others, America might still be a racist and segregated place.

Optional: Include text from the quote in the box in your conclusion.

Fill up both pages.

Tip:
Go with the flow.
Notice that although the student initially stated in his introduction that he would talk about two examples, the student found a 'flow' with his first example and decided to continue with this example in his second body paragraph. If you similarly find a flow while writing an example, go with it, since writers who write with flow almost always write at their best.

Timing Your Essay

Budget your essay time this way:

3 - 4 minutes:
Read the prompt and
THINK about your examples.

IMPORTANT!
Do NOT start to write right away.
Force yourself to take the time to <u>think first</u> about your examples. This way you are more likely to come up with good examples and to avoid having to change them in the middle of the essay.

20 minutes:
Write your essay.

To keep the essay examples balanced, you need to spend about the same amount of time on each example, so budget your writing time accordingly.

Tip:
At the 5 minute warning, start your conclusion. This will ensure that you have enough time to finish your essay strongly.

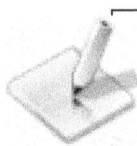

1 minute:
Edit for punctuation, grammar and spelling.

Take a minute to quickly edit your essay for these mistakes.

SAT Essay Quick Review

SAT Essay

General
- Always Section 1.
- **Read 'Assignment:' FIRST!**
- Fill up both pages (more is better!).
- Write in No. 2 pencil (no mechanical).
- Stay within margins.
- You can write about *anything*.
    - Write about what you know.
    - Don't worry about factual errors.
    - Fallback: MLK, Gandhi, or make something up.
- Come up with examples; then pick ONE side.
- Use either one or two examples.
  If two examples, keep balanced.
- Relax.

Organization

Paragraph 1: Short Introduction
   Sentence 1: Rewrite the prompt.
   Sentence 2: Throw the other side a bone
         (begin with 'while' or 'although').
   Sentence 3: Introduce your examples.

Paragraph 2: (BETTER example).
   Just the facts.
   Detail. Detail. Detail.
   Conclude by referring back to the prompt.

Paragraph 3: (2nd example or extension of first)
   Start with transition sentence.
   Detail. Detail. Detail.
   Conclude by referring back to the prompt.

Paragraph 4: Conclusion
   ALWAYS conclude your essay.
   Optional: refer to the quote in the box.

Timing
   3-4 minutes: THINK about your examples.
   20 minutes: Write essay (at 5 minute warning, start conclusion).
   1 minute: Proofread.

SAT Unlocked II

The Night Before

Do NOT study the night before the test.

Studies consistently show that people who cram the night before standardized tests do WORSE than people who do other things.

Instead, gather together everything you will need for test day:

- ☐ SAT Admission Ticket
- ☐ Photo ID
- ☐ No.2 Pencils (no mechanical pencils!)
- ☐ Calculator (check your batteries!)
- ☐ Snacks
- ☐ Drinks
- ☐ Watch (turn off the alarm!)
- ☐ Backpack (to put everything in)

Do NOT bring to the test:

- ☒ scratch paper
- ☒ notes, books, dictionary
- ☒ compass, protractor, ruler, or any other aid
- ☒ highlighter or colored pencils
- ☒ portable listening or recording devices
- ☒ camera or other photographic equipment
- ☒ timer or watch with audible alarm.
- ☒ Cell phone, pager, personal digital assistant, or other digital/electronic equipment.

Tip:
The SAT will not let you make any calls during the breaks and will most likely cancel your score if they catch you with a cell phone.
If you must bring a phone, <u>turn it OFF during the test</u>.

SAT Test Day

 **Relax.**

Watch a movie. Play a video game. Just do something that will let you relax and take your mind off the test for a little while.

 Eat a substantial dinner.

You will need energy for the test. You get this energy from food. Eating a big dinner (as opposed to a big breakfast) gives your body time to absorb and store the food's energy. It will also help you sleep.

 Drink lots of fluids.

You brain functions best when your body has a lot of water in its system. Drink a lot of water the night before to hydrate your system.

 Go to bed early.

Read a book if you can't sleep.

 **Set your alarm!**

Give yourself plenty of time in the morning to get ready and travel to the test.

The Morning Before

Wear layers.

You never know how hot or cold the test room will be. Wear layers of clothing to be sure you can be comfortable regardless of the temperature.

Eat a NORMAL breakfast.

Your stomach needs something in it, so it won't distract you during the test.

Tip:
Eat what you usually eat. Don't surprise you stomach with a greasy eggs and sausage breakfast if you usually just have cereal.

Tip:
Even if you don't usually eat breakfast, **eat something!**
A banana, muffin, even a chocolate chip cookie will help you do your best.

Drink fluids in moderation.

Drink, but don't overdo it.

Try a little exercise.

A few push ups, jumping jacks, or sit ups will help work out some of that nervous energy and let you relax for the test.

SAT Test Day

At the Test

**Arrive at the test center
at least 15 minutes before they tell you.**

Avoid the crush. Get there early.

Stay calm.

Once you get to the test center, register, find your seat, chill out.

Tip:
While waiting for the test to start, think about essay topics to write about. *Remember, the essay always comes first on the SAT. Get your brain working by thinking up possible essay topics, so you are ready to go when the test starts.*

During the Test

Keep your own time.

Don't trust the test proctors to tell you how much time you have. Before each section, set your watch to 12:00 and start it when the section starts. This way you can easily know exactly how much time you have left.

At breaks, stand up!

Sitting cramped over a desk for almost four straight hours sends all your blood to you feet rather than your head. Get your blood moving back to you brain by standing up, stretching, and taking a few deep breaths.

Drink fluids and eat snacks during breaks.

These will give you the energy to keep going.

Start each section fresh.

If you have trouble on a section, just let it go and start fresh with the next. Don't let one supposedly bad section spoil your whole day.

Keep moving!

Remember, every question counts the same. Skip questions you are stuck on and come back to them at the end.

Power through each section.

Everybody gets tired. The ones who score the best are those who can keep concentrating through the end of each section.

Finish strong.

Too many students don't do as well as they should simply because they let themselves lose focus during the last few sections.

Tip:
Be sure to turn to the last page of the test!
There will always be two to four Writing multiple choice questions (Sentence Improvements) on the back page of Section 10.
Don't accidentally skip these because you are in a hurry to finish.

After the Test

Go celebrate! You earned it!

GOOD LUCK!!!

SAT Quick Review

SAT

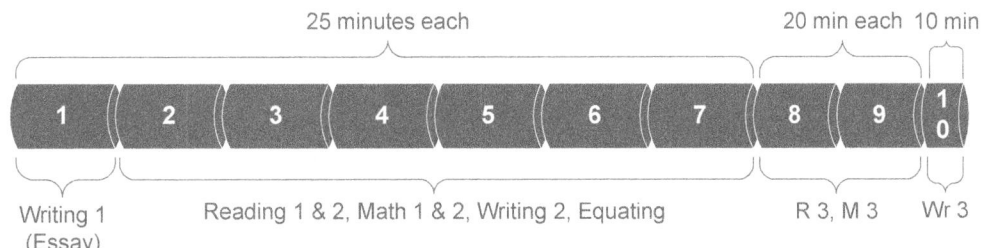

SAT Reading

SAT Math

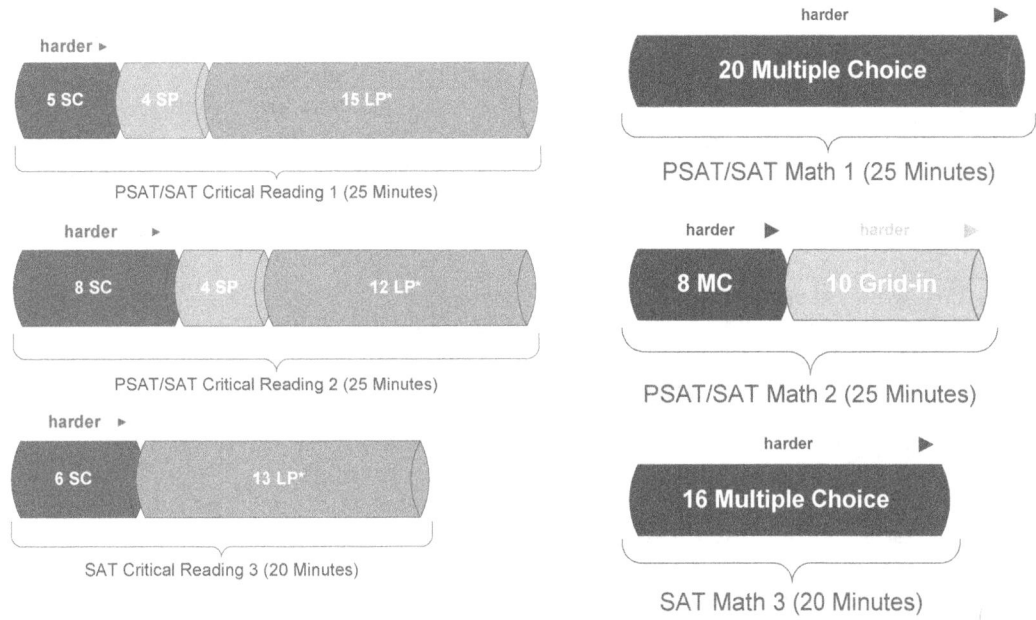

SAT Writing

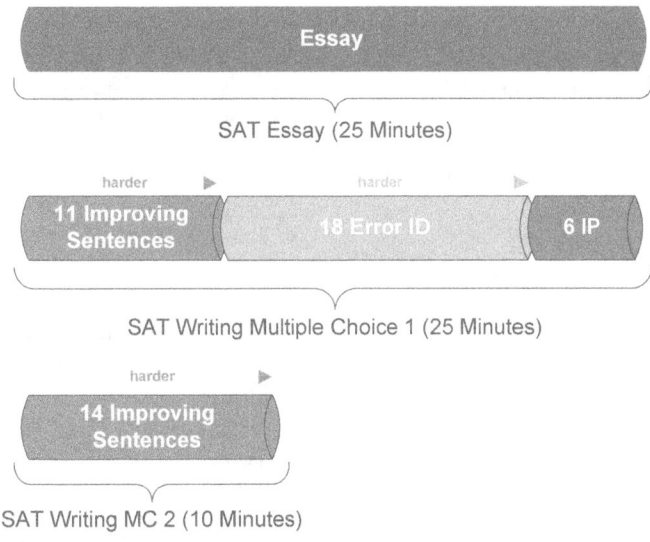

SAT Essay	SAT Critical Reading

General
• Always Section 1.
• **Read 'Assignment:' FIRST!**
• Fill up both pages (more is better!).
• Write in No. 2 pencil (no mechanical).
• Stay within margins.
• You can write about *anything*.
   ○ Write about what you know.
   ○ Don't worry about factual errors.
   ○ Fallback:
     MLK or make something up.
• Come up with examples;
  then pick ONE side.
• Use either one or two examples.
  If two examples, keep balanced.
• Relax.
 	
Organization
<u>Paragraph 1: Short Introduction</u>
  Sentence 1: Rewrite the prompt.
  Sentence 2: Throw the other side a bone
           (begin: 'while' or 'although'.).
  Sentence 3: Introduce your examples.
 	
<u>Paragraph 2: (BETTER example).</u>
  Just the facts.
  Detail. Detail. Detail.
  Conclude by referring back to the prompt.
 	
<u>Paragraph 3: (2nd example or extend first)</u>
  Start with transition sentence.
  Detail. Detail. Detail.
  Conclude by referring back to the prompt.
 	
<u>Paragraph 4: Conclusion</u>
  ALWAYS conclude your essay.
  Optional: refer to the quote in the box.
 	
Timing
<u>3-4 minutes:</u> THINK about your examples.
<u>20 minutes:</u> Write essay
           (at 5 minute warning,
           start conclusion).
<u>1 minute:</u>   Proofread.
	Sentence Completions
	• Don't waste time (30-45 seconds per q).
	• Qs appear in order of difficulty
	  (easy to hard).
	• Look carefully for clues in question.
	• Play positive/negative.
	• Right answer fits <u>well</u>.
	• On double answer Qs,
	  work one side then the other.
	• Skip hard Qs if you can't eliminate
	  any answers.
	
	Passage Reading
	<u>Reading the Passage:</u>
	1. Mark question line numbers.
	   Circle key words.
	2. *Always read the italicized introduction
	   and any asterisked (*) notes.*
	3. Read the passage, <u>underlining</u> one
	   or two things in each paragraph.
	
	<u>Answering the Questions:</u>
	4. Read the question carefully.
	5. Eliminate the three DUMB answers first.
	6. Re-read the question.
	7. Eliminate ATTRACTOR answer
	   (look for 'clunker').
	   Extreme words ('all', 'never', 'always',
	   'none', etc.) usually attractors.
	8. Whatever remains is CORRECT answer.
	   ('pragmatic' usually correct.)
	
	<u>Double Passage Sets:</u>
	1. Mark line numbers & circle Q #s
	   that ask about BOTH passages.
	2. Read Passage 1.
	3. Answer the questions for Passage 1.
	4. Read Passage 2.
	5. Answer the questions for Passage 2.
	6. Answer questions about both passages.
	
	<u>Question Tips:</u>
	• Primary Purpose: Look for 'big picture' that
	                       mentions <u>facts</u> of
	                       passage.
	• Most nearly means: Substitute answer for
	                       word in the passage.
	• Line #: Always read a few lines
	                       above and below.
	• Tone: Avoid:
	                       emotional words and
	                       words that don't take a
	                       stand ('ambivalent').

SAT Math

General
- Qs in order of difficulty (easy to hard).
- Concentrate on first 2/3 of Qs.
- If stuck, skip Q and come back.
- Grid-Ins:
  - Grid-Ins FIRST!
  - Always Answer! (no guessing penalty)
  - Start in the far left column.
  - Last resort: write in number of Q.
  - Answers never negative.
  - Can have multiple answers or range (0<x<1).
  - Improper fractions are proper (reduce!).
  - Decimals: carry repeaters to end.

Important terms
- Integer: whole number.
- Prime: div only by 1 & itself (1 NOT prime).
- Remainder: amount left over when dividing.
- Fraction 'of' a value = multiply frac by value
- Percentage 'of' a value:
  - Convert percentage to decimal.
  - Then multiply decimal by value.
- 'x in terms of y': solve for x.

Numbers & Operations
- Plug in Answers: "which of the following" or "what is the value".
- Plug in Numbers: Q or A contains variables
  - Pick easy numbers
  - Check all answers!
- Number lines: estimate values of points.
- Sequences: write out the missing values.
- Word problems: make 'x' thing to find.
- Combinations: Use factorials for specific places (4! = 4x3x2x1).
- Ratios (parts): "the ratio of x to y", add x and y to find total number of parts.
- Direct and Inverse Proportions:
  - "x is directly proportional to y" = $\frac{x}{y}$

    (di: think division)
  - "x is inversely proportional to y" = xy

Data/Stats
- Average (Arithmetic Mean) find total = avg. times # of terms.
- Median = middle number.
- Mode = number most often.
- Combinations: easy: multiply terms
  hard: factorial! (4x3x2x1)
- Probability = what you want / total.

Geometry
- Formulas on first page.
- Write down everything you know.
- Assume enough information to answer.
- Assume figure drawn to scale.
- If figure says NOT to scale, don't trust.
- Irregular figures: draw lines to create triangle and/or rectangle.
- Triangles:
  - Know formulas.
  - Isosceles: If two sides =, opp angles =.
  - Equilateral: If three sides =, angles = 60°.
  - The sum of two sides greater than third.
  - Right Triangles:
    - Pythagorean Theorem $c^2 = a^2 + b^2$.
    - Know 'special' formulas.
    - Look for 3-4-5 (6-8-10, etc.).
  - Similar Triangles: If angles =, sides proportional.
- Circles
  - 2x radius = 2x circumference but 4x area.
  - Circle Arc Length and Sector Area: divide angle by 360 to find fraction.
- Graphing
  - Slope = $\frac{rise}{run}$.
  - y = mx + b: m = slope, b = y intercept.
  - Perpendicular slope = negative reciprocal.

Algebra & Functions
- Exponents & Roots:
  - Simplify roots by squaring both sides.
  - Square roots positive or negative.
  - If both sides squares or cubes, take roots of BOTH sides.
  - Simplify negative exponents: 'flip' exponent.
  - Factor out squares from within square roots.
  - To set exp bases =, factor larger number.
- Absolute Value: |x| always positive.
- Where combination of variables = value, plug in combination.
- Always factor difference of two squares: $a^2 - b^2 = (a+b)(a-b)$
- Functions $f(x) = y$
  - Whatever inside parens, plug into equation.
  - Whatever function =, set = to equation.
  - If multiplied by function, divide out first.
- Function Graphing:
  - Value equal to function $f(x) = y$ value.
  - Value inside the parentheses = x value.
- Symbol Functions: Q will tell you what values go where.

SAT Writing Multiple Choice		
Improving Paragraphs (Answer First!) • Qs do NOT appear in order difficulty. • Scan Qs for sentence numbers and circle in passage. • Read passage quickly. • Many Qs are like Improving Sentences. • <u>Context</u> is key for others.	**Improving Sentences** • Q's appear in order of difficulty. • Trust your gut. • Try to spot issue before looking at answers. • When practicing, read the question out loud. • Start shortest answer first. • Answer choice (A) is always 'no error'. • Don't be afraid to pick (A).	**Error IDs** • Qs appear in order of difficulty. • Read the sentence completely answering. • Answer choice (E) is always 'no error'. • Expect 3 to 4 E's. • Don't skip Error IDs! <u>Just</u> answer (E). • Check E's at the end if you have time.

SAT Writing Multiple Choice Grammar Rules				
Improving Sentences Rules		**Example**		**Tips**
Wordiness	Extra pronouns and forms of 'to be' almost always INCORRECT.	Incorrect:	Payment in advance, **it is being** required by the campsite.	'to be' always incorrect
		Correct:	The campsite **requires** payment in advance.	
'Because'	Use 'because' to show cause and effect or to make a sentence less awkward.	Incorrect:	**Being that** her car was in the shop, is the reason **why** Jesse took the bus to work.	'because' often correct
		Correct:	**Because** her car was in the shop, Jesse took the bus to work.	
Sentence Fragments	Complete sentences always contain both a subject and main verb.	Incorrect:	Jesse Owens, the first man to win four gold medals in a single Olympiad, and **setting** world records in three of four events.	
		Correct:	Jesse Owens, the first man to win four gold medals in a single Olympiad, **set** world records in three of four events.	
Combining Sentences	Use comma + conjunction OR semi-colon/colon	Incorrect:	Sam studied hard**,** the test was not difficult.	'FANBOYS': For, And Nor, But, Or Yet, So
		Correct:	Sam studied hard**, so** the test was not difficult.	
			Sam studied hard**;** the test was not difficult..	
Rewriting Sentences	Rewrite so that one clause is no longer a sentence on its own.	Correct:	Sam studied hard for the test, **which** was not difficult.	
Introductory Phrases	Whatever follows the comma must be exactly who or what the phrase describes.	Incorrect:	After throwing for hours, **Jake's dog** finally learned to catch a Frisbee.	Watch out for possessives ('Jake's dog')
		Correct:	After throwing for hours, **Jake** finally taught his dog to catch a Frisbee.	
Spotting Contrasts	show the contrast between opposing things.	Incorrect:	Many are called, **and** few are chosen.	'although', 'however', etc.
		Correct:	Many are called, **yet** few are chosen.	
Error ID Rules		**Example**		**Tips**
Adverbs	Don't leave the 'ly' off the end of an adverb.	Incorrect:	Researchers examined the <u>constant changing</u> river bed.	
		Correct:	Researchers examined the <u>constantly changing</u> river bed.	
Idioms				
Dual Phrase Idioms	either … or neither … nor not only … but also between … and (me)	Incorrect:	**Neither** Chris **or** Lara arrived at the party on time.	'between' always takes 'me'
		Correct:	**Neither** Chris **nor** Lara arrived at the party on time.	
'Verby' Idioms & Prepositions	Watch for funny sounding prepositions.	Incorrect:	Josh's <u>preoccupation in</u> video games has hurt his grades.	
		Correct:	Josh's <u>preoccupation with</u> video games has hurt his grades.	

Rules for Both		Example		Tips
Parallelism				
Parallelism & Lists	Similar phrases must be written in the same (or 'parallel') grammatical form.	Incorrect:	A talented basketball player, Sarah can run quickly, pass crisply, and <u>is an accurate shooter</u>.	Prepositions must also be parallel
		Correct:	A talented basketball player, Sarah can run quickly, pass crisply, and <u>shoot accurately</u>.	
Parallelism & Dual Phrases		Incorrect:	The last few years have seen a sharp decline **not only** in crop production **but also** <u>textiles that are manufactured</u>.	
		Correct:	The last few years have seen a sharp decline **not only** in crop production **but also** <u>in textile manufacturing</u>.	
Verbs				
Verb Agreement (VA)	A verb and its subject must agree in number.	Incorrect:	'Brothers Karamazov' <u>are</u> a book by Fyodor Dostoevsky.	
		Correct:	'Brothers Karamazov' <u>is</u> a book by Fyodor Dostoevsky.	
VA & Prep Phrases	Words within prepositional phrases are NEVER the subject.	Incorrect:	The management of the apartments <u>have</u> installed air conditioning.	Draw lines through prep phrases
		Correct:	The management ~~of the apartments~~ <u>has</u> installed air conditioning.	
VA & Parenthetical	Words in parenthetical phrases, set between commas, are NEVER the subject.	Incorrect:	The artifacts, including a bronze cup, <u>was discovered</u> in an attic.	Draw lines through parentheticals
		Correct:	The artifacts, ~~including a bronze cup~~, <u>were discovered</u> in an attic.	
VA & Compound Subjects	For compound subjects, verb must be plural.	Incorrect:	The bass guitarist and the drummer <u>plays</u> the rhythm.	
		Correct:	The bass guitarist and the drummer <u>play</u> the rhythm.	
VA & Inverted Subjects	Watch out for subject placed after the verb.	Incorrect:	Along the highway across from the airport <u>is</u> a flashing light and roadside signs warning of the construction zone.	
		Correct:	Along the highway across from the airport <u>are</u> a flashing light and roadside signs warning of the construction zone.	
Verb Tense	Non-underlined verbs tell you the tense of the underlined verb.	Incorrect:	King Arthur continued his search for the Holy Grail after he <u>can find</u> knights to join him on his quest.	
		Correct:	King Arthur continued his search for the Holy Grail after he <u>found</u> knights to join him on his quest.	
Verb Tense & Dates	Use the date to figure out the tense.	Incorrect:	In 1890, the frontier <u>is</u> declared officially closed.	Dates usually sign of past tense
		Correct:	In 1890, the frontier <u>was</u> declared officially closed.	
Verb Tense & '-ing'	Verbs ending in '-ing' are often errors.	Incorrect:	Rachel knew a lot about how <u>fixing</u> old cars.	
		Correct:	Rachel knew a lot about how <u>to fix</u> old cars.	

Pronouns				
Ambiguous Pronouns	If you can't tell who or what an underlined pronoun refers to, the pronoun is INCORRECT.	Incorrect:	Harry, Chuck, and Dick met at the coffee shop, where he ordered mocha.	Watch out for random 'they'.
		Correct:	Harry, Chuck, and Dick met at the coffee shop, where Harry ordered mocha.	
		Incorrect:	The clown was so funny that they laughed out loud at his antics.	
		Correct:	The clown was so funny that the audience laughed out loud at his antics.	
Pronoun Number Agreement	A pronoun must agree with the person, place or thing in number.	Incorrect:	Although the **country** had a long history of peaceful relations, their leaders nevertheless voted to go to war.	'each of' and 'one of' are singular.
		Correct:	Although the **country** had a long history of peaceful relations, its leaders nevertheless voted to go to war.	
Pronoun Consistency	Do not mix 'you' and 'one' in the same sentence.	Incorrect:	One can never be a great musician unless you practice daily.	
		Correct:	You can never be a great musician unless you practice daily.	
Who vs. Which	'Who' refers to people. 'Which' refers to animals and things.	Incorrect:	The best **baseball players** are those which can hit, catch, and throw.	
		Correct:	The best **baseball players** are those who can hit, catch, and throw.	
Pronoun Case	Subjective: subject of a verb. Objective: everything else.	Incorrect:	Alice drove to the store with Sandra and I.	Cross out other people. (usually obj.)
		Correct:	Alice drove to the store with ~~Sandra and~~ me.	
Other Rules				
Noun Agreement	Nouns referring to other nouns must agree in number.	Incorrect:	Alma and Christie both found jobs as a lifeguard for the summer.	Q's about jobs test this rule.
		Correct:	Alma and Christie both found jobs as lifeguards for the summer.	
Faulty Comparisons	Watch out for comparisons of things that are not the same type.	Incorrect:	The novels of Patrick O'Brian are more detailed than CS Forester.	
		Correct:	The novels of Patrick O'Brian are more detailed than the novels of CS Forester.	
		Correct:	The novels of Patrick O'Brian are more detailed than those of CS Forester.	
Two vs. Three or More	Two things: - er Three or more things: - est	Incorrect:	Of the **two** instruments, the bass is largest, but the trumpet is loudest.	
		Correct:	Of the **two** instruments, the bass is larger, but the trumpet is louder.	
Redundancies	Watch out for extra words where they are not needed.	Incorrect:	The windows are more cleaner than they were before.	
		Correct:	The windows are cleaner than they were before.	

Preparing for Test Day

What to Bring

- ☐ SAT Admission Ticket
- ☐ Photo ID
- ☐ No.2 Pencils (no mechanical pencils)
- ☐ Calculator (check your batteries)
- ☐ Snacks
- ☐ Drinks
- ☐ Watch: Turn off the alarm!
- ☐ Backpack (to put everything in)

Do NOT bring:

- ☒ scratch paper
- ☒ notes, books, dictionary
- ☒ compass, protractor, ruler, or any other aid
- ☒ highlighter or colored pencils
- ☒ portable listening or recording devices
- ☒ camera or other photographic equipment
- ☒ timer or watch *with audible alarm*
- ☒ Cell phone, pager, personal digital assistant, or other digital/electronic equipment. **Turn OFF cell phone!**

The Night Before
- **Do NOT practice questions**! (reviewing these notes is OK)
- Gather together everything you will need for test day.
- Relax...
- Eat a big dinner.
- Drink a lot of fluids.
- Go to bed early.
- Set your alarm!

The Morning Before
- Get up early.
- Wear layers of clothing.
- Eat a normal breakfast.
- Eat what you usually eat, but eat something!
- Drink fluids in moderation.
- A little exercise helps with nerves.

At the Test
- Arrive at the test center 10-15 minutes *before they tell you*.
- Stay cool.
- Think about essay topics you might want to write about.

During the Test
- Keep your own time.
- At breaks, stand up!
- Drink fluids and snacks during breaks.
- Start each section fresh. (Don't worry about previous sections).
- Power through each section. (Keep moving!)
- Finish strongly.

After the Test
- *Go celebrate! You earned it!*

GOOD LUCK!!!

SAT Vocabulary

Definitions

Word	Part	Definition
abate	v	reduce
aberration	n	not usual
abnormal	a	not conforming to a standard type
abrupt	a	sudden or unexpected
absolutist	n	believer in unrestricted government power
abstract	a | n	theoretical | summary of a text
abstruse	a	hard to understand, baffling
absurd	a	senseless; illogical
accentuate	v	emphasize
accessible	a	obtainable; easy to approach
accumulate	v	gather; collect
acknowledge	v	recognize
acumen	n	keen insight; shrewdness
adept	a	skilled; expert
administer	v	manage
admonish	v	warn, caution; advise against
adroit	a	cleverly, resourceful, or ingenious
advantageous	a	furnishing convenience or opportunity
advocate	v	speak or write in favor of
aesthete	n	someone who appreciates beauties of art
aesthetic	a	sense of the beauties of art or nature
affable	a	friendly
afflict, affliction	v, n	cause mental or bodily pain
affluence	n	wealth
aggregation	n	group of distinct or varied things
agitate	v	disturbed, troubled
agnostic	a	undecided - often about the existence of God
agreeable	a	enjoyable; pleasant
alacrity	n	quickness; promptness
allege	v	assert without proof
alleviate	v	make easier to endure; lessen
allusion	n	passing reference
aloof	a	disinterested; reserved
altruism	n	unselfish concern for others
amalgam, amalgamation	n	mixture or combination
amass	v	collect, gather
amateurish	a	inexperienced or unskilled
ambiguous	a	having different possible meanings
ambition	n	desire for achievement
ambivalent	a	undecided
ameliorate	v	improve; make more bearable

amiable	a	pleasant, good-natured
amused	a	pleasurably entertained or occupied
anachronistic	a	not in the correct historical time
analogy	n	comparison
analytical	a	breaking into parts to study
anatomy	n	the structure of an animal or plant
anecdote	n	short story
animate, animated	v | a	make lively | give life to
animosity	n	strong dislike
anomaly	n	deviation from normal
antagonize, antagonistic	v, a	make hostile or unfriendly
anthropology	n	science of human civilization
anticipate	v	realize beforehand, foresee
antipode	n	direct or exact opposite
antiquated	a	old-fashioned
apathy, apathetic	n, a	lack of interest, passion or emotion
apolitical	a	not interested in politics or government
apologetic	a	sorry
appalling	a	causing dismay or horror
apparition	n	supernatural appearance
appreciation	n	gratitude, thankful recognition
apprehend	v	arrest by legal authority
apprehension, apprehensive	n	fear, fearful
aptitude	n	capability; ability; talent
arbitration	n	settlement of a dispute by a third person
arboreal	a	living in or among trees
arcane	a	understood by very few; obscure, esoteric; secret
archaic	a	marked by the characteristics of an earlier period
argumentative	a	fond of disagreeing
aroma	n	scent, smell
arrogance	n	offensive display of superiority or self-importance
articulate	a | v	speaking easily and fluently | say clearly
artistry	n	skillfulness in the arts
ascertain	v	find out definitely
aspersion	n	damaging remark, smear, slander
assess	v	judge the value
associate	v | n	connect; relate | ally
assuage	v	make less severe; relieve
astute	a	clever
attain	v	reach, achieve, or accomplish
audible	a	loud enough to hear
augment	v	make larger
aural	a	relating to the ear or sound
auspicious	a	promising success; favorable
authenticate	v	establish as genuine
autobiography	n	person's life history written by that person

autonomy	n	independence; freedom
avuncular	a	friendly, helpful
awakened	a	aroused or activated
backfire	v	opposite result to what is planned
baffled, baffle, bafflement	a, n, v	confused, bewildered, perplexed
banal	a	lack of freshness or originality, trite
bankrupt	a	unable to pay bills, insolvent
barrage	n	overwhelming quantity
barter	v	trade with goods rather than money
beautiful	a	intensely pleasing to the mind
beautify	v	make pleasing to look at
begrudge	v	envy, resent; be reluctant to give
belabor	v	worry about or work more than necessary
belie	v	show to be false; contradict
belittle	v	regard or portray as less important
bellicose	a	eager to fight; aggressively hostile
belligerent	a	warlike, aggressively hostile; pugnacious
beneficial	a	helpful, advantageous
benevolent	a	with goodwill or kindly feelings
benign	a	showing kindness; favorable; not malignant
bereft	a	deprived; lacking
bewilder	v	confuse or puzzle completely
bifurcation	n	division into two branches
bolster	v, n	support; reinforce; strengthen
bombastic	a	pretentious
boomerang	n | v	bent throwing club that returns | backfire
boorish	a	crude, insensitive
breakthrough	n	significant advance, development, or achievement
brevity	n	shortness of time; briefness
bucolic	a	rural, pastoral
bureaucracy	n	administrative structure of a large organization
bypass	v	avoid
byzantine	a	complex, intricate
cacophony	n	harsh sound
callous	a	insensitive, indifferent; hardened
candid	a	honest; impartial
cantankerous	a	grumpy; disagreeable; contentious
capricious	a	erratic; random; whimsical
catalogue	n | v	list | enter into a list
catalyst	n	something that brings about an event or change
catastrophic	a	disastrous
celebrated	a	renowned, well-known, famous
censure	v	criticize in a harsh manner
chaotic	a	completely confused or disordered
charity, charitable	n, a	generosity toward the poor, ill, or helpless
chicanery	n	trickery, deception

Word	Part	Definition
chide	v	express disapproval of
churlish	a	rude or surly
circulate	v	distribute
circumscribe	v	limit; enclose within bounds; confine
circumvent	v	bypass; avoid
clairvoyant	n, a	able to tell the future
clarify	v	make clear
cleanse	v	make unsoiled
coalition	n	temporary alliance
coddle	v	treat tenderly or indulgently; pamper
coerce	v	compel by force or intimidation
cognition	n	something known or perceived
collaborative	a	accomplished by two or more people
comely	a	pleasing in appearance, attractive
commendable	a	worthy of praise
compassionate	a	feeling sympathy and a desire to help
compensate	v	counterbalance, offset
complacent	a	contented, satisfied
complimentary	a	expressing praise or admiration; given free
compound	n, v	combination; mixture
comprehensive	a	of large scope, covering all
compress	v	press together; force into less space
compromise	v | n	agree; expose to danger | trade-off, concession
compulsive	a	compelling; irresistibly impulsive
conception	n	notion, idea; origination, beginning
concession	n	something given by an authority
conciliate, conciliatory	v, a	reconcile; create agreement
concise	a	expressing much in few words
conclusive	a	final; ending
concord, concordance	n	agreement
concur	v	agree
condemn, condemnation	v, n	pronounce guilty; punish; publicly criticize
condensed	a	reduced
condescending	a	snooty; snobbish; disdainful; supercilious
conditional	a	made or allowed on certain terms
condone	v	excuse (an offense); give approval to
conducive	a	helpful, favorable
confess	v	admit or own up to
confine	v	enclose within bounds; limit or restrict
confirm	v	establish the validity of, verify
conflagration	n	fire
conformity, conformist	n	following the group
confound	v	perplex, confuse, baffle
confrontational	a	eager for conflict
congenial	a	pleasant
conjecture	n	statement or conclusion based on guesswork

conscientious	a	meticulous, careful, painstaking, particular
consecrate, consecration	v, n	make or declare sacred
conservatism	n	preserving what is established and traditional
considerate	a	showing kindly awareness for others' feelings
console	v	alleviate the grief of
consolidate	v	concentrate; combine
conspicuous	a	attracting attention
constructive	a	promoting further development or advancement
consume	v	destroy or expend by use; eat
consummate	v | a	complete | perfect
contagious	a	spread from person to person
contaminate	v	make impure or unclean
contempt, contemptible, contemptuous	n, a	hatred, anger
contend	v	compete; assert earnestly
contradict	v	assert the opposite of
contrast	v	show differences
convene	v	meet formally as a group
conventional	a	ordinary
converge	v	meet at the same point
conversational	a	informal language
conviction	n	a fixed or firm belief; the act of proving guilty
convince	v	persuade
convivial	a	friendly; agreeable
convoluted	a	complicated; confusing
cooperation	n	working together (agreeably)
copious	a	plentiful
corollary	n	easily drawn conclusion; immediate consequence
corrective	n	a fix
correlation	n	similarity; link
correspond	v	in agreement; conformity; analogous; similar
corroborate	v	make more certain, confirm
corrosive	a	eroding or eating away; harmful, destructive
cosmopolitan	a	mixing many cultures or ethnicities; cultured
counsel	n	advice
counterfeit	a	fake
courteous	a	having good manners, polite
cowardice	n	fear, lack of courage
credence	n	belief as to the truth of something
credulity	n	willingness to believe or trust too readily
criticize, critic	v, n	judge or evaluate, usually negatively
critique	n	critical review or commentary
cryptic	a	mysterious in meaning; ambiguous
culminate	v	reach the highest point or degree; climax; finish
cultivate	v	farm; promote growth by labor and attention
cumulative	a	sum total
curative	a	restores health

curious	a	eager to learn or know, inquisitive
cursory	a	hasty; superficial
curtail	v	cut short
customary	a	typical; usual
cynical, cynicism	a, n	negative; pessimistic; skeptical; jaded; distrustful
dalliance	n	flirtation
deafening	a	stunningly or overwhelmingly loud
dearth	n	inadequate supply, scarcity, lack
debacle	n	complete collapse or failure
debilitate	v	make weak or feeble
debunk	v	expose as false
deceit, deceive	n, v	lie; falsehood; trick; chicanery
decimate	v	destroy a great number or proportion
decipher	v	discover the meaning; decode
decisive	a	confident
decorous	a	dignified
defer, deferment	v, n	put off an action to a future time
deference, deferential	n, a	respectful submission or courteous regard
defiance	n	resistance; strong opposition
deficient	a	lacking
deficit	n	lack; shortage
definitive	a	most reliable or complete
deflate, deflation	v, n	release air from; reduce in size; fall in prices
deft	a	skillful
degrade	v	reduce in value
dehydration	n	extreme loss of water from the body
deleterious	a	harmful, injurious
deliberate	a	carefully weighed or considered; studied
deliberation	n	careful consideration before decision
delineate	v	trace the outline of; describe with precision
delusion	n	a false belief or opinion
demolish	v	destroy or ruin
demonstrative	a	open expression of emotions; explanatory
denial	n	disbelief in the reality of a thing
denounce	v	condemn or censure openly or publicly
denude	v	make naked or bare, strip
denunciation	n	public condemnation (see denounce)
dependent	a	relying on others; weak
depersonalize	v	make impersonal; deprive of personality
derail	v	cause to fail or go off track
derelict	a	deserted, abandoned
derision	n	ridicule
derivative	a	changed from the original
derive	v	receive or obtain from a source or origin
descend	v	go downwards
desolate	a	barren; uninhabited; lonely

despair	n	hopelessness
despoil	v	strip of possessions, plunder, pillage
detach	v	unfasten and separate; disengage
determined	a	resolute; decided
deterrent	n	discourages or restrains from acting
devious	a	shifty or crooked; tricky
devoid	a	completely without; not possessing
devotion	n	profound dedication or earnest attachment
diaphanous	a	sheer, nearly see-through
dichotomy	n	division into two contradictory parts
dictum	n	an authoritative pronouncement; a saying
didactic	a	instructive
diffidence	n	lack of self-confidence; shyness
digression	n	moving away from the main topic or purpose
dilatory	a	delaying; procrastinating
dilettante	n	amateur
diminish	v	cause to seem smaller or less important
diplomatic	a	skilled in dealing with people; tactful
disarming	a	using charm to remove hostility or suspicion
discard	v	cast aside or dispose of
discern	v	distinguish or discriminate; perceive
disclaimer	n	statement that denies responsibility
disclose, disclosure	v	make known, reveal
discrepancy	n	inconsistency
discriminating	a	recognizing differences
disdain	n	contempt; scorn; hatred
disguise	v	change appearance
disillusion	v	deprive of belief or idealism
disinclined	a	lacking desire or willingness
disingenuous	a	lacking in candor, insincere
disintegration	n	deterioration, decay, falling apart
dismantle	v	disassemble, take apart
dismay	v	upset; sadden
dismiss	v	discharge, remove; send away
disparage	v	speak of negatively; belittle
dispassionate	a	lack of emotion or bias
dispatch	n	promptness or speed
dispel	v	cause to vanish; alleviate; debunk
dispense	v	distribute
disperse, dispersive, dispersion	v, a, n	spread in various directions
disposal	n	getting rid of
disposition	n	attitude; feeling about
dispute	n	argument, debate
disregard	v	ignore; leave out of consideration
disrepute	n	low regard, disfavor
disrupt	v	interrupt; cause disorder in

disseminate	v	spread widely
distention	n	expansion; swelling
distill	v	extract the essential elements; refine
distinctive	a	having a special quality, notable
distort	v	twist ; deform
diverse	a	of various kinds or forms
divert	v	turn aside from a path or course; deflect
divisive	a	separating into parts, groups, sections
docile	a	easily managed or handled
dominate	v	control; rule over
dowager	n	wealthy widow
drab	a	dull or faded
dramatize	v	express vividly, emotionally, or strikingly
drenched	a	thoroughly wet, soaked
dubious	a	doubtful
duplicate	n	exact copy
durable	a	able to resist wear and decay; enduring
duration	n	length of time
dwindle	v	become smaller and smaller; waste away
ebullient	a	bubbly
eccentric	a	peculiar or odd
eclectic	a	selecting from various sources
edible	a	fit to be eaten
edify	v	Instruct, benefit
efface	v	erase
effusive	a	gushing, overflowing
egalitarian	a	belief in the equality of all people
egotist, egotistical	n, a	conceited, self-centered
elaborate	a | v	intricate or excessive detail | explain more fully
elevate	v	raise
elitist	a	snobbish, supercilious
elliptical	a	ambiguous, cryptic, obscure
elusive	a	hard to express or define; cleverly evasive
emancipator	n	liberator; rescuer
embellish	v	add to; ornament; adorn
embitter	v	make angry or hostile
embody	v	express, personify, or exemplify in concrete form
embrace	v	to hug; to receive eagerly
empathy or empathetic	n	understanding the feelings of another
emphatic	a	strongly expressive
empiric	a	derived from experience or experiment
enact	v	make law
encompass	v	include everything
encounter	v	come upon or meet with, especially unexpectedly
encroach	v	advance beyond established limits
endanger	v	place in peril

endorse; endorsement	v	approve, support
engage	v	occupy the attention or efforts of another
enhance	v	raise a higher degree, intensify
enigma	n	mystery; puzzle
enlighten	v	impart knowledge; explain
enormous	a	huge
ensure	v	make certain
entangle	v	involve in difficulties; complicate; confuse
enthusiasm	n	lively interest
entourage	n	group of attendants or associates
entreat	v	ask or plead
envelop	v	surround entirely; wrap in a covering
envious	a	jealous
envision	v	picture mentally
ephemeral	a	short lived; fleeting
epitome	n	perfect example; embodiment; template
equanimity	n	emotional stability or composure
equitable	a	just and right; fair; reasonable
equivocal, equivocate	a | v	unclear; uncertain | avoid an issue, evade
eradicate	v	remove or destroy utterly
erratic	a	unpredictable; inconsistent
erroneous	a	incorrect, mistaken
erudition	n	knowledge through study; learning; scholarship
esoteric	a	obscure detail; special knowledge or interest
estrange	v	alienate affections; make unfriendly or hostile
ethical	a	right or moral
eulogy	n	praise of a person or thing (often of the dead)
evaluate	v	judge or determine the quality of, assess
evolve	v	develop gradually
exacerbate	v	increase the severity of; make worse
exasperation	n	extreme annoyance
excessive	a	beyond the usual, necessary, or proper
excise	a	internal tax on goods
exclude	v	shut or keep out
execute	v	carry out, accomplish; murder
exemplar	n	an example to be imitated
exhilarating	a	invigorating, stimulating
exonerate	v	clear of wrongdoing
exorbitant	a	highly excessive
exotic	a	strikingly unusual; of foreign origin or character
expeditious	a	prompt, quick
expendable	a	not worth keeping; disposable
experiment	n, v	try or test to discover or prove
exploit	v	use selfishly, especially for profit
expose	v	make known, disclose, or reveal; present view
exposé	n	public exposure or revelation

express	v	show, reveal
extant	a	in existence
extirpate	v	destroy totally
extol	v	praise highly
extract	v	take out
extrapolate	v	infer an unknown from something that is known
extravagant	a	excessive; overly elaborate
extremist	n	fanatic, radical
fabrication	n	untruthful statement; lie
facetious	a	sarcastic
faction	n	group within a larger group
famished	a	extremely hungry; starving
fastidious	a	very careful; fussy; meticulous
fathom	v	comprehend, understand
feign	v	fake
fertilize	v	enrich (as soil); make pregnant
fervent	a	having intensity of spirit; enthusiastic
fickle	a	likely to change; not constant in affections
fidelity	n	loyalty; strict observance of promises
filial	a	pertaining to a son or daughter
finagle	v	achieve by trickery or manipulation
finesse	n	skill in handling a difficult or sensitive situation
fitful	a	recurring irregularly
flabbergasted	a	overcome with surprise; bewildered; astounded
flashback	n	vivid memory or vision of a past event
flotsam	n	floating material, trash
flourish	v	thrive, prosper
foil	n	person or thing that makes another seem better
folly	n	senseless action
foreboding	n	feeling that something bad will happen
foresee	v	know in advance
foreshadow	v	show or hint beforehand
foresight	n	act of looking forward
formidable	a	forceful, powerful
forthright	a	truthful; direct, frank; outspoken
fortify	v	strengthen; protect against attack
foster	v	promote development; further; encourage
founder	v	fail utterly, become wrecked; sink
fraud, fraudulent	n, a	deceit for profit or for unfair advantage
frisky	a	lively, frolicsome, playful
frugal	a	prudently saving or sparing; economical
funerary	a	pertaining to a funeral or burial
furious	a	extremely angry; irate
further	v	help forward (as a cause or undertaking)
furtive	a	sly, shifty, secret
futile	a	ineffective; useless; impossible

gaiety	n	merriment, liveliness
garish	a	gaudy; tacky; flashy
gaudy	a	excessively showy; garish
generalization	n	broad conclusion
generate	v	bring into existence, produce
gesture	n	expression by movement of the body or face
glacial	a	cold; stony; frozen
gloomy	a	dark; dismal or depressing
glorify	v	honor
gluttonous	a	eating & drinking excessively; greedy, insatiable
graceless	a	lacking elegance or charm
grating	a	irritating or unpleasant; harsh
gratuitous	a	done without charge or payment
grimy	a	dirty
groundbreaking	a	pioneering a new endeavor
guarantee	v	secure; ensure
guarded	a	careful
gullible	a	easily deceived or tricked
hackneyed	a	commonplace, trite, banal
harmonic	a	agreement, congruity; combination of tones
harvest	v	gather, reap
hasten	v	hurry
haughty	a	overly proud; snobbish
hilarity	n	extreme humor, cheerfulness, merriment
hinder	v	cause delay, hamper, impede
holistic	a	complete, whole
hospitality	n	friendly reception or welcoming of guests
hubris	n	excessive pride; arrogance
humane	a	tender; compassionate; sympathetic
humiliate	v	publicly embarrass
humility	n	a modest opinion of one's own importance
humorous	a	funny
husbandry	n	careful or thrifty management; conservation
hybrid	n	combination of different sources
hypothesis, hypothetical	n, a	unproven theory
hysterical	a	uncontrollably emotional
iconoclast	n	critic; unbeliever; heretic; non-conformist
idealize	v	praise as perfect
idiosyncratic	a	peculiar characteristic or habit
ignominy	n	disgrace, dishonor, public contempt
illegible	a	unable to read or decipher
imaginative	a	creative
immersion	n	being deeply engaged or involved
immune	a	protected; exempt
impenetrable	a	incapable of being understood
imperative	a | n	absolutely necessary or required | command

imperial	a	of an empire; kingly; commanding; domineering
impermanent	a	temporary
impersonal	a	emotionless; unfriendly
impetuous	a	impulsive, rash
implacable	a	unable to be appeased, unbending
implement	v	perform, carry out, put into effect
imply	v	indicate or suggest without explicitly stating
imprecise	a	not defined or exact
impression	n	effect, feeling or image received from experience
impressionable	a	easily influenced
improbable	a	unlikely to happen
imprudent	a	not careful in providing for the future
impudent	a	rude; offensively bold
impugn	v	challenge as false; cast doubt upon
impulsive	a	swayed by sudden emotions
inaccessible	a	not able to be used or entered; not attainable
inadequate	a	not sufficient; inept or unsuitable
inane	a	lacking sense or significance
inattention	n	negligence; lack of care or consideration
inaudible	a	incapable of being heard
incarnate	a	personified or typified; in the flesh
inclination	n	liking or preference toward something
inclusive	a	including a great deal or everything
incoherent	a	baffling, without logical connection, disjointed
incompetent	a	lacking ability or qualification
inconclusive	a	not resolving fully all doubts or questions
inconsequential	a	of little or no importance
inconspicuous	a	hidden, unnoticeable
incorrigible	a	bad beyond correction or reform
indecent	a	offensive; not in good taste
indecipherable	a	unable to be read or understood
indecisive	a	uncertain; unable to decide
indict	v	charge with an offense or crime
indigence	n	poverty
indigenous	a	native
indignant	a	offended
indiscernible	a	unable to be understood
indiscriminate	a	random; lacking in selectivity, judgment, or care
indistinguishable	a	imperceptible
indomitable	a	cannot be subdued or overcome
induce	v	persuade; bring about
induction	n	placing in office, position; initiation
ineffable	a	indescribable
inept	a	without skill or aptitude
inevitable	a	certain; unable to be avoided
infatuated	a	foolishly in love; obsessed

infelicity	n	unhappiness; bad luck
inferior	a	lesser grade or level
infighting	n	fighting within a group; fighting at close range
inflexible	a	rigid, unyielding
informal	a	casual; familiar; without ceremony
informative	a	instructive
infusion	n	injection; pouring into
ingenious	a	cleverly inventive or resourceful
inhibit	v	hinder or restrain
innate	a	native to; born with; existing in
innocuous	a	harmless; inoffensive
innovation	n	new ideas or methods
inquiry	n	questioning, investigation, request for information
insecurity	n	lack of confidence or assurance, self-doubt
insensitive	a	lack of feeling or consideration; callous
inseparable	a	incapable of being parted or disjoined
insightful	a	perceptive
insipid	a	boring; without interesting or distinctive qualities
insolent	a	rude
insolvent	a	unable to pay debts; bankrupt
inspire, inspiration	v, n	arouse; encourage; stimulate
instantaneous	a	occurring at the same time
instinct	n	natural impulse or tendency
instrumental	a	necessary, important; useful, helpful
insubstantial	a	not solid or real; imaginary; weak
insure	v	guarantee against loss or harm
insurrectionist	n	one who rises against civil authority
integrate	v	bring together or incorporate parts into a whole
integrity	n	having moral and ethical principles
intellectual	a	smart; intelligent; brainy
intemperance	n	excessive appetite or passion; lack of restraint
intensify	a, v	make stronger
intercept	v	interrupt or halt the passage of something
interfere	v	oppose; get in the way; meddle
intermittent	a	alternately stopping and starting again
interrogation	n	questioning
intricate	a	complicated; detailed
intrigued	a	interested, curious
intrude	v	barge in; interrupt rudely
intuition, intuitive	n, a	perceive truth without reasoning; hunch
invaluable	a	priceless; infinitely valuable
invariable	a	not capable of change; static, constant
invocation	n	earnest call for help or aid
irate	a	very angry
irony	n	intending the opposite of what is stated
irrefutable	a	cannot be disproved

irrelevant	a	not applicable, insignificant, unimportant
irreproachable	a	free from blame
irresolute	a	not determined, doubtful, weak willed
irreverence	n	lack of respect
irritable	a	easily annoyed
jaded	a	dulled by overindulgence; cynical
jeopardize	v	risk, imperil
jingoism	n	loud and excessive patriotism
jocular	a	funny, humorous
jubilant	a	very happy
judgmental	a	overly critical
judicious	a	wise, sensible
juxtaposition	n	placed side by side
knack	n	special skill, talent, penchant
lackadaisical	a	lazy; without interest or determination
laconic	a	using few words, terse, concise, succinct, brief
languid	a	slow; lacking in vigor; lacking in spirit or interest
lassitude	n	weariness, lack of energy
lax	a	slack; lenient
legislation	n	laws; statutes
legitimate	a	accepted; authorized; official
levity	n	humor; silliness
liable	a	legally responsible; susceptible; likely or apt
libel	a	false writing that damages a person's reputation
liberate	v	set free
liquefy	v	make liquid
lithe	a	flexible, supple
lobby (for)	v	campaign for; argue for
loquacious	a	talkative
loyalist	n	a supporter of the existing government
lucid	a	clear, easily understood
lucrative	a	profitable
lugubrious	a	mournful, dismal, gloomy
lush	a	luxurious, rich, opulent; abundant
magnanimous	a	high-minded; generous
mandate	n	authoritative order, command
manifesto	n	public declaration of objectives or motives
manipulative	a	influencing others for one's own benefit
mar	v	damage; harm; scar
maternal	a	motherly
mawkish	v	extremely sentimental; sappy
meager	a	scanty; inadequate; very small
meddle	v	interfere; intrude
mediocre	a	average
mellifluous	a	sweetly or smoothly flowing; sweet-sounding

melodramatic	a	exaggerated emotion; histrionic
mentor	n	wise or trusted counselor or teacher
mercenary	a	acting merely for money
mercurial	a	volatile; fickle; erratic
metaphor	n	comparison
meticulous	a	precise, detailed, very careful, fastidious
miffed	a	irritated; angered
militant	a	aggressive, combative; belligerent; pugnacious
mischievous	a	sneaky; devilish, wicked
misconception	n	mistaken idea
miscreant	n	villain, evil-doer
misfortune	n	adverse circumstances, bad luck
misguided	a	misled, mistaken
misinterpret	v	understand incorrectly
misnomer	n	misapplied or inappropriate name
mitigate, mitigator	v, n	lessen in force or intensity, moderate
mock, mockery	v, n	make fun of; scoff
moderate	a	reasonable; calm; mild
modicum	n	small amount
mollify	v	pacify, soothe, calm
momentous	a	very important
momentum	n	force or speed of movement
monarchical	a	kingly; regal
monotonous	a	boring; repetitious
monumental	a	exceptionally great; of enduring significance
morbid	a	gloomy; diseased
motley	a	mixed; varied
multifaceted	a	many sides or abilities
multifarious	a	numerous; varied; diverse
mundane	a	common, ordinary, banal, unimaginative
mute	v	muffle, tone down; silence
myopic	a	shortsighted, tunnel vision; narrow minded
naïve, naïveté	a, n	lack of experience; gullible
nefarious	a	extremely wicked or villainous
negate	v	to deny; to cause to be ineffective
negligent	a	careless, indifferent
negligible	a	insignificant; almost nothing
negotiate	v	deal, bargain
nonchalant	a	casual
nondescript	a	undistinguished, commonplace
nonpartisan	a	neutral; impartial; not political
nostalgia	n	fond memories
noteworthy	a	worthy of attention; remarkable
notorious	a	dishonorable, lowly
obligated	a	morally or legally bound
obliterate	v	destroy completely

obscure	a	unclear, ambiguous, vague
obsequious	a	submissive; fawning
obstinate	a	stubborn
obtrusive	a	pushy, obvious
occlude	v	close or cut off
odoriferous	a	smelly
officious	a	self-important, dictatorial
offset	v	counterbalance, compensate for
omnipotent	a	all-powerful
onerous	a	burdensome, oppressive, troublesome
onset	n	beginning, start
opportune	a	lucky; favorable; appropriate
opportunism	n	taking advantage of a situation
opt	v	choose
opulent	a	wealthy; abundant; rich; lush
orderly	a	methodical, organized
ornate	a	elaborately and often excessively decorated
ossified	a	rigid, inflexible
ostentatious	a	showy, gaudy
oust	v	expel, remove, kick out
outlook	n	point of view
outspoken	a	forthright; unreserved
overhaul	v	restore; fix
overjoyed	a	feeling great delight, elated
overt	a	in plain sight; clear
pacifist	n	peace-lover; opposed to war or violence
painstaking	a	meticulous, thorough; diligent
palpable	a	plainly seen, heard, or felt
panacea	n	remedy for everything, cure-all
partisan	a	partial; biased
passion	n	love; enthusiasm
pathos	n	deep sadness; pity
patronage	n	support; condescension
paucity	n	small amount
pedagogical	a	related to teaching methods
pedestrian	a	lacking imagination; commonplace; dull
peevish	a	annoyed, irritated
penchant	n	knack; fondness, inclination
penurious	a	extremely stingy; extremely poor
perceive	v	become aware of
perfidy	n	disloyalty
perquisite	n	benefit over and above regular income; perk
persistent	a	determined; continuous; enduring
personification	n	giving human qualities to non-human things
pertain	v	refer or relate (to)
peruse	v	examine; scan; look over

petty	a	trivial, insignificant, trifling; picayune
petulant	a	irritable over petty things
phenomenon	n	unusual occurrence
philanthropist	n	charitable donor; humanitarian
philosophical	a	thinking deeply; reflective; conceptual, theoretical
phlegmatic	a	easy going; not easily excited
phobia	n	persistent, irrational fear
picayune	a	trivial, insignificant, trifling; petty
pilfer	v	steal
placid	a	calm; peaceful
plaudit	n	enthusiastic approval, applause, acclaim
plausible	a	possible; believable
pliable	a	bendable
pliant	a	easily influenced; obedient
polarized	a	divided into sharply opposing factions
politicize	v	apply a political meaning
postpone	v	delay; put off to a later time
pragmatic, pragmatism	a, n	practical
praiseworthy	a	deserving congratulations; commendable
precision	n	accuracy, exactness
preclude	v	make impossible
precursor	n	something that comes before something else
predilection	n	favorable tendency; preference; knack
preeminent	a	above or before others, superior
premature	a	done too soon; before the proper time
prestige	n	fame, influence
presumption, presumptive	n, a	taken for granted, assumed, or supposed
presumptuous	a	unwarrantedly bold; arrogant
pretentious	a	conceited; self-important; haughty
prevail	v	succeed, win out
privilege	n	a special right, immunity, or benefit
procure	v	obtain; get
prod	v	poke; rouse, incite
profiteer	n	greedy person
profound	a	intellectual, thoughtful, deep
prognosis	n	forecast, especially regarding a disease
prohibit, prohibitive	v | a	forbid; prevent | impossible
prolific	a	highly productive
prolong	v	extend, draw out; delay
prominent	a	leading, important, or well-known; conspicuous
propaganda	n	political messages
propensity	n	a natural inclination or tendency
prophecy, prophetic	n, a	prediction, foretelling
proponent	n	supporter, advocate
prosaic	a	common; dull, unimaginative
prospectus	n	brochure or other describing document

proverb	n	short saying; catch phrase; axiom
provoke, provocative, provocation	v, a, n	incite; anger; arouse
proximity	a	nearness
prudent	a	careful
psychiatry	n	study of mental and emotional disorders
publicize	v	make widely known; promote
pugnacious	a	aggressive, combative; belligerent; militant
punctilious	a	careful, exacting; formal
purvey	v	provide, supply
puzzlement	n	mystery; confusion
quell	v	suppress, subdue
quixotic	a	romantic, idealistic, visionary; unrealistic
quizzical	a	questioning
raiment	n	clothing
rambunctious	a	loud, energetic, boisterous
rancorous	a	full of hatred, malice, resentment
ratify	v	confirm, authorize
rational	a	reasonable
rationalism	n	accepting reason as the supreme authority
raze	v	demolish
rebate	n	refund
rebuttal	n	argument against
receptive	a	openness
recessive	a	passive, inactive
reciprocate	v	give or feel in return
reclusive	a	unsociable; secluded; shy
recollect	v	remember
reconcile	v	settle a quarrel; make compatible or consistent
reconnaissance	n	exploration, inspection, observation, survey
recriminate	v	blame, accuse
rectitude	n	rightness, decency, virtue
recurring	a	happening again and again
rediscover	v	find or gain knowledge of again
refute	v	prove false; argue against
regal	a	royal, stately, splendid
regenerate	v	renew; revive
regressive	a	backward; less advanced
regret	v	feel sorry or upset about
rehash	v	work up (old material) in a new form
reinforce	v	make stronger
relevant	a	applicable; appropriate; connected to
remiss	a	negligent, careless, slow
remonstrate	v	urgently argue against
renovate	v	restore, redo
renown	n	fame
repeal	v	revoke, withdraw, annul

repertory	n	collection (usually of songs)
repetitive	a	continuous; boring; repeats over and over
replicate	v	duplicate
reprehensible	a	very bad; shameful; blameworthy
repressive	a	keeping down; suppressing
reprieve	n	temporary relief; delay punishment
reprimand	v	rebuke severely
reputable	a	honorable, respectable, estimable
resentment	n	hatred
resignation	n	act of quitting; acceptance of one's fate
resilient	a	springing back; recovering readily from adversity
resolute	a	set in purpose or opinion; determined
resource	n	supply
resourceful	a	ingenious; inventive; adroit; clever
respite	n	rest; temporary relief
retain	v	keep; hire
reticent	a	silent; reserved
retract	v	withdraw; take back
retrench	v	cut down, reduce; remove
retrieve	v	recover; regain
reverence, reverential	n, a	deep respect; awe
revisionist	n	advocate of amending or altering
revisit	v	come back to
revitalize	v	give new life to
rhetoric	n	speech; use of language
rhetorical question	n	question that assumes an answer
rigorous	a	demanding; difficult
robust	a	strong and healthy; rude
rousing	a	exciting, stirring
rudimentary	a	simple; elementary; undeveloped; primitive
rustic	a	living in the country; unsophisticated
salvageable	a	able to be saved
sanctimonious	a	hypocritical show of religious devotion
sarcasm	n	harsh or bitter irony; ironical taunt; facetiousness
satire, satirical	n	mocking or making fun of something serious
saturate	v	wet or drench completely
scandalous	a	shameful; shocking; improper
scarce	a	insufficient, not abundant
scholarly	a	academic
scoff	v	mock; make fun of harshly
scorn	n	contempt; hatred
scour	v	thoroughly cleanse; polish
scrupulous	a	principled; careful
scrutinize	v	examine in detail
scuttle	v	run with quick steps, scurry; destroy
secluded	a	hidden; alone; withdrawn from social activity

sedate	v	calm; put to sleep
seditious	a	rebelling against a government
sedulous	a	diligent; persevering
self-serving	a	selfish
serene	a	calm, peaceful, tranquil; unruffled
sermonize	v	preach
setback	n	a check to progress; reverse, defeat
shrewd	a	smart in practical matters; tricky, cunning
shroud	v	cover, hide from view
sinister	a	evil; threatening harm or trouble
skeptical, skepticism	a, n	questioning; doubtful
slipshod	a	careless, untidy, slovenly; seedy; shabby
smug	a	cocky; supercilious; conceited; self-satisfied
sneer	v	show scorn or contempt
solace	n	comfort; alleviation of distress
solicitous	a	show interest; eager to please
somber	a	sad
sophistry	n	false argument
soporific	a	causing sleep; boring
sparse	a	scanty; meager; little amount
speculate	v	guess
spellbinding	a	enchanting, fascinating
spontaneous	a	unplanned; acting upon sudden impulses
sporadic	a	irregular; scattered
sprawling	a	spread out
spurn	v	reject
squander	v	spend wastefully
squelch	v	suppress, silence
stature	n	height; level of achievement
status quo	n	the way things currently are
steadfast	a	fixed in place or direction; unwavering
stifling	a	stuffy; suffocating
stimulate, stimulating, stimulus	v, a, n	invigorate; incite to action
stipulate	v	agree to a fact or demand
stockpile	v	accumulate
straightforward	a	direct; plainspoken
stratify	v	place in layers
streamlined	a	designed for efficiency; compact; simplified
stringent	a	strict; severe; rigorous
stunt	v	cut short; slow or stop growth
subdue	v	overpower by superior force; overcome
subordinate	a	lower rank; less important
substantiate	v	prove
subversive	a	rebellious; undermining
succinct	a	expressed in few words; concise, terse
sullen	a	moody; depressed

sundry	a	various; diverse
supercilious	a	haughty; contemptuous; pompous; conceited
supplant	v	take the place of another
supple	a	bending without breaking, flexible
supplement	v	add to; complete
supportive	a	providing sympathy or encouragement
supposition	n	assumption
suppress	v	keep in or repress (as a feeling)
surfeit	n	excess
sustenance	n	means of supporting life; nourishment; livelihood
symbiotic	a	cooperative or interdependent relationship
syncopate	v	shorten word; change rhythm
systematic	a	involving a method or plan
tacit	a	unspoken, unstated; implicit
tactful	a	diplomatic; careful not to offend
tactile	a	touchable, tangible
tangential	a	off topic; unrelated
taunt	v	make fun of in an insulting manner
taut	a	tight
temperamental	a	moody, irritable, or sensitive; unpredictable
temperance	n	self-control
temperate	a	moderate; mild
tempered	v	lessened in force or intensity
temporize	v	indecisive or evasive to gain time; procrastinate
tenable	a	reasonable; defensible
tenacious	a	persistent; never giving up
tentative	a	uncertain; hesitant
tenuous	a	lacking a sound basis; thin; perilous
terminate	v	bring to an end; dismiss from a job
testify	v	give evidence
theorem, theory	n	proposition to be proved
thesis	n	primary argument or proposition
thought-provoking	a	stimulating mental activity
thrive	v	grow or develop vigorously; prosper
thunderous	a	producing a loud noise
timeworn	a	showing the effects of age
totalitarian	a	dictatorial; authoritarian
toxic	a	poisonous
transitory	a	lasting a short time, temporary
transmit	v	send; pass, spread
treacly	a	overly sentimental; sappy
tremulous	a	trembling; timid, fearful
tribulation	n	serious trouble, severe suffering
tribute	n	gift, compliment
trite	a	unoriginal; boring
trivialize	v	cause to appear unimportant

truce	n	suspension of hostilities
truculent	a	aggressively hostile, belligerent
unabashed	a	not concealed or disguised; obvious; unashamed
unanticipated	a	not realized beforehand or expected
unapproachable	a	not accessible; not easy to meet
unconcern	n	indifference
undermine	v	attack by secret or underhanded means
understatement	n	describing in restrained terms or as less than it is
unemphatically	a	without emphasis
unequivocal	a	clear; having only one possible meaning
unforeseen	a	not known in advance
unhindered	a	unrestrained; not slowed or blocked
unimpressive	a	not arousing awe or admiration
unintelligible	a	not capable of being understood
unprecedented	a	not occurring previously; novel
unrelenting	a	continuing; not easing or stopping
unsubstantiated	a	unproved; unverified
unsuitable	a	unfitting; inappropriate
unswerving	a	straight, direct course; steadfast
unvarying	a	constant; not changing
unwarranted	a	lacking justification or authorization
unwitting	a	unaware; ignorant; oblivious
unyielding	a	steadfast; stubborn; firm; hard
uprising	n	revolt
vacillate	v	waver; go back and forth
validate	v	substantiate; give official approval
valor	n	bravery, courage
variable	a	changing
variegated	a	varied, diverse; patches of different colors
vector	n	direction; bearing; heading
venality	n	openness to bribery or corruption
venerable	a	commanding respect
verbalize	v	express in words
verbose	a	wordy, long winded
versatile	a	capable of different tasks; having many uses
viable	a	practical, workable; livable
vicarious	a	imagined experience of others
vicious	a	readily disposed to evil; malicious
vigilant	a	careful, watchful; alert; on guard; wary
vindicate	v	clear from accusation; justify
vindictive	a	hateful, revengeful
virtue	n	moral excellence, goodness, righteousness
vitality	n	liveliness; energy
vivid	a	intense; clear
vocation	n	career; occupation
voluminous	a	of great size, fullness, or volume

vulgar	a	crass; rude; obscene
vulnerable	a	open to attack; weak; helpless
wane	v	decrease in strength, intensity, etc.
wary	a	suspicious; alert; on guard; vigilant
waver	v	begin to fail or give way; show indecision
whimsical	a	unpredictable; playful; spontaneous; capricious
widespread	a	extensive; broadly distributed
winnow	v	separate valuable from worthless parts
wordplay	n	witty or clever verbal exchange
worldly	a	experienced; knowing; sophisticated
wrath	n	strong anger
wrongheaded	a	wrong in judgment or opinion; misguided

SAT Unlocked II

Work Sheets

OSSG	Word	Definition
Page: Question:		
Page: Question:		
Page: Question:		
Page: Question:		
Page: Question:		
Page: Question:		
Page: Question:		
Page: Question:		
Page: Question:		
Page: Question:		
Page: Question:		
Page: Question:		
Page: Question:		
Page: Question:		
Page: Question:		
Page: Question:		
Page: Question:		

OSSG	Word	Definition
Page: Question:		
Page: Question:		
Page: Question:		
Page: Question:		
Page: Question:		
Page: Question:		
Page: Question:		
Page: Question:		
Page: Question:		
Page: Question:		
Page: Question:		
Page: Question:		
Page: Question:		
Page: Question:		
Page: Question:		
Page: Question:		
Page: Question:		

OSSG	Word	Definition
Page: Question:		
Page: Question:		
Page: Question:		
Page: Question:		
Page: Question:		
Page: Question:		
Page: Question:		
Page: Question:		
Page: Question:		
Page: Question:		
Page: Question:		
Page: Question:		
Page: Question:		
Page: Question:		
Page: Question:		
Page: Question:		
Page: Question:		

Get more help online at: SATunlocked.com

OSSG	Word	Definition
Page: Question:		
Page: Question:		
Page: Question:		
Page: Question:		
Page: Question:		
Page: Question:		
Page: Question:		
Page: Question:		
Page: Question:		
Page: Question:		
Page: Question:		
Page: Question:		
Page: Question:		
Page: Question:		
Page: Question:		
Page: Question:		
Page: Question:		

About the Author

Founder of Marin SAT Prep, Adam Piacente is a former attorney and legal writing teacher who designed academic course materials at two law schools. He is also the author of a number of instructional texts, including the official launch guide for the lexis.com legal research service.

Transitioning from law, Adam started tutoring the SAT. He soon found that he really enjoyed helping students prepare for the test and quickly began developing new and more effective prep methods. These methods have proven so successful that Adam wrote *SAT Unlocked II*.

Adam also writes about the SAT on the web at **SAT Tutor's Blog** (http://sat-tutors-blog.com).

www.ingramcontent.com/pod-product-compliance
Lightning Source LLC
Chambersburg PA
CBHW082034230426
43670CB00016B/2651